Herefordshire's River Trade

Herefordshire's River Trade

Craft & Cargo on the Wye & Lugg

by

Heather Hurley

Logaston Press

LOGASTON PRESS
Little Logaston, Logaston,
Woonton, Almeley, Herefordshire HR3 6QH
www.logastonpress.co.uk

Published by Logaston Press 2013
Copyright © text Heather Hurley 2013
Copyright © illustrations as acknowledged

ISBN 978 1 906663 75 9

Typeset by Logaston Press
and printed and bound in Poland
www.polskabook.pl

Contents

Sources of Illustrations

Herefordshire Record Office
5, 9t, 31t, 35b, 46, 49 58b, 70b, 82, 92b, 109, 114b, 119, 121t, 122, 137t, 139, 140, 142t, 143t, 144,147, 149, 154, 158

Herefoird City Library
2, 16, 18, 19, 20, 27, 33, 47t, 103, 112t, 123t, 125, 128b, 135t & b, 137b, 141, 146, 156, 160t, 162r

Dean and Chapter of Hereford Cathedral
99 (HCA B.5.236), 126 (HCA 5715/3/150, 161 (HCA B.3.16/2)

The National Archives
3, 46

Gloucester Record Office
24 (Q-RR/1)

Wye Valley Area of Outstanding Natural Beauty, 'Landscape Origins' project
166

Hereford Museum	**Monmouth Museum**	**TWNFC**
63, 142b	72t, 161t	145l
Ross Old Books	**Tim Ward**	**Fred Druce**
94	91t	65, 74
Colin Gibbons	**Simon Clarke**	**Ridgebourne Archives**
78	86	95

All others from the Hurley or Logaston collections.

Introduction & Acknowledgements

This book is concerned with the river trade and transport on the Wye and Lugg which ceased over 155 years ago. Its writing would not have been possible without studying the barge accounts digitally copied by the Landscape Origins of the Wye Valley project and examining similar records from other sources. The findings from these documents combined with investigating the banks of both rivers has led to a greater understanding of the river trade, enabling the Wyeside wharves to be located, cargoes to be identified, bargemen, owners and masters to be named, as well as providing details of the barges, boats and trows. Even so it has been a challenge to interpret the river trade with its colourful barges, elusive bargeman and the almost unknown hauliers who towed the laden vessels both upstream and downstream. Whilst the trade is shrouded in romanticism, in reality it was a tough, tedious and dangerous occupation.

The principal contributors to our knowledge of the river trade are Samuel Ireland and John Price in both word and print, Herefordshire's own 'sketcher' James Wathen, the artist Edward Dayes and the flowing words of Charles Heath. Their accounts, combined with the wider material, not least the barge accounts, have revealed a scene of bustling wharves, stacks of cargo, flights of barges, industrious bargemen, hard-working hauliers and views and descriptions of the unpredictable rivers.

My acknowledgements and thanks to Jon Hurley, who spent many interesting days with me exploring the banks of the Wye and Lugg, to David Lovelace for copying and transcribing an invaluable document from The National Archives, to Jean Dobson for information from her research and to Tim Ward for use of a ledger in his possession. I am grateful for references from David Clark, John Eisel and P.J. Pikes, help and advice from Colin Green and Angus Watson and information from Colin Gibbons and Roz Lowe. My thanks extend to the friendly service of Rhys Griffith at the Herefordshire Record Office, Rosalind Cairns at the Cathedral Archives, Lauren Price and Annemarie Dossett at Hereford Library, Andrew Helme at Monmouth Museum, Catherine Willson at Hereford Museum, and the staff at Gloucester Record Office. Not forgetting help and advice from Andy and Karen Johnson of Logaston Press.

The book contains a comprehensive list of archives, books, maps, journals and newspapers which will serve as a stepping-stone for future researchers to expand certain topics.

Heather Hurley
Hoarwithy, 2013

1   RIVERS WYE AND LUGG NAVIGATION

The River Wye follows a meandering course of 157 miles along the Welsh Borders from its source on the barren and rocky slopes of Plynlimon in mid Wales. As a mountain spring it leaps over rocks as a fast upland stream, before widening into a river that was once navigable from Glasbury and then passing the market towns of Hay-on-Wye, Hereford, Ross-on-Wye and Monmouth to reach Chepstow and its confluence with the Severn. It is the fifth longest river in the United Kingdom, designated as an SSSI along its entire course and now only navigable by canoe from Glasbury to Chepstow with a few pleasure craft on the lower Wye. The Lugg rises above Presteigne and was once navigable from Leominster to its confluence with the Wye at Mordiford.

Early River Transport
From early times river valleys provided a means of trade, transport and communication, although there is no direct evidence to suggest when man first utilised water transport. At Symonds Yat early man inhabiting caves and rock shelters possibly traded along the Wye in open boats capably of carrying cargoes of about 3 tons.[1] The Romans used ships to transport stone on the Thames, but despite Roman sites on the Wye at Huntsham and Kenchester there is little evidence to support their using the Wye for navigation. It has been suggested that they would have used the Wye for transport upstream from Huntsham at least as far as Kenchester, but what evidence there is at Huntsham suggests trade with Gloucester to the east and down the river to the lower Severn, rather than northwards.[2] Nevertheless, it is possible that the remains of Roman masonry on the river bank at New Weir near Kenchester may have been associated with a wharf or landing stage.[3]

By the time of the Domesday survey the lower Wye was known to have been used for transport. During the 13th century wine from France and venison from Ireland were transported in boats up the Wye from Bristol to Monmouth, then transferred onto land carriage to Goodrich Castle. A wharf was recorded at Hereford Castle in 1256, but probably used only to aid transport of goods across the river, as it was unlikely that any boats would have reached Hereford from the lower Wye at that date. On the Monnow, a tributary of the Wye, archaeologists identified a wharf at Skenfrith dating from the 13th century, but again no evidence exists to support any kind of trade up or down the river and the wharf was probably used to land goods brought from the opposite river bank.[4]

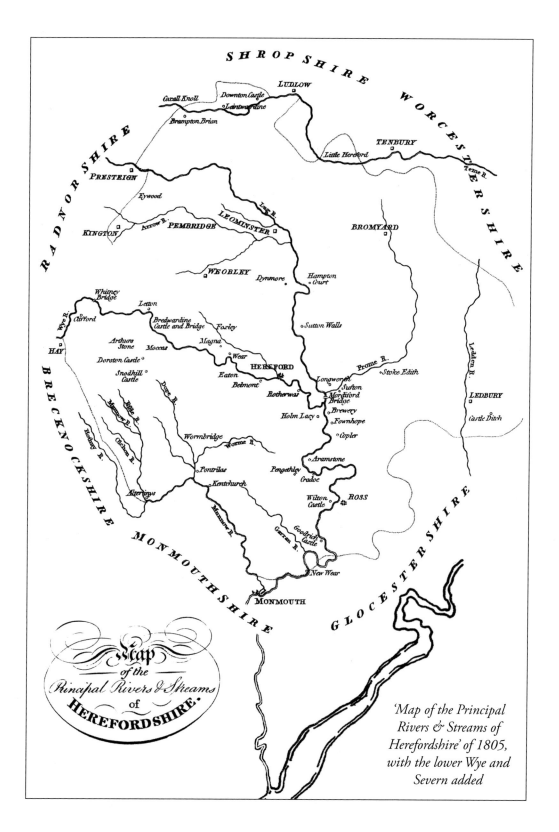

'Map of the Principal
Rivers & Streams of
Herefordshire' of 1805,
with the lower Wye and
Severn added

April 18. Worcester. Commission to John Buteturte and William de Mortuo Mari to survey the weirs, dykes and stakes in the water of Weye between Hereford and Monemuth, as it appears that ships and boats cannot pass as they were wont by reason of the erection thereof so that they extend into the channel, Henry de Lancastre and the sheriff of Hereford will provide a jury out of the liberty of Munemuth and the county respectively.   By pet. of C.

Top: Record in the Patent Rolls of a commission to survey the Wye in 1301
Below: A printed summary

Whilst traffic on stretches of other rivers in England gradually grew, the main hindrance to improving and extending the navigation of at least the lower Wye was the obstruction of the river by innumerable weirs that had been constructed to provide power for the medieval mills and forges, coupled with fish garths for the breeding of fish.[5] In 1215 Magna Carta ordered that rivers were to be kept free from obstructions, and this led to a series of petitions, Statutes and Acts to ensure that the navigation on rivers should be kept free of weirs and other hindrances. In 1301 a commission was set up 'to survey the weirs, dykes and stakes in the water of Weye between Hereford and Monmouth, as it appears that ships and boats cannot pass as they were wont by reason of the erection thereof so that they extend into the channel'.[6] In 1315 Henry of Lancaster (subsequently the 3rd Earl of Lancaster) was seeking 'the removal of a fish weir from the River Wye which is causing damage and disruptions to boats using the river'. On the Thames an Act of 1350 prohibited obstructions, and in 1377 there was a complaint 'that the Severn is restricted by fish weirs so that boats cannot easily pass and many have been lost'.[7] In Hereford the Dean and Chapter's mills and weir on the Wye were in continual repair as recorded by the 'keeper of the mill'. His accounts from 1396 to 1415 show that all carriage of materials was by land and not river.[8] In 1527 the weir and mills were 'thrown down and destroyed' and had to be rebuilt under the terms of the 1555 Hereford Mills Act, which made no mention of boats or barges on the Wye. In the meantime, from the 15th century trows had been carrying wheat, malt and flour on the Severn, and small craft were being built in the Forest of Dean for use at least on the lower Wye.[9]

In order to protect timber for naval use during the Tudor period The Timber Preservation Act was passed in 1559 to prevent trees being converted into charcoal for the iron-making industry. It prohibited the felling of timber trees for iron-making (as its potential for shipbuilding was recognized) within 14 miles of the banks of the Severn, Wye, Thames and other rivers, where the carriage of timber was 'commonly used by boats or other vessels to any parts of the sea'.[10] From 1570 wine, oil, iron, soap, raisins, linen, pitch, hops and fish were amongst the many goods conveyed up the Severn as far as Bridgnorth from Bristol, whereas barley, malt and peas came downstream. Timbers for shipbuilding were floated down the Severn from at least 1575, and a year later salt was recorded as a cargo on the same river.[11]

Transport in the Seventeenth Century

From the beginning of the 17th century there was a new enthusiasm for improving river navigation, partly due to the poor condition of roads that meant that 'wheel carriage was twelve times dearer than inland water carriage'. This was possibly an exaggeration, because in 1603 a cargo of salted fish was sent up the Thames from London to Burcot for 16s 8d, whereas the shorter land carriage would have cost 7s 8d.[12] The Oxford to Burcot Commission was appointed in 1605 to improve this stretch of the Thames, but as its results were not forceful enough another Act was introduced in 1624 giving the Commissioners 'full power to cleanse and make navigable the River' and 'the right to open, prepare, or make all necessary weirs, locks and turnpikes'.[13]

In 1622 the Monmouth Weir on the Wye was causing a problem, which the commissioners of sewers took seriously. They interviewed 'a group of boatmen whose average age was about 90. They all agreed that Monmouth weir had been there a long time and caused no interference. William Roberts, aged 85, remembered the weir being built at the end of Queen Mary's reign and there were no through boats under Monmouth Bridge. Wines were brought from Bristol to Monmouth and unladened below the bridge and then carried by wain to Hereford. Boats were drawn by line by men up the river to Monmouth from Brockweir.' Another boatman confirmed that the weir was built on the foundations of an earlier one, and that the Wye was navigable for woodbushes (rafts) and long trows from the Severn to Brockweir. A fisherman reported that he had seen 'timber being carried from Whitchurch to Lydbrook in small boats'.[14]

On the Severn the Bewdley merchants of 1630 were shipping wool and hides, and in 1635 a trow from Bristol delivered soap, bottles of wine and a cloak-bag to Shrewsbury, made possible by the cutting of barge gutters around the fish weirs.[15] At Worcester 'sons of Arnold Bean plied the river from Chepstow and Bristol carrying Gascony wine in the *Alice* and *Anne*'.[16] Around this date authorization had been given to construct locks on the Warwickshire Avon, a tributary of the Severn, to enable boats to reach Stratford from Tewkesbury. Although it was understood that the work was not completed for a number of years, it was recorded that 'the industrious Mr. Sandys did in three years make the Avon passable for barges of 30 tons to Stratford-upon-Avon, through foul and low bottoms, purchasing with excessive charge mills, meadows and other grounds to cut a course for the watery work'.[17]

In the early years of the 17th century bark was being conveyed on the lower Wye together with Forest coal and minerals from Lydbrook, 'carried out of the Forest by horses, donkeys and mules, and loaded on boats and barges plying on the river Wye and Severn'. This use of water carriage was probably in part due to the state of the local roads.[18] In Herefordshire the roads were certainly in a 'wretched state', 'overhung by trees with

Accounts of 1641 detailing costs of carriage of paper between the Scudamores' house at Holme Lacy and London

the mire of January hardly dry by Midsummer, in other places the bare rock worn into inequalities by heavy rains, rose in ascents in ledges like stairs'. Yet despite the roads being 'impenetrable and impassable, churned into mud by horses hooves and deeply rutted by wheeled vehicles', there is no evidence to suggest that the Wye above Monmouth was yet being used to carry goods.[19]

Before and during the 17th century cumbersome wagons and packhorses carried a wide range of raw materials, manufactured goods, fresh food and beverages from one part of the country to another along the neglected roads. Wagons that carried heavy loads such as timber were drawn by teams of up to 12 horses and travelled at an average speed of 2mph. Other vehicles were drawn by oxen, whilst two-wheeled carts pulled by a single horse or pony were used for lighter and local deliveries. The goods conveyed along the Herefordshire roads included stone, lime, coal, brick, poles, corn and manure.[20] During the 17th century the Scudamores at Holme Lacy paid £1 5d for 'Five quires of Royal paper, carriage of it from London'; 4s for 'ye carriage of 6 bushels of wheat to Gloucester'; 2s 2d for 'carrying 4 hampers from London' and 10d to 'carriers of corn and cider to Gloucester'.[21]

Over hilly and mountainous countryside, where winding and narrow tracks followed gradual gradients, it was more convenient to use packhorses, which were often driven in long 'trails'. Packhorses were ponies under 14.2 hands (smaller than a driving horse), had firm hooves and could cover between 25 to 30 miles a day.[22] In parts of Herefordshire sure-footed packhorses were a faster and more reliable form of transport, carrying a variety of goods including wool, malt, pottery, lead, coal, textiles and even wine in panniers slung across the animal's back. Ancient routes from Droitwich were used by packhorses to transport salt used for manufacturing paper, soap, dyes and medicinal products. At Wellington '17 measures of salt at 30 pence' came from Droitwich in the 11th century, and at Hartpury in Gloucestershire the tenants of the bishop of Gloucester had a duty to deliver salt from Droitwich.

Difficulties of River Navigation

As interest in river navigation increased, shipment of goods along many rivers remained difficult due to the number of weirs. The most vivid description of these obstructions was provided by the 'Water Poet' John Taylor. A Gloucester-born, self-educated, eccentric Thames wherryman, Taylor wrote and published numerous pamphlets and verses describing his travels by river, road and sea throughout Britain between 1618 and 1653.[23]

In July 1641 Taylor set out from London on one of his expeditions with 'two men and a brace of boyes' with a 'scullers boate' to explore the Thames, the Severn, the Wye and the Warwickshire Avon. On the Thames between London and Oxford his boat had to be pulled over or through locks and other obstructions which hindered his passage, although barges negotiated the locks with the help of capstans. On the Severn, Taylor found the river 'almost as much abus'd as us'd' with rubbish from the coal mines 'whiche by neerenesse of the river is all washed into it. And makes as many shallows, that in time Severne will bee quite chocked up, and all passage stopped'. From Tewkesbury Taylor noted the Avon, 'which by the great change and industry of Master Sands is made navigable, many miles up into the country'.

An illustration of Taylor's journeys that accompanied a printed record of his voyages

Between rivers Taylor hired a wain to transport his boat, men, boys and luggage, and in August 1641 he reached Chepstow to start his journey on the Wye. He headed upstream passing Tintern, Monmouth, Lydbrook and Ross to Hereford where he ended his 'painful' journey and contemplated selling his boat and returning to London by land, but changed his mind and returned via Ingestone to Lydbrook. He found his journey 'debard of all passages with boates, by 7. weares, 2. of them are Monmouth Weares, and Wilton Weare, the other 5. are Inkson Weare [Ingeston at Foy], Carrow [Carey], Founehope [Fownhope], Hancocks [Hancock's at Bolstone] and Bondnam Weare [Bodenham's mills in Hereford]'.[24]

In 1653, during the Commonwealth that followed the Civil War, a petition was made by Hereford City 'for the removal of weirs on the rivers Wye and Lugg, which have caused flooding of adjoining meadows and pastures, and have carried away hay crops, and which, although in the reigns of Elizabeth I and James I were ordered to be demolished, remained, probably, it was suspected, due to the dishonourable dealings in high places; and the

The Wye at the site of Hancock's Weir

absence of which would render the rivers more easily navigable'.[25] A year later – in 1654 – Parliament ordered the Wye to be made navigable and appointed a committee to put forward an Act which was secured by money from the sale of land belonging to the Dean and Chapter of Hereford.[26] It was not until 1662, following the Restoration, that the Rivers Wye and Lugg Navigation Act was passed.

Under the terms of this Act, Sir William Sandys, Windsor Sandys and Henry Sandys had the authority 'for the making navigable or passable by Barges, Boates, Lighters or other Vessells, the said Rivers of Wye and Lugg and the Rivuletts, Brookes and other water courses falling into them, and so falling into the said River Severne' and 'To cutt such and soe many new Channells from, by, or in any of them as may be fit for Navigation into the said River of Severne'. It was an ambitious scheme to remove all impediments, to provide wharves and ways for hauling boats and barges by foot or horses, to erect locks and weirs and to repair the bridges from Chepstow to Hereford.[27] However, due to lack of capital and engineering expertise the proposed work was never completed.

Although this first attempt at making navigable the Wye and Lugg proved unsuccessful, other rivers were gradually becoming commercial waterways. Amongst those confirmed as being navigable at this date were the Warwickshire Avon to Stratford, the Severn to Shrewsbury and the Thames to Abingdon. The Wye is also considered to have been navigable to Monmouth.[28]

Following the failure to achieve the aims of the Act of 1662, other attempts to improve the navigation of the Wye followed. Although the Sandys family had carried out a considerable amount of work, they lost interest in the Wye, so a further scheme was put forward by 'a local consortium' in Hereford in 1664. This caused a number of petitions for and against the proposals for 'making navigable the Rivers of Wye and Lugg' including one announcing 'That the Mayor of the City of Hereford hath clandestinely prevailed upon William Williams, a poor Boatman, and several other poor Men of the Town of Monmouth, to subscribe a Paper, purporting their Approbation of making the Rivers Wye and Lugg navigable', saying that 'since corn was brought to Monmouth on horseback the market would be destroyed as boats would pass through without stopping'.[29]

Other petitions were in favour. One from the inhabitants of Ross stated that 'the making of the Rivers Wye and Lugg navigable will be a great Advantage ... And praying that the said Mills and Weirs may be taken down'. The merchants and traders of Bristol described their 'Commerce with the County of Hereford, by the Conveniency of carrying Goods to and fro' by Water, but that of late Years, by reason of the Mills and dams now on the Rivers Wye and Lugg, and the excessive Rates of Land-carriage, their Communication is, in a manner lost'.[30]

Nothing was, however, done and in 1673 Hereford's Quarter Sessions recorded the projected rates and prices of 'Toll & Tunnage' for 'Lyme and Cole brought upp' on the Wye:

> To Hereford per Tunne............................ 0 1 0
> To Mordiford per Tunne......................... 0 0 9
> To Hancox and Cary.............................. 0 0 6
> To Horewithy... 0 0 5
> To Ingeston and Wilton.......................... 0 0 4
> Wood and all other heavy Carriage from
> Fownhope to Hereford per Tunne.......... 0 0 2 [31]

A few years later the Quarter Sessions listed all the weirs associated with 'Corn & Woollen Mills' on the Wye and Lugg,[32] maybe in consideration of the need to transport the 3,650 tons of coal considered to be required by the inhabitants of Hereford. 'Eight boats would be needed and it would sell for more than fifteen shillings a ton – half the price charged if it came by road transport'.[33]

In due course a second 'Rivers Wye and Lugg Navigation Act' was passed in 1695 with similar objectives to those stated in the previous Act. The financing was however transferred from private individuals to the county. All 'the mills with their weirs and all the fishing weirs were to be removed and the shallow places deepened', but due to the importance of iron-making at New Weir in Whitchurch, this weir was allowed to remain providing the Duke of Kent (as owner) 'make and maintain a good convenient and sufficient lock' and build a house 'for the perpetual habitation of a person rent free, to keep the said lock, and constantly to attend the opening and shutting thereof'. The Act also made due provision 'for the building of warehouses or storehouses' on the site of Hereford Castle.[34]

Although the weirs – with the one exception noted – were to be demolished under the terms of the Act, it is interesting to read Daniel Denell's survey of the 'Weirs, Mills, Fords and Shallows' of 1697.[35] His detailed account of the Wye from Chepstow to Monnington, and of the Lugg from Mordiford to Leominster describes a number of weirs standing at heights between five and nine feet, together with the decayed state of the locks, fish traps and mills. The Wye's width, depth, shallows, tides and channels were noted, along with the boats, cargoes, quays and fishing. At Chepstow Denell recorded that 'Ships of 250 tunns may safely rest at Anchor near the Town wall below the Bridge', noting several vessels so moored 'amongst which were 2 laden with Copper-ore from Cornwall bound for Redbrook'. He also recorded that Chepstow was a 'safe place for a key [quay] for

The problem of weirs. These pictures show a weir on the River Monnow at Kentchurch.
The top photograph shows it in 1900, that at lower left in 2010 and that at lower right in 2012
after it had been demolished to improve fishing and prevent flooding

Brockweir wharf on the Wye in 2009

Vessels', whilst lying at anchor at Brockweir were '16 Boats & Barges which Trade to Bristol with Corn and goods of wood great and small' with 'Vessels capable of carrying 40 or 50 Tunns'.

Denell described the Duke of Kent's weir at New Weir as 'built out of loose stones thrown into ye river [with] stakes and turfs behind them with a hedge on the top', the highest part of the weir being over nine feet and the lowest about six feet. At 'the East end of this Wear is a Locke of 13 foot wide ... in Reasonable good repair' and 'there is a Forge lately built upon ye West End of ye Wear'. Below Wilton Bridge there was a weir of six foot topped by a hedge belonging to Lord Chandos. If a cut 'of about 20 foot [was] made in ye Wear, there would be a good Passage for vessels of any Burthen as could be desired', but the lock was 'utterly decayed'. At Hampton Bishop 'there might easily be made a very good Passage for vessels of 30 Tunn and upwards at most times of the year', whilst at Hereford, Sugwas and Monnington there were weirs of between five and eight foot in height.

From Mordiford the River Lugg was found to be partly obstructed and unsuitable for boats due to the lowness of its bridges. Denell thought that one arch of the Mordiford Bridge needed to be raised, but 'Vessells of 12 or 14 Tunns or more may pass as we Judge most part of Summer'. At Shelwick there were '3 mills and a Stone Weare of about 9 foot high'. The three mills at Kings Mills above Moreton Bridge belonging to a London vintner 'had no Wear but floodgates', whereas at Hampton Court Mills there was a stone weir 'in very good repair' which caused 'the greatest difficulty of making a good passage' and 'the Stone Bridge there is very low'.[36]

In 1677 Andrew Yarranton had published *England's Improvement by Sea and Land* in which he wrote 'For Herefordshire, part of the County is already well improved; First it

Extensive wharves at the inland port of Bewdley on the Severn in Worcestershire.

hath a Navigable river unto the City made by Art; but imperfect at present'. He wrote that bottled cider from Herefordshire was 'sent to Gloucester, from thence to Lechload [Lechlade], and so to London by Water' on the Thames, which had become a busy navigable river. Around the same period on the Severn at Worcester John Chance 'carried wine, but in addition transported malt, hops, wool, cloth, herrings, hides, lead and groceries'. At Madeley north of the River Severn in the Severn Gorge in Shropshire there was John Hagar, a trowman who owned 'one Barge & all her Rigging', at Broseley Edward Dawley was a barge owner with 'one old Barge and all thereunto belonginge' and William Ashwood, a trowman at Madeley, had 'one old Barge with materials thereunto belonging'.[37] From Bewdley barges were importing and exporting cargoes of ironware, glass, pot clay, timber, coal, bricks, paper and wine, and on the Warwickshire Avon the Countess of Plymouth in 1696 was paying tax on river-borne coal brought down the Severn and up the Avon.[38]

Despite improvements on other rivers, by the late 1690s the Wye and Lugg still suffered from major difficulties for those wishing to navigate the river above Lydbrook, although accounts exist of pig iron being transported from Redbrook to Hereford, Bishopswood to Brockweir and Redbrook to Brockweir in 1692.[39] From 1697 Lord Scudamore of Holme Lacy was making regular payments to 'Lug and Wye', referring to the tax collected by the Wye and Lugg Commissioners, and during 1698 his accounts list items such as 'halling Timber for the House', 'halling timber to Wye for Prossers barn' and 'Ropes to tow timber down the Water'. There was also many payments for work carried out repairing Hancock's Weir in Bolstone parish, including for 'making 3,500 faggots for the Weare' and 'for cutting Polls and stakes for the Weare work'.[40] The weirs built across the Wye formed a massive barrier built of turfs and stones held in place by stakes and poles, with a staked hedge planted on top. The weirs stood anything from 5 feet to 9 feet high above the water level.

But gradually the commissioners appointed under the Act of 1695 began to make improvements. Accounts dating from 1696 to 1700 show various items of expenditure: 8d was paid for 'bringing the iron drag from Fownhope', 4s 6d for 'Notices when the trees were cut down', £5 9s 3d for '7 days work in cutting down ye trees and Bushes on the River side from Fownhope to Ross and Lydbrook', £4 11s 6d for 'making the broach in Suggas Weare', 9s for 'bringing the barge to Hereford Wear for drawing the stakes', £2 14s 3d for 'work done at Lea Brink', 15s for 'going down the River with Wm. Williams & Ed. Williams in the barge to view the River', 7s 6d 'to take up the gravell out of ye fords' and 32 5s for 'carrying 150 tun of gravel at 3d per tun'.[41]

That there was a need to take up the gravel of the fords indicates how these were an obstruction to the barges. Some of these fords were paved and built as causeways on the river bed, and were sited at wide and shallow parts of the river where it was deemed acceptable to wade across at armpit depth. Horses were ridden across up to chest height and cattle were driven across. When the Wye was made navigable and the fords at least partially cleared, more were replaced by ferries. At some crossings two boats were kept, one for foot passengers and a larger horse boat for conveying goods and livestock.'[42]

Before the end of the 17th century it was understood that there was no difficulty in taking small barges to Redbrook on the tide and boats with a shallow draught were able to reach Monmouth. Further upstream 'the carriage of iron from Whitchurch in small boats' was noted and there is a suggestion of a 'flat-bottomed boat of 4 tons drawing 1 foot 4 inches of water, which could ascend the Wye to Hereford'.[43] In general, however, the possibility of using the upper Wye for commercial river traffic was still 'frustrated by landowners who wished to use the river for mills or fisheries'.[44] One of the first known traders based above Ross was Daniel Kerry at Kings Caple. Shortly after his friend John Harris opened an inn called the Old Boar in 1695, 'they made a tying up place, where barges could safely tie up and load the hogsheads of cider, sacks of corn and anything else which could go down the river and be sold in Bristol for a better price'. The piece of land became known as 'Kerry's Lockstock Boat Place'.[45]

Eighteenth Century Progress

In 1700 substantial parts of the nation were 'more than 15 miles from navigable water' and the 'greater the distance from navigable water, the more water transport lost its advantage of lower charges through the cost of carriage to and from the wharf'. Charges for river carriage were about one penny per ton-mile compared with rates of 8 to 13 pence per ton-mile by wagons or 9 to 18 pence by packhorse.[46] Although the barges that were beginning to convey goods on the upper Wye were small, such a barge could carry 30 tons if towed by man or horse compared with the capacity of under one ton for a wagon, and just one eighth of a ton for a packhorse.[47]

From the early 1700s evidence suggests that the Wye and Lugg became more regularly used as a navigable waterway, with William Williams, Luke Hughes, William Welch, Thomas Hall and Joseph Reginald recorded as bargemen on the Wye.[48] Locks on the Lugg were built at Mordiford, Tidnor and Hampton Court, and on the lower Wye pig iron was shipped from the Forest of Dean to Chepstow and Bristol.[49] At Holme Lacy the Scudamores were carrying out maintenance on 'weare works' paying tax for 'Rivers Lugg & Wye', and were busy hauling or carrying timber and bark from their woodlands. Further upstream Thomas Pennoyre at Clifford was selling charcoal produced from '500 cords of timber' to Thomas Church and Samuel Bullock at Hereford, which may have been loaded onto barges.[50]

By 1714 the Trustees of the Wye and Lugg Navigation had purchased Tidnor Mills on the Lugg and instead of demolishing the weir and two watermills, leased it to John Smallman. The rent of £30 per annum was then used to improve navigation as the 'River Lugg continues still unprofitable to the Country by not being made navigable'.[51] In the Wye Valley, the timber from its woodlands had became very valuable for the iron-making industry run by a business partnership between Thomas Foley and William Rea. Amongst their purchases was the 'timber out of Hom Park' and 'Rudge Wood in Fownhope belonging to the Dean and Chapter of Hereford' which was 'sent down the Wye' and delivered to furnaces and forges at Newent, Bishopswood and Lydbrook.[52]

In 1727 the third Rivers Wye and Navigation Act was passed to make the navigation more 'effectual' above Ross by re-building the weirs, as their pulling down had been found to 'prejudice the Navigation of the said Rivers, by occasioning very great Shoals and Flats, so that at low Water the said Rivers are not passable in many Places'.[53] It seems unlikely that any weirs were re-built, however, but trade on the Wye continued to improve with 'a good trade' at Ross, whilst Leominster was noted as 'a large and good trading town on the River Lug. This river is lately made navigable by Act of Parliament, to the very great profit of the trading part of this country, who have now a very great trade for their corn, wool, and other products of this place, into the river Wye, and from the Wye, into the Severn, and so to Bristol.'[54]

A wharf was built at Hereford in 1728 for 'Trows, Boats, Barges and other Vessells' by Joseph Trumper and Philip Symonds, another was built at Wilton by Luke Hughes in 1735, and a meadow was rented from the Scudamores at Holme Lacy to haul timber to the Wye, the meadow's bank being used to load timber onto barges or make timber rafts to float downstream.[55] By 1739 the Wye was navigable to Hay as the bells from Llywel Church (brought to the river bank at Hay from beyond Sennybridge) were conveyed to Chepstow, and in 1772 the river was navigable to Glasbury Bridge.[56] Although this evidence shows a reasonable use of the Wye for transporting goods, it was not an easy task due to the variable water levels, with shallows in summer and floods in winter. Conveying goods downstream was less of a problem than taking them upstream, when even five or six men hauling a barge carrying 20 tons could run into trouble against the flow.

The sinuous Lugg posed great difficulties and whilst, like the Wye, it was prone to flooding, its limitations restricted the size of barges and trows used on the upper Wye. In 1777 a number of ambitious schemes were proposed to connect Leominster by canal to either Stourport, Hereford or Bridgnorth but the difficulties involved and vast cost prevented any of them being developed, leaving the Lugg 'being rather ineffectual when compared with certain other rivers'.[57]

Into the Nineteenth Century

With a growing population in Hereford needing coal, it was resolved in 1790 to cut a canal 'which might open communication with the Severn at Gloucester, and, by passing through the collieries, afford the city of Hereford and its neighbourhood a more regular supply'.[58] This was an ambitious project which took many years to complete, a time during which the majority of the county's roads were improved through the introduction of turnpike trusts. In the meantime, in 1801 James Teague constructed an early horse-drawn tramroad leading from a mine at Perch Hill in the Forest of Dean to a wharf on the Wye at Lydbrook. This was followed in 1810 by an extension of the Severn & Wye Railway, as it was called, to a wharf at Bishopswood. The purpose of these tramroads was to carry coal from the pits 'for shipment by barges upstream to the City of Hereford and elsewhere'.[59]

These improvements were made despite a growing awareness of the threat that the Gloucester to Hereford Canal posed to the trade on the Wye, and there was concern therefore to improve the river's navigation, for barges still had to deal with both high and low water levels which could prove fatal to navigation. As described in 1804: 'The latter is experienced during the greater part of every dry summer, when shoals barely covered with the stream, occur very frequently: in winter, heavy rains, or snow dissolving on the river's banks, within the county, have the effect of gradually adding a few inches to the depth, but when these rush into its channels, from the mountains of Brecknock and Radnorshire, they occasion an almost instantaneous overflow, and give it a force which defies all the ordinary means of resistance and control.'[60]

In 1805 an engineer was 'engaged to make a report on the practicability of scooping out channels through the principal shoals which obstruct the navigation at low water; of confining the current in those places within narrow limits; and for making a towing path for horses instead of men'.[61] The proposed route between Hereford and Tintern was surveyed by Henry Price in 1805, the same year that a 'Report on the Improvements of the Navigation of the River Wye' was put together by William Jessop. He concluded that the construction of a horse towing path would lead to 'a saving to the Public of about £4,233 per Annum, exclusive of the advantages arising from dispatch and regularity, and that of restoring 500 Men, who are now substitutes for Horses, to more useful Employment'.

This led to a further Rivers Wye and Lugg Navigation Act in 1809 which made provision for a 'Horse Towing-path on certain Parts of the Banks of the said River Wye'. Under the terms of this Act a 'Towing-path or Roads for Horses' was to be made and maintained by the Trustees, the path running from the 'City of Hereford to a certain Place in the Parish of Welch Bicknor, in the county of Monmouth opposite to Lidbrook, in the county of Gloucester'. The rates for using the towpath was 'the Sum of Sixpence per Mile for every Mile' for every beast 'drawing any Barge, Lighter, Boat or other Vessel'. Under the terms of the Act the River Wye Horse Towing Path Company was to 'build Houses and Stables for Collectors of the Tolls', to 'keep Ferries for carrying over the Draft Horses and Drivers etc.', and to 'let horses to Hire'.[62]

The first horse-drawn barges were recorded two years after the passing of the Navigation Act in 1809 – on 15 January 1811. The first such barge passing under Wilton Bridge was Jonathan Crompton's barge the *Henry*, carrying a cargo of coal and William

Hoskins as master. The second such barge was the *Fanny*, with Thomas Jones as master and also owned by Jonathan Crompton; each barge was pulled by two horses. (The Crompton family were prominent barge owners and coal merchants in Hereford, see chapter 10.) However, surviving barge accounts of this period hardly mention horses, and few images show horses towing barges on the Wye and Lugg. At Lydbrook in 1814 the Horse Towing Path Company were still collecting tolls 'Taken by Mr. Henry Thompson, at the Ferry Boat, at Lidbrook; and all persons are hereby desired to take Notice, That before any Horses or Horses are employed on the said Towing Path, for the purpose of Drawing any Boat, Barge, or Wherry, they must apply to the Boatman for a Ticket'.[63]

One improvement made in 1825 was the removal of the New Weir at Whitchurch to encourage the use of steam barges, and a proposal was made to deepen 'the bed of the streams, to render the river navigable at the lowest water for barges carrying ten tons'.[64] From 1825 to 1827 one company's accounts reveal a good trade on the Wye upstream to Hereford, although trolleys, carts and wagons were also used. Despite organised opposition from barge owners and others with vested interests in trade on the Wye, the horse-drawn tram carrying coal from south Wales reached Hereford in 1829. This was followed by the completion of the canal from Gloucester to Hereford in 1845, the opening of the Newport, Abergavenny and Hereford Railway in 1854 and the Hereford, Ross and

A house built at Careyboat by the Horse Towing Path Company
to collect tolls and provide shelter

An illustration by De Wint c.1820 of bow hauliers and a barge on the Wye with the ruins of Goodrich Castle in the background

Gloucester Railway in 1855, events which abruptly ended the navigation on the upper Wye and Lugg.[65]

In 1873 John Lloyd reflected that although the course of the Wye from Chepstow to Glasbury was never a regular conveyance, 'the navigation has proved of great service to the county of Hereford ... most of the coal consumed in Hereford and its neighbourhood was brought up in barges after a flood. Various other heavy articles, such as grocery, wines, and spirits, having been first conveyed from Bristol to Brockweir in large vessels, were carried up thence in barges at a much easier rate than land carriage. In return the boats were freighted with the valuable oak timber, bark, cider, wheat, flour, and other produce of the county.'[66]

2   BARGES, BOATS AND TROWS

The flat-bottomed boats that worked the river were known variously as trows, sloops, snows, frigates and brigantines, but were generically known as barges on the upper Wye, whereas trow appears to have been the preferred name on the lower Wye. The barges on the Wye varied in size and included the 'common' barge of 1763 which could carry between 18 and 20 tons, and measured 50 feet long and 11 feet broad. In 1805 such a barge was recorded as carrying between 18 and 40 tons.

Properly described, a trow was a wooden sailing vessel used on both the Severn and the Wye, typically measuring between 60 and 70 feet long and between 12 and 20 feet broad, with a shallow draught and a flat bottom. It had decks at the bows and the stern, with an open cargo hold amidships. It had a square rig and made use of the wind and tide where possible, but in confined waters could be towed by gangs of men, and later horses. A sloop (also known as a cutter or smack in the Bristol Channel) was a single masted trow with a different rig, having a fore and aft main sail, whilst a snow was a two-masted vessel which carried square sails on both masts. According to Defoe a snow was the largest of all old two-masted vessels. A brig was a merchant vessel with a square rig on its two masts (of which the main mast was the one at the rear), whilst a brigantine also had two masts but with a square rig only on the foremast and fore-and-aft rigging on the mainmast, and was somewhat similar to a snow. A frigate was a name sometimes applied to smaller single masted trows on the Severn, presumably with tongue in cheek as the name usually referred to fast three masted naval ships that carried between 28 and 35 cannon.[1] On the Severn barges and frigates varied between 40 to 60 feet in length, had a single mast with a square sail and could carry between 20 and 40 tons of cargo.[2]

Also plying the Wye were schooners and hoys. A schooner was a fore-and-aft rigged sailing vessel having at least two masts, with the foremast usually the smallest. The *Endeavour*, a trow of 65 tons in 1763, was later rebuilt as a schooner, and in 1828 the *Castle* was built as a schooner at Chepstow. A hoy was the name given to either a small sloop-rigged coasting ship or a heavy barge used for freight. The 48-ton *Abbey* was built as a hoy in 1744 at Bristol, but re-registered as a trow of 68 tons by James Madley of Redbrook in 1804.[3]

On the Severn the difference between a barge and a trow was more clearly defined in 1758: 'the lesser barges and frigates being from 40 to 60 feet in length, have a single mast, square sail and carry from 20 to 40 tons; the trows, or larger vessels, are from 40 to 80 tons burthen; these have a main and top mast, about 80 feet high, with square sails, and some have missen [mizzen, or middle] masts, they are generally from 16 to 20 feet wide and 60 in length being when new and completely rigged worth about £300'.[4]

Some boatmen owned several different vessels, such as Thomas Gower on the Severn in 1728 who had 'One Trow, One Barge, One Frigate, with Ropes, Masts, Sails, Shafts, Oars, planks and all other Materials', or Richard Clarke in 1731 who owned a 'Trow, old Barge and old Frigate'.

Boats on the Wye faced more difficult operating conditions than those on the Severn, and due to the comparatively shallow water and receiving less help from the tide, many cargoes were transhipped at Brockweir from larger vessels onto flat-bottomed barges. Brockweir was 'one of the most important ports on the river and the waterfront is still of archaeological interest thanks to the fact that its stone wharf, which lies upstream of the present road bridge, has survived almost intact'.[5] Another transhipment point was at Mordiford where coal and lime-coal was 'measured' and 'put out' at the mouth of the Lugg, which suggests that cargoes were either transferred onto smaller barges before continuing upstream or loaded onto trolleys, carts and wagons for easier and quicker transport to Hereford and Leominster.[6]

The Wye barges were described as being 'continually at work, keel-less, flat-bottomed vessels of great dimensions, drawing but little water'. They were fitted with a tall mast, which could be lowered by a small winch carried on the forward decking to allow the vessel to pass under bridges. Although most barges carried a single square sail hung on a cross yard on the mast, it was not always possible to use this method of propulsion. Lack of wind,

Men towing a barge into Hereford in 1778

breeze in the wrong direction and riverside trees all conspired against the sailing vessels, so the best means of progress was provided by teams of men known as bow hauliers.

Bow hauliers were 'engaged, probably at Brockweir, to haul barges up the sometimes shallow reaches of the river to Monmouth and beyond and were known as rough, tough and lawless. Generally speaking six to eight men were needed to deal with a barge against the current, although up to twenty men were occasionally employed on a particularly large vessel.'[7] It was hard and dangerous work which required working as a team, especially when bridges had to be negotiated. High up the mast was a block through which the tow-rope was run, a spare being coiled on the stern decking near the captain who also acted as steersman. The tow-rope was fixed to the mast rather than the bows of the vessel so that it was less likely to become entangled in any undergrowth on the river bank. Each bow haulier had a leather breast-strap with a small harness rope which he could attach to the tow-rope. The men attached themselves to the tow line about five yards apart and the captain could pay out or shorten the length of tow-rope as required. On approaching a bridge the hauliers would clamber up the bank and onto the bridge with the long tow rope attached to the top of the mast. When the barge reached the bridge the mast was lowered, the skipper released the rope and a single man hauled in the boat end from the bridge and dropped the rope back onto the barge on the opposite side of the bridge to be refastened. Deeply cut grooves made by the barge ropes are still visible on some Wye bridges.[8]

'The barge's bow was bluff and the sides protected with tarpaulins so that they could carry downstream in a freshet a load which allowed only a few inches of free-board.' Most barges also carried oars to help with propulsion and poles to help push the barge over shallows, and also an anchor for 'Landing & Standing', the latter when they might need

Men towing a barge at Belmont in 1800 (a detail from the illustration on p.141)

A barge below the Doward as depicted by Edward Dayes in 1792.
The earliest images of barges and boats on the Wye appear on estate maps dating from 1721
at Hereford and Fawley, from 1755 at Wilton, on Taylor's Map of 1754 and in a survey of
New Weir in 1755

to wait out a flood or, alternatively, an increase in the river's spate to help carry them over shallows.

During the 1790s payments were made for 'housing for the men', 'drink for the men' and 'housing & hauling', suggesting that use was made of riverside overnight accommodation. On the trows, accommodation was known to be 'cramped and uncomfortable frequently cold and wet' with limited opportunities for cooking hot food. Other payments made were for 'work in the river towing', 'expenses for Handling & Wharehousing', and 'to the porter taking the bags'.[9]

Another method of transportation used for timber was to create a raft and float it downstream. On the Severn mature oak trunks for shipbuilding were carried down in floats from as early as 1575, and floats on the Wye were used from 'Hom Park to Chepstow' in 1719. Such floaters, as they were called, were unwieldy and difficult to steer and after several accidents and loss of life on the Severn during the 18th century they were discontinued, and heavy timber was instead carried on barges.[10] On the Wye, however, the method was still in use at the beginning of the 19th century when 'tree trunks were placed side by side in the water, dogs [grappling-irons] were driven in them and they were then roped together, zigzag across the raft. They were made narrow enough to pass through the bridges and were sometimes two or more sticks long'.[11]

An incident involving such a timber floater was reported in 1806. 'On Monday last, as five men were conducting a float of timber down the Wye, near Ross, in attempting to pass through Wilton Bridge, by some accident (the waters being extremely high) they

A raft or float of logs being navigated on the Severn towards the Welsh Bridge in Shrewsbury as depicted on Lord Burleigh's map of the town of c.1575

ran against one of the Piers, when three of them were instantly washed off and drowned; another was also carried off by the force of the current, but fortunately taking hold of an oar, he floated, in a most perilous situation, nearly a mile and a half down the river, when, by the humane exertions of Mr. Pearce, of this city, and two others, he was got out and his life saved.'[12]

Barge Names

Barges were named according to ownership, place and type of craft as well as for identification and registration purposes. After the Merchant Shipping Act of 1786 the owners of ships 'with a deck and of more than 15 tons burden' were required to be registered with the Customs Officers in the ship's home port. Many of the barges using the Wye were thus registered, although those built prior to 1786 or of a smaller size avoided the requirement.[13]

Named vessels were plying the Severn from as early as the 1570s, often bearing personal names or names of places near the river. From 1673 John Beale was well established in

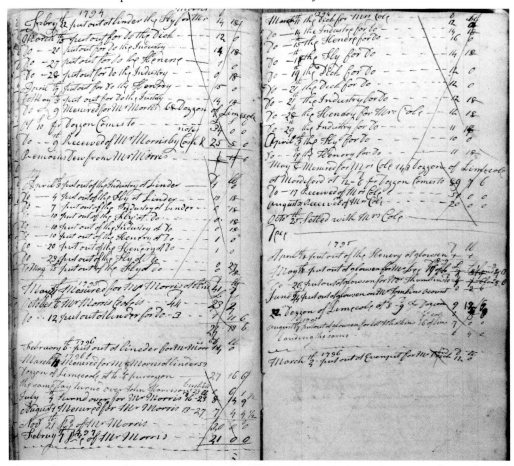

A page from unnamed barge accounts for the year 1794, which shows the names of several vessels including the Dick, Fly, Industry *and* Henery *(Henry)*

the river trade between Bewdley and Bristol using trows named *George, John* and *Margaret*. Beale was also associated with the Wye, purchasing 19 tons of pig or bar iron from Thomas Nourse of Walford. Before the end of the 17th century on the Severn there was the *Elizabeth* and *Primrose* of 1675, the *Walton* and *Joyce* of 1689 and the *Joan* of 1692. Edward Lloyd was a trowman at Madeley who owned 'One Ould Trow called the *Eastop* & all her appurtenances' and 'One Ould Barge called the *Nicholls* with all materials belonging to her'.[14]

The earliest name of a craft associated with transport on the Wye was the *Scudamore*, a galley built at Chepstow for the carrying of timber by the owner in partnership with the Scudamores at Holme Lacy. (The galley was a type of vessel known at Gloucester on the Severn between 1710 and 1764, and propelled by oars.[15]) The launch at Chepstow was an important occasion when the ship's carpenter and his men, the sail makers, rope makers and those employed in rigging the ship were all invited to an entertainment organised by a local innkeeper.[16] From 1719 this vessel carried bark from Chepstow to Cork, cordwood to the furnaces and forges at Bishopswood and Lydbrook, and timber from Holme Lacy and Fownhope to Plymouth. Presumably the *Scudamore* was therefore a sea-going vessel similar to the *York*, a galley of 1739 bound for Maryland and steered by Daniel Bridge from Ross, that would have been supplied with timber brought down the Wye in barges.[17]

Around 1719 there was also a sloop called the *George*, 'the good ship the *Tyrall* of about 300 tons' and the 90-ton *Arts of Bristol*, which were all employed in carrying timber from Chepstow.[18] An advertisement in 1725 named the '*Kent Snow* ... Burthen 90 tons, four Guns, Men answerable, now riding at Anchor in the River Wye, Chepstow, takes in Cyder, or any other goods, and the Master may be spoke with next week at Mr. Forde's at the Red-streak Tree, or at the Ship and Castle in Hereford'.[19] (Such a large vessel wouldn't have come up the Wye, but the master would have made the journey to drum up trade for his ship.) Barges recorded but not named include the 'Trows, Boats and Barges and other Vessels' mentioned as being at Hereford in 1728, the 'Barges & Boats on ye river Wye' at Wilton in 1735, and 'Wheastone's Barge', 'Wm. Yem's Barge' and 'Francis Philips Barge' of 1772 and 1773 at Whitney.[20] It would be interesting to know which barges used the 'meadow and wharf' at Fownhope in 1775, or the 'free

The **LIBERTY**, A NEW VESSEL, from NEWNHAM, Capt. Morgan, will be at CHEPSTOW the 10th inft. to take in Cyders and other goods for London.
April 3, 1777.

From the Hereford Journal *for 10 April 1777*

HEREFORD.

TO BE SOLD BY AUCTION, BY JOHN FREECE,

On Friday, the Third day of Auguft, 1798, at the dwelling-houfe of William Greenly, known by the name of the Saracen's Head, in the city of Hereford, unlefs difpofed of by private Contract,

THE BARGE VALIANT, of Hereford, meafures 50 feet on the fpear, and 13 feet on the beam; carries 30 tons, at a feet 9 inches of water.

Alfo, The BARGE DAN and ANN, of Hereford, meafures 50 feet on the fpear, and 12 feet on the beam; carries 25 tons, at a feet 5 inches of water.

The property of Daniel Pearce.

The above Barges are in complete repair, and fit for the Severn Trade.

An advertisement in the Hereford Journal *for 15 July 1798 regarding the barges* Valiant *and* Dan and Ann

mooring' at Wilton in 1780. Then there was Biss's trow – so called because of its owner – which carried rum from Bristol in 1785 and barges were mentioned at Bishopswood Wharf in 1788.[21]

Between 1791 and 1850 a range of named barges were recorded trading on the Wye between Hay and Symonds Yat. Amongst them were the *Nancy, Flora, Sally, Eliza, Prudence, Martha* and *Penelope*, which may have been named after female owners who were active in the river trade, whereas those called *William, Thomas, Henry, George, Dick* and *James* may have reflected a male ownership. Combinations such as *John and Mary, Dan and Ann, Ann and Peggy* and *Mary and Elizabeth* suggest a joint ownership. The *Farmer, Industry* and *Trader* describe the intended use of the barge, and *Wellington, Hereford, Lydney Trader* and *Monmouth* represent an association with a place; *Agincourt* possibly just nationalistic pride, or a connection with Agincourt Square in Monmouth. One can only speculate on barges named *Liberty, Fly, Macaroni, Valiant, Friends, Bolivar, Rival, Mayflower* and *Happy Returns*.[22]

The *Industry* was built at Tintern in 1772 as a 57-ton trow, 52 feet long and 16 feet wide. Between 1791 and 1804 she was used to convey coal, 'loaded on board' and towed by '11 men and boys'. The *Industry* worked together with the *Henry*, a sloop of 76 tons, and three unregistered (and so presumably small) barges called the *Fly, Dick* and *Fisherman*. The *Sally* was another of this period, a 40-ton barge, 56 feet long and 12 feet wide, built at Rhydspence near Hay around 1780. She carried coal and lime, and was recorded at both Dinedor and 'Lindor' (near Foy) in 1799. The *Flora, Farmer* and *Nancy* were lime carriers when, in December 1799, nine shillings was paid for 'New sacks lost', ten shillings for 'detaining the *Nancy* and *Flora* 1 day each' at Tintern, and five shillings for 'Taking the *Flora & Farmer* to Abbey - 10 men 6d each'.

There was a *Willan* of 1811 that carried lime and tiles, and a *William* of 1815, a 40-ton barge built at Fownhope by the Wheatstone family.[23] Between 1825 and 1827 a number of named barges plied the Wye including the *Ann*, a 30-ton barge with one mast delivering bark

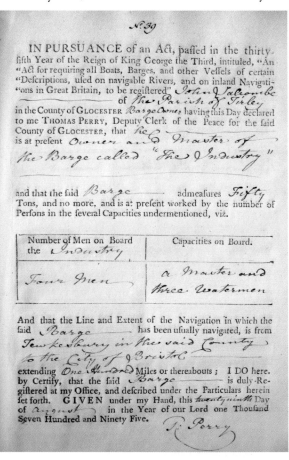

The registration certificate for the barge Industry

from Canon Bridge to Chepstow; the *James*, a 50-ton sloop carrying timber from Canon Bridge to Brockweir and Bristol; and the *Hereford*, a sloop of 54 tons carrying a mixed cargo to Hereford. In 1827 the 31-ton *Paul Pry* was introduced to the Wye as a steam-propelled barge, whilst the *Trader* was a small sloop of 16 tons measuring 31 feet long and 11 feet wide that was built at Chepstow. Although the steam barge was unsuccessful, the *Trader* was immediately used for carrying cargoes that were collected at Mordiford 'to be put onto ship' at Brockweir.[24]

From 1830 there were several barges plying the Wye downstream from Hereford with names including the *Jane* at Bishopswood, the *Water Witch* and the *Thomas and Mary* at Hereford in 1831. Two years later there was the *Mary* at Bishopswood, and the *George* at Hereford in 1834. The *Liberty* was at Hay, the *Martha* at Hereford, the *Rival* at Wilton, the *Mary and Elizabeth* at Bullinghope, the *Betsy* at Lydbrook, the *Nelson* at Fownhope and the *William* at Hereford during 1836. The *Bee* of 1837, the *Prudence* of 1845 and the *Hereford* of 1847 were at Hereford, and the *Ann and Peggy*, the *Lady Alma* and the *Monmouth Trader* were recorded at Fownhope and New Weir between 1854 and 1856.[25]

> **How a tun of wine became a ton of displacement**
>
> A ship's capacity was originally reckoned on the number of tuns of wine she would carry, a tun being a cask containing 252 old wine gallons, or 210 imperial gallons. This was expressed as so many tons burden. The tun measurement eventually became acknowledged as 1,000 cubic feet of capacity, the equivalent of a gross ton.

Accidents, Smuggling & Robbery

There were accidents reported of barges sinking, cargoes getting lost, and bargemen drowning in the Wye. From as early as 1621 there was concern over the dangers of the weirs which at that time 'presented a hindrance to boats, and a cause of deaths by drowning'.[26] In 1795 a barge sank and the 'Sail Beam left by the men' was sold for £1 15s. A year later William Jenkins 'a bargeman of Ross, in attempting to leap from the bank to a barge lying near Foy, fell into the river Wye, and was unfortunately drowned'. In 1804 a man drowned when 'a coal barge sank at Eign below Hereford', and the same year another was killed 'unloading coal at a Hereford wharf'.

The *Abbey*, originally a hoy of 48 tons that was re-registered as a trow in 1804, traded in the lower Wye as a barge under the ownership of James Madley of Walford. Under a previous owner, J. Pritchard, the *Abbey*, then working out of Tintern, 'laden with grain was swamped and run aground at Wye mouth. No lives were lost and a greater part of the cargo was saved'. Another vessel from Tintern, the *Sampson*, a barge of 45 tons registered in 1805, 'was lost on a voyage to Bristol' a few years later. In 1806 a barge sank under Wye Bridge at Monmouth and three men were drowned.[27]

An inquest was held in 1809 'on the bodies of W. Watters, captain of a barge belonging to Mr. Porter of Wilton, who was drowned in the Wye about a month since, in consequence of a pole with which he was pushing forwards a barge, breaking, and letting him in'.

An accident involving the ferry boat at Goodrich was reported in the *Hereford Journal* for 17 December 1814. Towards the end of the day some people returning from Ross hailed the boat, then on the Goodrich shore. He crossed the river and picked up his passengers, disaster striking on the return journey. 'Owing to the darkness of the night, and the rapid current of the river, Mr. Welling, the renter, being with the boat himself, the rope by she is hauled across slipped above the roller, and he was dragged overboard; yet, by clinging to the rope with his hands, he warped himself on shore; but unhappily, just as he had recovered his footing, and was looking after the fate of the boat from the quay, a stone on which he stood gave way, and he was again precipitated into the river, where, from extreme darkness, and no person being near, he perished in a dead part of the stream close to the shore. His body was not found till three hours after the accident ... The boat was carried down by current as far as the Kern, where the passengers, by laying hold of some sally boughs, stopped her further progress, and got safe on shore.'

A barge sank in 1819 near Fownhope, an accident in which five men lost their lives, and in 1825 a boat capsized at Whitchurch causing the death by drowning of James Daniels. At Monmouth a vessel capsized in 1825 with loss of life when the *Monmouth*, a snow of 111 tons, was being launched at the mouth of the Monnow. 'She lurched and threw several persons into the water, two boys being drowned.' In 1828 a barge that 'was travelling on the river Wye collided in fog, with a pier of Wilton Bridge', causing the death of Joseph Thackway of New Weir.[28]

An Inquest was held at the Green Man at Fownhope on 26 December 1826 after a fisherman had pulled out a body from the river. 'The corpse was laid out in the pub for all to see. Two witnesses gave evidence. Richard Batchelor recalled that he had been driving two horses on the tow path to pull a barge. They had called in on the right bank at Dinedor at 8.30 in the morning on Dec 8th to pick up John Philpott. As the barge moved on it was turned by the force of the current and wind, filled with water and quickly sank. The master Robert Crompton who was at the helm end managed to swim ashore but both Philpott and John Meredith were instantly drowned. Batchelor stated that all the crew were sober. John Wigley [a fisherman and boatman] gave evidence that the body had been in the water for some time and there was no other marks to suggest any other cause than drowning. The jury concluded that John Meredith had drowned instantly through suffocation.'[29]

Bargemen assisted during the floods of 1831 that caused havoc in both Hereford and Ross. 'Passengers were obliged to be conveyed in boats and carts through the currents on the road beyond St. Martin's Street' in Hereford, which was impassable to foot passengers. At Ross 'the Wye continued rapidly rising and the communication between the town and Wilton became hourly more difficult and dangerous ... In consequence of the circumstance several persons on horseback, and an individual in a cart, were precipitated into the hollow formed by the water, but they were extricated by the prompt assistance of boats and boatmen.' It was noted that despite the floods, 'several sailing boats were manoeuvring about upon sheets of water, near the town'.[30]

In 1844, during the 'ravages of a storm, the river had overflowed its banks. The meadows were flooded, and the ferries were impassable; neither Fidoe or Wigley [Fidoe was the ferryman at Hoarwithy] would venture across. Near Mordiford, a large barge was stranded; the top of the mast only was to be seen above the water; two lives were lost.'[31] Just before the arrival of the railway which ended the trade on the Wye, a flood in 1852 damaged

Barge transferring cargo at New Weir in 1815

several Hereford barges, so a subscription was commenced in the city and neighbourhood 'to raise a fund to repair some of the barges which were injured by the late flood. We feel assured, considering that the owners are poor but industrious persons, that this will meet with that assistance'.[32]

In mid January 1852, a 9-year-old boy, the son of a Mr. Levason, a dentist, was playing on the river bank below the Bridewell on Castle Green with another boy, when they tried to get into a barge or large boat moored near the shore. As he caught hold of the barge, it drifted away from the shore and he fell into the water which was then running high and fast. He was quickly carried out into the current, where no-one could help him. The body had still not been found a few days later.[33]

A fatal accident occurred in 1866 a few years after the barges had ceased plying the Wye. It concerned a pleasure boat operated by William Newton, a Ross innkeeper and boat proprietor who had conveyed the Rev. W. Temple from Ross to Welsh Bicknor. On his return to Lydbrook, William Newton met two men hauling a boat owned by John Evans and steered by Thomas Hodges. 'Newton asked them to allow him to fasten his boat to theirs, and they did so. He then got into Mr. Evans's boat, which was a large one, and the whole party proceeded towards Ross. They had not gone a mile, before the men who were pulling the boat found that something was wrong. On looking round they saw that the boat had struck against one of the salmon cribs, and that Mr. Newton was not in.' Although a diligent search was made that day, the body was not recovered until the following morning.[34]

Danger was sometimes premeditated. The trade in wine, spirits and tobacco created opportunities for smuggling, which certainly happened at Chepstow, although there is little evidence for it on the upper Wye. On the Severn 'it was generally supposed that the sailors of Bridgnorth added to their income by a little smuggling, more particularly of brandy, which they obtained out of bond from the ships at Bristol'.[35] Barges were, however, subject to forms of piracy. The *Hereford Journal* in April 1796 reported that a barge belonging to Mr. William Wall of Old Forge in Hereford, was seized by men when it was at a place called Water's Cross in the parish of Ruardean in Gloucestershire. Three of the felons were identified as William Pritchard, a basket-maker of Walford, and Thomas Burgum the elder and Thomas Burgum the younger, labourers of Lydbrook. They made away with several bushels of barley and other bags containing unspecified goods. Pritchard was caught, but escaped, and Wall offered a reward of 7 guineas for the apprehending of any of the thieves, payable on a successful prosecution.[36]

Rioting occurred in the Forest of Dean when the foresters opposed the scarcity and high price of wheat and corn which led to the Bread Riots of 1795 and 1801. These were years of unrest in the Forest (the French Revolution was underway, adding to people's fears of revolution in England), and the *Hereford Journal* reported another, larger case of piracy in April 1800. 'On Wednesday morning last, three barges laden with grain, for Bristol, were stopped on the River Wye, at Lidbrooke, by the colliers and other inhabitants of the Forest of Dean. From their numbers, and the threats of the ringleaders, it was deemed necessary to have recourse to military aid; when a detachment of the Berkshire Fencible Cavalry, quartered at Ross, proceeded to the spot, attended by the Rev. Mr. Williams, of Goodrich, one of the Magistrates of that district. The violence and clamour of the mob, precluded the possibility of reasoning with them; and the Riot Act was read, without inducing them to disperse. On the contrary, they began throwing stones, when some of the soldiers were compelled to fire in their own defence, and one of the most daring of the rioters was shot through the shoulder, but not dangerously. It was even with difficulty that the barges were then suffered to proceed on their voyage; and the mob only dispersed, under a threat of intercepting them farther down the River.'[37]

A few years later the foresters opposed the inclosing of Crown land in 1831 when, led by Warren James, the rioters were found guilty of throwing open the inclosures and were transported to Tasmania. They were later joined by a group of convicted Chartists who sailed from Chepstow to Tasmania in 1840. At Brockweir, the *Friends*, a 106-ton trow valued at £600, was destroyed by fire by a group opposing the Poor Law Amendment Act in the 1840s.[38]

3 BARGE OWNERS, MASTERS AND MEN

An incredible assortment of people from different backgrounds were involved in the river trade on the Wye from the late 17th century. They comprised four main groups – the owners, the masters or captains, the bargemen and the bow hauliers. The barge owners were mainly merchants and tradesmen having a vested interest in distributing and selling their wares, although a few are known to have been lawyers, surgeons, naval officers, and even some gentlemen; many only had a small share in a barge, whilst others were sole proprietors. The masters captained and navigated the vessels and occasionally had a part share in ownership or served jointly as owner and master. The bargemen served as the crew who were hired by the master, and the hauliers and later horse-handlers were taken on as required.

There is little evidence of women working on the barges, but women were recorded as barge owners and masters, usually inheriting the business from their deceased husbands. The women involved in the river trade included Mary Platt in 1795, Elizabeth Llewellyn in 1797 and Susannah Biss in 1835 – all from Wilton. There was Ann Crompton at Hereford in 1810, Ann Hughes at Wilton in 1811, and lower down the Wye there was Elizabeth Lambert at Monmouth in 1826, Mary Williams at Llandogo in 1825 and Susannah Chapman at Chepstow in 1810.[1]

Barge Owners

The Wye barges were mainly owned by merchants trading in goods ranging from timber and bark, coal and iron, cider and wine, to lime and stone, together with those dealing in agricultural products. The earliest known trader on the Wye was probably John Beale, active on the lower Wye in 1662 and in the 1670s on the Severn delivering pig iron from the Forest of Dean.[2] The Beales 'were probably the most dominant family in Bewdley's river trade in the 17th and 18th centuries' and had become well established by 1673 on the Severn between Bewdley and Bristol.[3] Apart from a few stray references to John Beale, few records exist of owners on the Wye until improvements were made to the navigation of the river as from the late 1600s. On the Severn, meanwhile, merchants were transporting timber and coal from as early as 1570 and during the 17th century grocers, mercers and vintners shipped grocery goods, tobacco, wine, spirits, salt, textiles and cloth.

During the early 18th century a few more barge owners associated with the Wye emerge from the records. In 1718 there was George Evans of Swansea, a ship's carpenter, who owned a sloop called the *George*, and John Hobbs, owner of the *Arts of Bristol*. William Smith, a timber merchant, and Mr. Paddison, 'a purveyor employed by the commissioners of his majesties navy', worked with the partnership of Thomas Foley and William Rea, who owned the *Scudamore* galley in the early 1700s mentioned in chapter 2.

In 1701 Luke Hughes, a 'bargeman', was admitted and sworn as a Freeman of the City of Hereford. He was the first person to establish himself as a barge proprietor at Wilton, where he was described as 'a bargeman, mariner, trowman and innholder' of the Bear – which later became the King's Head – at Wilton.[4] A few years later the first known traders to own barges in Hereford were Joseph Trumper, a glover, and Philip Symonds, a mercer. In 1725 Symonds leased a 'piece of ground formerly inclosed into a garden' at Castle Hill, where the two partners built a wharf for their 'Trows, Boats, Barges and other Vessels'.[5]

Edward and Joseph Tamplin at Whitchurch were involved in the iron-making trade in 1744, and although the type of carriage was not recorded, ore was probably transported on the river in their own barges. The following year Richard Wheatstone was shipping lime from Lydbrook, where he built a house opposite a wharf in 1759. These two names were the start of a long association by these families with trade and transport on the River Wye at Wilton, Fownhope and Whitney.[6] By 1759 William Baker had established himself as a flourishing barge owner in Hereford, occupying 'Buildings, Warehouses, Dye house Yards, Gardens and Appurtenances' where he kept his 'Trow and three Barges'.[7]

On the borders of Fownhope and Mordiford a property called the Pitthouse was leased to John Greenly, a barge owner, in 1771. The following year the owner of 'Wheatstone's Barge' was carrying timber and bark from Whitney to Chepstow, when payments were made for 'Twelve pounds Twelve shillings being in full for the carriage of fourteen Ton of bark to Chepstow' and 'Twenty eight pounds five shillings being in full for the

carriage of 28 Ton 10 feet of Timber to Chepstow'. Other barge owners based at Whitney were Francis Phillips, who received 'Seven pounds twelve shillings being in full for the carriage of 8 Ton to Chepstow at 19 shillings per Ton', and William Yem, who loaded his 'Barge now at Whitney – Fifteen Tons Timber planks'.[8]

In 1775 Nathaniel Purchas leased a 'meadow and wharf' at Fownhope that he used to trade his wines, spirits and bark.[9] He also took a part share in a barge and shipped large quantities of bark, pipes of wine, small casks, hampers, baskets and empty bottles down and up the Wye. His first known barges were the *Jupiter*, a large brigantine of 120 tons that he shared

Accounts for Nathaniel Purchas in 1795 showing charges for freighting pipes, casks and bottles of wine, as well as paying 1s 6d to men for 3 days spent in Chepstow

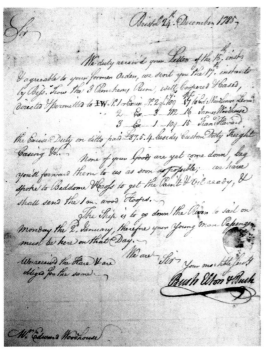

A letter from the firm of Bush, Elton and Bush in 1785 confirming a shipment that included '3 pancheons rum, well-coopered' on the Biss

An advertisement in the Hereford Journal *for 2 May 1798*

with other merchants from Chepstow and Tidenham, and the *John*, a 90-ton brigantine shared with Chepstow and Newnham merchants.[10]

During the last two decades of the 18th century several barge owners were recorded, including Daniel Pearce from 1783 with his fleet of four at Hereford. John Jones of Ross part owned *Fanny*, a 125-ton brigantine, in 1784 and the *Wilton*, a sloop of 65 tons that had been built at Chepstow in 1785. Meanwhile the firm of Bush, Elton and Bush from Bristol were shipping consignments of rum in their barges up the Wye and Lugg destined for Edward and James Woodhouse at Leominster.[11] In 1793 two other barge owners emerged in Hereford: James Biss, a corn factor and carrier, and Jonathan Crompton, who was involved in the porter trade.[12] At Wilton, William Porter, although a corn factor, was shipping deal, cloth and lime in 1795 in a barge named the *Wilton* which he shared with other traders.[13]

Chepstow's timber trade flourished during the Napoleonic Wars and John Bowsher, James Hodges and Richard Watkins formed a firm which they claimed 'supplied the government with one half of the timber used in building ships for the navy'. Bowsher, Hodges and Watkins 'had shares in nearly one hundred ships during the years when Chepstow's prosperity was at its height'.[14] During the late 1790s the company was shipping quantities of timber and bark from Wilton; '11 ton from Hoarwithy' and 'Elm Planks from Foy' to their timber yards at Chepstow.[15] Their vessels, often shared with others, included the *Fanny*, the first brigantine to be registered at Chepstow, the *Charming Peggy*, a sloop of 63 tons, and the *Ann* of 67 tons.[16]

Other Chepstow timber traders and barge owners involved in the upper Wye were the Buckle family. George Buckle had a wharf in Hereford from 1801 and was transporting burr stones (mill stones made from a particular rock imported from France) up the Wye a few years later. Although he was the sole owner of the *Perseverance*, a brigantine of 85 tons, this

An advertisement of 1822 for the 'conveyance' of goods from Hereford to Bristol

family of shipbuilders, wine merchants, maltsters, ropemakers and coopers owned many vessels. In 1809 he was shipping timber from Wilton and Canon Bridge. This year also saw George Morse trading from his wharves at Lydbrook using the *Eliza*, his 40-ton barge, and Henry Pewtner shipping goods on the *Betsey*, a 37-ton barge, from New Weir.[17]

The last years of the upper Wye navigation was monopolised by Messrs. Easton, Swift, Cooke, Pearce, Pulling and Bunning of Hereford. In 1822 there was a weekly 'Conveyance by Water to Bristol, John Easton's Barges, from the Castle wharf, and John Cooke's, and Swift & Co.'s, from the Commercial wharf'. Downstream at Bishopswood there was James Ward, a coal merchant and part-owner of barges from 1823. Between 1825 and 1827 the Liverpool & Bristol Company operated regular 'traders' up and down the Wye. In 1847 Messrs. Pulling were importing wines and spirits on their schooner the *Friends*, and the *Ann* mastered by Charles Wheatstone.[18]

A barge moored at Hereford

A barge at Hereford in the mid 19th century, as the trade is declining

Barge Masters

Little is known about the lives of the Wye barge masters who were often co-owners and traders, but their way of life would have been similar to those working on other rivers and a useful account relates to masters on the Thames at Taplow towards the end of the 18th century. Here, 'the master of any vessel breaking the law could be fined up to £5' and at the beginning of the 19th century the steersman (captain) was assisted 'by bargemen, who with large ashen poles, from 14 to 19 ft. in length, with incredible dexterity, keep the barges in the proper navigation channel. The occupation of a bargeman requiring not only strength and activity, but considerable experience and local knowledge, is very lucrative. The number of persons requisite to work the largest barges, is six men and one boy. One of the men, who has the care of the vessel, and who defrays the tonnage etc., is called cost bearer, or captain.'[19]

From 1719 on the Wye there were a few known masters of timber barges that were associated with the river at Chepstow. Daniel Disney of Yarmouth was 'master of the good ship *Tyrall*' in 1719, and in 1721 Robert Ford was 'master of the ship *Scudamore*' succeeded by John Whittaker 'in going master of the *Scudamore* galley', while Samuel Jones, a mariner, in 1726 served 'as mate and pilot'. A few years later the Hughes, Tamplin and Wheatstone families appear on a long list of masters and trowman trading on the Wye.

The Hughes family came from Wilton and Monmouth. Luke Hughes, the barge owner met with earlier, may have overstretched himself as he took out a couple of bonds in

An advertisement in the Hereford Journal *for 23 April 1772*

1752 and 1754 for £140 and £40. After his death in 1755, his son William inherited 'his messuages, tenements at Wilton known as the New Bear and the Turnpike House' but his river trade was taken over by Thomas, who in 1772 was advertising for barges 'to convey a large quantity of plank and converted navy timber from Whitney to Chepstow for Mr. Stallard at Hardwick'.[20] Between 1795 and 1800, Thomas was master of the *Farmer*, and after his death in 1817 his son continued to run the Bear Inn until he retired to Gloucester in 1824. It is not known whether grandson James was involved in the river trade whilst victualler of the Bear at Wilton, but in 1810 and 1811 a James Hughes of Ross was shipping slate, pantiles and deals from Bristol, and a Mrs. Ann Hughes from Wilton was conveying agricultural produce.[21]

In 1761 the barge owner Edward Tamplin was associated with Edward Llewellyn, a trowman at Wilton, where Tamplin had built a 'quay or landing place' and a warehouse used by Elizabeth Llewellyn in 1780. Whether or not of the same immediate family, a Thomas Tamplin in 1791 was master of the *Wilton*, a 65-ton sloop, and the *Endeavour*, a 65-ton trow, in 1798. He was followed by two other Tamplins as masters: William in 1827 and John in 1829.[22]

From the late 17th century the Wheatstone family were involved in the river trade as owners, masters and traders. At Lydbrook, Richard Wheatstone was active in the iron-making and coal industries from 1745, built a house with a wharf in 1759 and shipped coal from his wharves in 1762. John, George and Richard Wheatstone were transporting timber, bark and planks to Chepstow from Whitney and Hardwick in 1772 when George Wheatstone was 'master' of a barge that worked out of Lydbrook before the family moved to Fownhope.[23]

From 1774 John Wheatstone leased a riverside site at Even Pits in Fownhope. Over 30 years later 'uncle John Whetstone', who was freighting coal in 1807, became master and co-owner of the *Eliza*, a 40-ton barge. During the next fifty years the Wheatstones were based in Fownhope at Even Pits, the Anchor Inn and Holyfast Croft. They served as masters and owners of the 40-ton *William*, the 46-ton *Mary and Elizabeth*, the 30-ton *Ann*, and the 17-ton *Nelson*. At Even Pits, Richard and William Wheatstone built three barges, and in 1849 Charles Wheatstone was master of the *Ann*, shipping chopped bark to Chepstow.[24]

Other prominent barge masters included the Crompton/Crumpton families who were associated with the Severn river trade from at least 1672, carrying iron ore in the 1720s,

An advertisement in the Hereford Journal
for 17 June 1801

From Richard Wheatstone's accounts for 1745

A receipt issued to Charles Wheatstone,
master of the Ann, *for bark carried*
for Messrs. Pulling & sons of Hereford in 1849

operating a ferry and running a public house in the Severn Gorge.[25] Jonathan Crompton kept the Crown and Anchor at Goodrich in 1728, but does not appear to have had any interest in the river trade, whereas Jonathan Crumpton of Mordiford owned barges and boats left in his will of 1774. At Hereford, John Crumpton was a bargeman and victualler at the Anchor in 1784 and Jonathan and Adam Crompton were barge masters in the 1790s.[26] By 1808 Jonathan was owner of the 33-ton *Kitty* built at Hereford and Henry Crompton was the master. Quite how the various members of the family were related is unclear.[27]

Although the Pearce family were connected with the river at Hereford, where Daniel Pearce was a barge owner with a wharf near the Wye Bridge, it was the Pearces at Lydbrook who were the barge masters. James Pearce was master of several barges from 1794 and in 1806 purchased land at Lydbrook from the Hill Court estate after the death of Jane Clarke, where he created a wharf.[28] He still occupied the premises in 1808 when 'two wharfs adjoining the River Wye situate at Lidbrook' were offered for sale. Before his death in 1827 he may have been the Pearce who was master of the 129-ton snow called the *William* and of the 44-ton barge called the *Victory*.[29]

After the opening of the horse towing-path in 1809,

William Hoskins and Thomas Jones were masters of the first horse-drawn barges that came 'through Wilton Bridge' in 1811. The barges named *Henry* and *Fanny* were hauled by 'two horses each' and carried coal from Lydbrook to Hereford. During the 1820s Hoskins was carrying timber from Hereford on the *Eliza* to the Chapmans' timber yard at Chepstow, and returning with wines and spirits on the *James* for Messrs. Pulling in Hereford. He also shipped timber from Canon Bridge on the *Charles* to John Easton, a timber merchant at Hereford.[30]

Other masters included William Watters, captain of a barge belonging to Mr. Porter of Wilton, who drowned in the Wye. The barge that he fell from is not recorded, but in 1806 he had been master of the *Briton*, a 25-ton sloop.[31] There was Francis Goodman, who carried goods on the *Ann*, the *Trader* and the *Wellington* from Hereford and Mordiford in the 1820s. He became master of the 32-ton barge called the *George* in 1834 and the 17-ton *Nelson* in 1836. One of the last masters on the Wye was 'Captain Prout' of 1846 from a family of masters and mariners who had worked the Wye from at least 1817 and had purchased the 79-ton *Duchess of Gloucester* in 1836 and the 59-ton schooner the *George and Francis* in 1850.[32]

Bargemen and hauliers

The bargemen and hauliers have proved even harder to trace, but stray references in leases, sale particulars, quarter sessions, newspaper reports, parish registers, freemen lists and census returns have located a few.[33] The first bargemen recorded on the upper Wye were William and Edward Williams in 1696, and Luke Hughes and William Welch in 1701, when the latter paid £10 for his freedom of the City of Hereford.[34]

On the Severn the bargemen were 'feared as dangerous, untrustworthy and inefficient, but they resisted all attempts to replace them with horses. In 1831 they behaved so badly at Bewdley that the Riot Act had to be read and a detachment of Scots Greys called in to restore order'. Delays in their journeys 'led to the trowmen's deserved reputation for dishonesty.' Because there was little room to store food and drink for the crew aboard a heavily laden trow, the men would quite possibly tap their cargoes for alcoholic beverages, make forays to harvest vegetables and poach rabbits and pheasants from the riverside.[35] Similar behaviour seems to have occurred on the Wye. At Hoarwithy trespass by 'trampling or walking over meadow-grounds' and illegal mooring of barges became such a problem in 1779 that the landowners announced they would 'commence actions against every person' found committing these offences. Another occurrence of trespass was recorded at Wilton in 1811, when Thomas Powell, master of Jonathan Hoskins' barge, led two horses 'a considerable way further in

TO BARGEMEN.

BARGEMEN wanting employment, will meet with encouragement, by applying to Mr. Davis, Clerk to the Coal Company, Hereford; or Mr. John Harrison, at Lidbrook.

N. B. A few steady Men, of good character, acquainted with the Navigation of the Wye, are wanted, as Masters of Barges, who will be treated with on liberal terms.

An advertisement looking for bargemen carried in the Hereford Journal *on 18 November 1801*

The former Anchor Inn at Hoarwithy in 1900

the Withybed meadow than they are allowed by the Act of Parliament in the Presence of William Thomas, William Price Waggoner and William Charles. A stake [was] driven in the ground at the time by William Price in the Presence of Mr. Thomas to show how far the horses went and Mr. Hoskins ordered the boy who led the horses to lay a land measure.'[36] At Hereford several bargemen were charged with 'stealing ropes, shafts etc. from different barges', something known to be a common practice in 1824.[37]

In 1804 Charles Heath noted that 'a curious custom prevails at all the ports on the River Severn, but only at Monmouth on the Wye, between the owners and the watermen. Every man, when hired for a voyage receives a pint of ale, as earned for his services, which is called Mugging, and if he does not perform the labour stipulated for, he is liable to three months imprisonment. Also, if the master refuses afterwards to employ the bargeman, the servant has power to demand the wages from him, as tho' he had performed the voyage.' The wages at that date were £1 8s per man to take cargo from Hereford to Chepstow, unload, and then return.[38] In 1830 the pay from Bishopswood to Brockweir wharf was 10s 6d, to Chepstow 16s 6d and Hereford 13s 6d. Bow hauliers were paid 7s or 9s per voyage depending on the load and state of the river, whilst the rate for horses from Lydbrook to Hereford varied from £2 to £2 10s for two.[39]

During the voyage the master and his crew would live on the barge sleeping in rolled sails or lie on straw-covered benches sheltered by a canvas awning on hooped poles in an area at the stern. Some warmth and means of heating food was provided by a protected brazier or a clay-lined hearth. As there was little room on board apart from this area in the stern and a small deck at the bows, the hauliers were usually hired on a daily basis as required, to avoid accommodating the men at night.[40] Alternatively the bargees could seek food, drink and shelter in local beer and cider houses that flourished along the waterways, but the valuable cargoes had to be guarded, a job usually taken on by young boys or disabled men.[41] Thus, along the Wye from Chepstow to Glasbury, inns, taverns, and cider houses lined the banks of the river at regular intervals. Those with names reflecting a definite association with the river trade were the Boat at Chepstow of 1789, and the Ship Anchor, Sloop, Severn Trow and Waterman's Boat at Tintern, Brockweir, Llandogo and Monmouth in the mid 19th century. At Goodrich and Ross there was the Boat, Crown & Anchor and Hope & Anchor in the 18th century, and at Foy the Boatman's Rest and the Anchor & Can served the bargemen in the mid 19th century. At King's Caple the Old Boar was established in 1696, the same time as the Anchor opened on the opposite bank at Hoarwithy in anticipation of the river trade. The Anchor at Fownhope was of a later date, but the Anchor & Can and the Ship in Hereford were recorded in the early 1800s. Further upstream there were Boat named inns which also catered for those crossing the river at Sugwas in 1818, at Byford in 1850 and at Whitney in 1801, the latter kept by Thomas Jones. There was also a Ship at Hay in 1815, and pubs flourished at Rhydspence, Llowes and Glasbury, although they did not bear nautical names. Along the Lugg there was the Crown and Anchor of 1813 at Lugwardine, and at Leominster the Anchor of 1830 and the Old Iron Boat Inn.[42]

As for the size of the crew, whilst between four and six men was considered normal, more specifically it was observed that '5 men can return with a barge unladen from Brockweir to Monmouth, but it requires the proportion of 15 men to 25 tons to haul it up when laden'.

The Hope & Anchor above the Dock at Ross

In the autumn of 1791 eleven men were required to haul the *Fly* carrying lime from Eign in Hereford, eleven men and one boy to haul the *Industry*, and nine men and one boy to haul the *Dick*. From these accounts it is 'noted that the same barge is listed after only three or four days' interval indicating that the vessel was in continuous use. Longer periods of absence in the accounts can be explained either by the barge carrying someone else's cargo, or lying idle through lack of cargo or due to poor river conditions'.[43]

An interesting account has survived from 1804 of an 81-ton sloop called the *Amity* which sailed into Chepstow to unload iron ore and reload with bark. The costs associated with the visit to Chepstow were listed as follows: pilotage £1, invoicing at the Custom House 2s 6d, discharging 6d per ton, allowance for discharging the ore 17s 4d, men employed for loading bark 3d per day, an allowance of 19s 6d (though for what is not mentioned), clearance at the Custom House £3 4s 10d, dockage 6s 8d and harbour dues 2s 4d. For a stay of 15 days at Chepstow the provisions for the crew included one hundred weight of potatoes costing 3s, greens 4d, half a hundred weight of bread 10s 6d, 45 lbs of beef at 5½d per lb, 10 lbs of salt 3d, 6 lbs of treacle 5½d and two cases of small beer.[44]

An account of 1805 states that the Wye barges were capable of carrying from 20 to 30 tons, but that this was reduced to between 13 and 16 tons when the draught was only 20 inches. Those which traded from Brockweir to Hereford carried 10 tons, had a master and four men with the boat, and five men more (possibly hauliers), paid at 15s each for 2½ to 3 days work. If the boats carried 20 tons, they hired ten men, or one man to every 2 tons. In conveying coal from Lydbrook to Hereford, extra hauliers were required at the rate of 9s per man for the one and a half to two day voyage. Before the passing of the Horse Towing Path Act of 1809 it was considered that one horse and a boy would be equivalent to six men hauling and therefore reduce the cost of conveying coal from Lydbrook to Hereford, but there is very little evidence to support the use of horses.[45]

Bargemen seeking employment were dependent on the state of the river, the quietest periods being during the summer months when the river was shallow and during the winter floods which made the Wye difficult to navigate. The men often had other seasonal occupations and generally lived an itinerant life as they sailed barges downstream as far as Bristol. They may have been hired at town and village wharves along the Wye, especially at Brockweir where cargoes were transhipped and at Mordiford where coal was measured for the occasional delivery up the Lugg. In the lower Wye it 'was quite a custom for a cart from Monmouth to meet barges at Bigsweir and take off the crew so they could reach their homes for the night. They were taken back the next morning so that the voyage could be resumed.'[46]

Amongst the bargemen at Hereford were Francis Price of 1719 married to Mary Gwillim; Francis Thomas, a carpenter in 1719 described as a bargeman in 1738; Thomas Roberts of 1739; William Symonds in 1753; William Baker in 1759, whose widow Elizabeth was left a legacy of £50 by Edward Cox; William Kyte of 1761; William White, also a victualler in 1761; John Greenway in 1766; John Vaughan of 1767 and William Davies in 1768. A rather shady character in 1770 was Richard Penny, sometimes known as Garnons, who owed John Darke a mercer '£2 6s & upwards for goods sold and delivered'. In 1789 Jude Preece, a bargeman of St. Owen in Hereford, received '£1 of the interest of the late Duke of Chandos donation of £500 interest for the poor Freemen of the City', but his 'eldest surviving son' became a labourer and a freeman of the city in 1820.

Outside the city there were Richard Probert of Hoarwithy, the eldest son of a staymaker in 1767; John Dale of Fownhope in 1771, who also worked as a labourer; William Crumpton of Brockweir in 1784; John Davis of Fownhope in 1789; Edward Moore, a bargeman working at Wilton for Elizabeth Llewellyn who left him £5 in her will of 1791; and William Jenkins of Ross who in 1796 'attempting to leap from the bank, to a barge lying near Foye, fell into the River Wye, and was unfortunately drowned' leaving 'a wife and two children'.[47] In 1811 another drowning was that of Edward Bayton, son of William, working at New Weir.[48]

As the 19th century progressed and navigation on the upper Wye declined, there was a notable decrease in the number of men associated with the barge trade. At Lugwardine there was Mr. Eddy, 'whose occupation is entered in the parish register as that of a mariner'. In 1841 John Thirkil was a 50-year-old bargeman at Walford, Samuel Terry a boatman at Fawley, Richard and William Wheatstone at Fownhope and William Goode, a 35-year-old bargeman living at Wyeside in Brilley. Ten years later at Fownhope there was William Tyler living with his wife at the Warehouse, William Wheatstone still living near the Brewery, and at Symonds Yat in Whitchurch parish there were 'two watermen and a barge master'.[49]

4   CARGOES SHIPPED ON THE WYE

Although John Taylor had commented that the people of Hereford were deprived of urgently needed coal in 1641, it was several years after the Civil War that the navigation on the Wye enabled barges to trade on the upper Wye to Hereford, Hay and up the Lugg to Leominster. From the end of the 17th century therefore, wharves were developed from which 'large quantities of wheat, barley, bark, lime, poles, hoops, seeds, timber, cheese, beer, cider, flax, paper and many other items including household furniture were transported down to Wilton, Monmouth, Chepstow, Bristol and onto Plymouth'. Some goods were taken down the Wye and up the Severn to Stourport. Goods brought upstream included coal, bricks, wine, rags and junk (old ropes) which were used for making paper.[1]

Coal and Iron

At the end of the 17th century it was estimated that 250,000 tons of coal per annum were shipped nationwide by river, and that 3,650 tons of coal were required each year by Hereford for industrial and domestic use. It was calculated that if transported by river, coal would sell for 'no more than fifteen shillings a ton – half the price charged if it came by road transport'.[2] Although coal was taken down the Wye from Lydbrook during the late 17th century, it was not until around 1719 that it was brought upstream into Herefordshire. From 1741 the Free Miners of the Forest of Dean who had their own barges were given preference in 'carrying their trade' under the mine law court regulating traffic on the Wye.[3] Certainly from 1744 William Jones, William Stevens, William Green, Thomas Morgan, John and William Mathews and Thomas Davis were recorded as colliers delivering coal either by land or river.[4]

The coal was of several different grades including fire coal, smith coal and lime coal, which, together with charcoal, were used for the iron-making and lime-burning industries. The Wye was well suited for iron-making, with motive power for hammers and bellows provided not just by the flow of the main river but also its tributaries such as the Angidy at Abbey Tintern, the Garren at Whitchurch and the Lodgegrove at Bishopswood. During dry seasons a water supply was stored in mill ponds on the Angidy and Lodgegrove. There was a ready supply of charcoal made in coppice woodlands, lime for flux from nearby limestone quarries and ore delivered by mule pack and river,[5] combined with access to coal

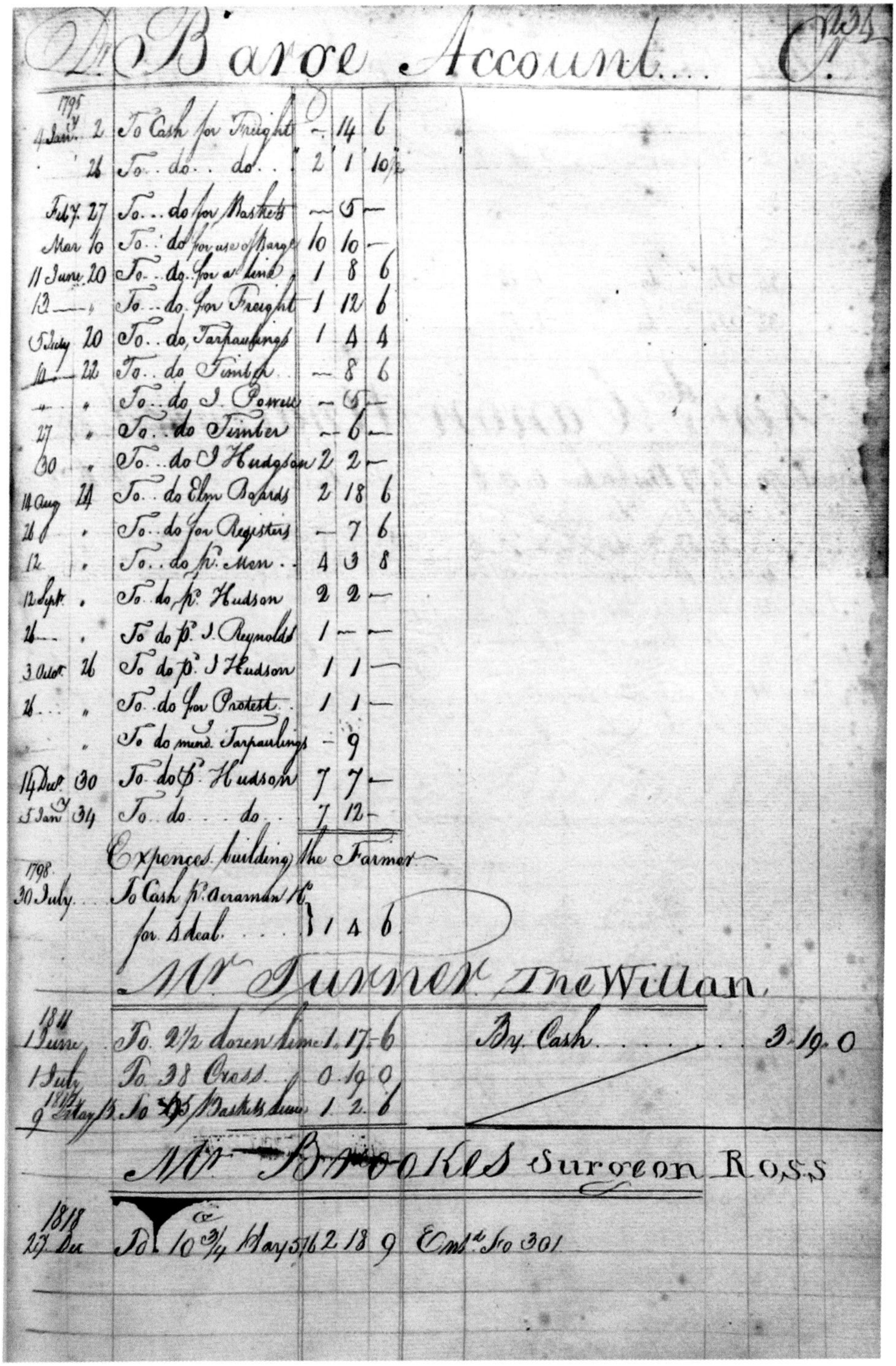

Barge Account...

1795				
Jan 2	To Cash for Freight	—	14	6
26	To.. do.. do..	2	1	10½
Feby 27	To... do for Baskets	—	5	
Mar 10	To.. do for use of Barge	10	10	
June 20	To.. do.. for a Line	1	8	6
13	To.. do for Freight	1	12	6
July 20	To.. do, Tarpaulings	1	4	4
22	To.. do Timber	—	8	6
	To.. do J. Powell	—	5	
27	To.. do Timber	—	6	
30	To.. do J Hudson	2	2	—
Aug 14	To.. do Elm Boards	2	18	6
16	To.. do for Registers	—	7	6
12	To.. do S. Men..	4	3	8
Sept	To.. do R. Hudson	2	2	
26	To do p. J. Reynolds	1	—	
Octr 26	To do p. J Hudson	1	1	
26	To.. do for Protest	1	1	
	To do mend. Tarpaulings	—	9	
Decr 30	To do p. Hudson	7	7	—
Jan 31	To.. do... do...	7	12	—
	Expences building the Farmer			
1798 30 July	To Cash p. Acraman & Co. for 5 deal...	3	1 4	6

Mr Turner The Willan

1811						
1 June	To 2½ dozen lime	1.17.6	By Cash..........	3. 19. 0
1 July	To 38 Cross	0.10.0		
9 May	To 25 Baskets due	1.2.6		

Mr Brookes Surgeon Ross

1811					
27 Dec	To 10 ¾ Hay 5/6	2 18 9	Entd. to 301	

*A page from the barge accounts listing deliveries of tarpaulins, lime and timber,
together with the names of people for whom goods were transported,
as well as 'Expences building the Farmer', a barge*

150

1745. Per Contra Cr £ s D

April 1st | By Halling Pigg Iron from wey & bar Iron to wey as ⅌ Note .. | 10 „ 14 „ 1½
July 2 | By Halling &c as ⅌ Note .... £ | 10 „ 12 „ 11
Sepr 10 | By a Rope &c .... | 1 „ 5 „ —
Octobr 7th | By Halling &c as ⅌ note .... £ | 5 „ 4 „ 7

A list of expenses in taking iron to the Wye for onward transport,
as well as for 'halling' (hauling) goods in 1745

from the Forest of Dean. Apart from the forges and furnaces in the lower Wye, there were iron-making sites on the river in Herefordshire at Bishopswood, Whitchurch, New Weir and Carey.

Several iron-works in the Forest of Dean, the Wye Valley and Herefordshire were controlled by the Foley Partnership which was established in the late 17th century by

A barge and boatyard at New Weir

Thomas Foley of Witley in Worcestershire, an industrial empire that passed to his second son Paul, a barrister, later of Stoke Edith in Herefordshire. In 1704 William Rea joined the partnership and in 1709 he became the managing partner, building a house for himself in Monmouth. Several years later, as a result of buying timber from the Scudamores at Holme Lacy, losses were suffered which left Rea in debt. This led to a series of Exchequer suits begun by Thomas Foley against William Rea, who was sacked in 1725, although the case lingered on until 1731.[6]

Between 1744 and 1746 the raw materials required for iron-working were provided by James Price and John Kear, who were paid for the delivery of 'Fire Cole' and by George White, who supplied 'Fire Cole for ye use of Lidbrook Forges' and the forges at Redbrook. Some goods went by road, some by the river, as entries in various barge accounts show: 'From Hom to Redbrook', 'Halling Pigg iron from Wey & bar Iron to Wey', 'Coles from Hom lacy to Lidbrook', '50 Tons of pig Iron by Freight' from the New Furnace, 'from the Boat to the Forge'.[7] Some of the transportation on the river was carried out by Edward Tamplin from Wilton where he had built a warehouse and a quay, and by Richard Wheatstone who was later associated with the river trade at Whitney, on the upper reaches of the navigation towards Hay.[8]

By 1767 coal was being unloaded at Hereford and at Fownhope and in 1770 it was reported that at 'Lydbrook is a large wharf where coals are shipped for Hereford and other places'. The barges operating from Lydbrook might have been of a distinctive design, though more likely they were simply adapted to the needs of handling their dirty ware.[9] By

The house that William Rea built for himself in Monmouth

1797 Lydbrook wharf was large and extensive, being the base for an expanding trade in coal to Ross, Hereford and elsewhere on the river, a business that involved a Mr. Thompson, James Teague and George Morse.[10] The barge accounts dating from this period also show that James Hughes, Mr. Prosser and Mrs. Wiltshire were shipping coal from Wilton, and at Hereford there was Mr. Pearce.

At Lugwardine on the Lugg, the corn grist mill and weir at Tidnor had not been destroyed by the navigation trustees and by 1776 had become an iron forge. 'Pig iron was brought by barge from the Forest of Dean and made into merchant iron bar [i.e. in finished bars, ready for sale]. During the Napoleonic wars there was an intense demand for naval equipment, and it is believed that some of the huge anchors and chains were made at Tidnor' and either carried by packhorses or freighted downstream to Mordiford and along the Wye to Chepstow and Bristol.[11]

From 1809 William Porter from Wilton, although a corn factor, was involved with Charles Bonnor, also from Wilton, in shipping small loads of coal to Wyeside wharves in Herefordshire and larger amounts to Bristol. Thomas Pearce and Mr. Davies, meanwhile, shipped lime and hard coal to Hereford. In 1811 Mr. Almond was selling coal at Hereford, the accounts indicating that he used horse-drawn barges, and coal was also transported as far as Lugg Bridge mills.[12]

In 1822 there were four coal merchants in Hereford, but as no known accounts survive for this period it is unclear how much of the coal was shipped from the Forest of Dean along the Wye or overland from south Wales. A horse-drawn tramway had reached Hay transporting coal from south Wales, and another eventually reached Hereford in 1829. In 1835 a visitor wrote: 'We saw a considerable number of barges and other craft moored at Hereford, when we were told that some of these vessels, drawing very little water, could, at certain seasons go twenty-five miles higher up, or nearly to the Hay. At other times, however, when the river is low, they have some difficulty even in getting as far as Hereford. Most of the coal and wood consumed in that city and its neighbourhood are brought up in barges from Bristol, Chepstow, and the Forest of Dean, after a swell in the river; and the inhabitants occasionally export by the same conveyance, their excellent Herefordshire cider.'[13]

Timber and Bark

Timber for the Royal Navy and bark for tanning were amongst the earliest recorded cargoes on the Wye. Tanning was a long and complicated process which converted raw hides into leather. Hides were brought to the tanyards where they were washed then soaked in lime pits to aid the removal of flesh, fat and hair. Before tanning, the pelts were de-limed then put through a series of tan pits full of solutions made from ground bark and water. After further washing the hides were taken to drying lofts, then to the currier, who made the final touches to the leather ready for the shoe and boot makers, saddlers, harness and glove makers.

The Scudamores of Holme Lacy made payments in 1698 for felling, cutting the cord and squaring the timber in their woods, to make rope 'to tow Timber downe the Water', and for 'halling Tymber to Wye'.[14] In 1701 Thomas Pennoyre agreed to sell 500 cords of timber

By the Nett Produce of the following
Woods Viz.ᵗ
Hom Lacy Park Timber Cut down in
1750, and Converted as follows.
by Mr. Thomas Griffitts in 1750 & 1751 _____ 1,018.11.2½
by the Commissioners of the Navy as pᵉ Contract
with them, sent to Plymouth Yard _____ 2,399.14.8½
by the Nett Produce of the Offal of saidᵉ
Timber _____ 1,130.13.7

Records of timber being felled at Holme Lacy and being sent to Plymouth in the 1750s

at Hardwick to Thomas Church and Samuel Bullock of Hereford. It was measured and turned into charcoal with provision made for the 'carrying away of the coles'.[15] Oak bark was supplied from the local woods and from 1713 taken downstream to Chepstow from where it was shipped to supply the rapidly expanding Irish tanning industry, Chepstow quickly gaining pre-eminence in this trade.[16] From around 1715 coppice bark from Chase Wood and Penyard Park was 'conveyed in barges down the river Wye to Chepstow and thence to Ireland and sold'. There was also a thriving tanning industry along the Wye itself. Bark houses were situated at many places along the banks of the Wye, including Tintern, Brockweir, Llandogo, Redbrook, Monmouth, Wilton, Hoarwithy and Fownhope. In late April and May the bark was stripped from the trees and made into large ricks, where women were employed to strip off the moss and outer skin. The bark was then taken into the bark house, where men cut it into pieces measuring about four inches in length. The chopped bark was then conveyed to the tanners by barges which could carry 20 to 25 tons of chippings, according to the state of the river.[17]

In 1719, when timber was being transhipped at Chepstow for the Foley and Rea partnership, there was 'timber out of Hom Park' and from the Fownhope woods, which were shipped either as cordwood for the lower Wye forges and furnaces or down to Chepstow and 'thence sent to Plymouth for the use of the navy'. The wood was also used for making hoops, laths and trenail pins (wooden pegs that swell when wet) for shipbuilding.[18]

During the 1720s and 1730s large amounts of money were recorded from the sale of timber from the Scudamores' woods in Herefordshire, including an entry in 1721 for £2,143 17s 1½d 'By Navy bills', and £660 paid in 1738 'By estimation Sixty Acres by wood measured 21 foot to the Lug fifty five Acres at 12 per acre'. Other accounts reveal 'Halling timber to Redbrook £6 11s' in 1744, '109 cords of wood £22 18s' and 'Cordwood as of Redbrook £118 11s' in 1745. Timber in Holme Lacy Park was felled in 1750 and purchased for £1,018 11s 2½d by 'the Commissioners of the Navy as per contract with them sent to Plymouth Yards', which would have been sent down the Wye to Chepstow and transhipped to Plymouth.[19] On the Lugg, 'cordwood and timber were conveyed downstream from Hampton Court' in 1756.[20]

46

Whitney Bridge in 1815

In the early 1770s John Stallard, a descendant of Thomas Pennoyre, was selling timber and bark from his woods in Hardwick and Whitney to Jaques and Dixon in Chepstow. During 1772 and 1773 tons of timber, planks, cordwood and chopped bark were shipped to Chepstow by the barges of William Yem, Francis Phillips and the Wheatstone family. Payments were made for hauling, measuring, cutting cordwood, paying the bargemen, surveying, squaring, carriage and delivery.[21] The first bridge at Whitney was built in 1774

Timber stacked at Whitney sawmills in 2011

Oak, Elm, Ash & Beech Timber.

HEREFORDSHIRE.

TO BE

SOLD by AUCTION

At the Beaufort Arms, Inn, Monmouth,

BY RICHARD BURTON,

On Saturday the Seventeenth day of JANUARY, 1824,

Between the Hours of FOUR & SIX in the Afternoon,

SUBJECT TO CONDITIONS OF SALE TO BE THEN PRODUCED,

THE

FOLLOWING VALUABLE

TIMBER

IN LOTS.

LOT 1.

No. 67 Maiden Oak Timber Trees, numbered with red paint, from 20 to 80, inclusive, growing on the Yew Tree Estate, in the parish of Garway.

LOT 2.

Eighty-nine Maiden Oak Timber Trees, numbered from 1 to 19, and from 87 to 156, growing on the above estate.

LOT 3.

Twenty Oak Pollards, numbered from I to 20, Sixteen Ash Trees, numbered from I to 16, and Ten Beech Trees, numbered from I to 10 ; all growing on the above Estate.

LOT 4.

Thirty-nine Maiden Oak Timber Trees, numbered from I to 39, and Thirty-six Oak Pollards, numbered from I to 36, growing on the New Ditch Estate, in the parish of Much-birch.

LOT 5.

Ninety-three Elm Timber Trees, numbered from I to 93 and Two Lime Trees, numbered from I to 2, growing on the last mentioned Estate.

LOT 6.

Thirty-eight Maiden Oak Timber Trees, numbered from I to 38, and Four Oak Pollards, numbered from I to 4, growing on the Bridge Estate, in the parish of Lanwarn.

LOT 7.

Forty-eight Elm Timber Trees, numbered from one to 48, Twenty-six Ash Trees, numbered from I to 26, One Ash Pollard and One Poplar Tree, growing on the last mentioned Estate.

LOT 8.

Fourteen Elm Timber Trees, numbered from I to 14, growing at Town's End Cottage, One Maiden Oak, growing at the Grove, Nine *Maiden Oak Timber Trees,* numbered from I to 9, One Oak Pollard, Nineteen *Elm Timber Trees,* numbered from I to 19, and 3 *Ash Trees* numbered from I to 3, growing on an Estate occupied by Mr. Rowland Walters, situate in the parish of Lanwarn.

LOTS 1, 2, 3, are situated near a good Turnpike Road, and distant about Seven Miles from Monmouth, and Ross. Lots 4, 5, 6, 7, 8, are distant about two or three Miles from the Navigable River Wye.

The above Trees are of very Fine Dimensions, Remarkably Good, and will be found worthy the attention of SHIP BUILDERS, TIMBER MERCHANTS, &c.

For a View of the Lots, Apply to the Respective *Tenants,* on the different Estates, and for further Particulars, to the *AUCTIONEER, MONMOUTH.*

AWBREY, PRINTER, MONMOUTH.

at a time when 'barges full of Forest of Dean coal were regularly coming up the river as far as Glasbury and often these barges would be lashed together for the return journey so that they could carry whole tree trunks down to the river mouth'.[22]

During the Napoleonic Wars 'John Bowsher, James Hodges and Richard Watkins owned or had shares in nearly one hundred ships during the years that Chepstow's prosperity was at its height and the timber yards occupied most of the river bank'. The earliest known freighting of timber, planks, bark and hurdles to Messrs. Bowsher and Hodges dates from 1795, the same year that Nathaniel Purchas, brewer and wine and spirit merchant, was shipping bark and hoops from Fownhope to Chepstow, and John Hatton and Richard Hole were delivering timber to the Young Colliers mine at Ruardean in the Forest of Dean. At Leominster in 1798 timber from Eye and Kimbolton was advertised for sale at 'an easy distance from water carriage' – referring to the Lugg.[23]

In 1809, according to one ledger 77 shipments were made by one operator, probably based in Wilton. Bark, timber, poles, wheat, beans, peas, rye, oats, boxes, lime, slate and coal were transported to and from Bristol, Chepstow, Brockweir, Wilton, Ross and Hereford including smaller sites at Backney, Lyndor and How Caple.

From the end of the 18th century, bark from Wilton, Backney, Hoarwithy and Fownhope was being shipped to Messrs. Bowsher, Hodges and Watkins and to George Buckle at Chepstow. Accounts for bark from 1800 to 1812 include 'gave five guineas for the barge going to Chepstow with his bark' in 1800, 'To freight 17 tons 4½ cwt Bark from Backney £11 3s 7d' and 'To freight 10 tons 6 Cwt of Bark from Wilton to Chepstow £7 14s 6d'. The timber accounts included 'To freight 9 ton 3 cwt Timber Crad [Caradoc in Sellack] to Chep £4 19s 9d', 'To Freight Poles from Wilton to Bristol 18 ton 6 cwt £9', 'To Freight Hurdle Stuff £2 8s 0d' from Sir Hungerford Hoskyns at Harewood and 'To Freight 14½ tons Poles from Lindor [Lyndor in Foy] to Bristol £11 4s 0d' with an import of '120 Deals from Chepstow to Wilton £6'.[24]

A bark rick at Kentchurch in 1900

During 1802 while touring south Wales Lord Nelson and his party visited the Forest of Dean where he did a survey and made a report to the Admiralty about his concern of the neglected state of the trees that would be needed for ship building. At Ross his party breakfasted at the Swan and Falcon, then decided to travel by boat to Monmouth instead of by carriage. On his journey he visited Chepstow, where he stayed at the Three Cranes Inn, and Hereford, where he was made a freeman of the city.[25]

Between 1825 and 1827, the Liverpool & Bristol Company was providing a freight service either by barge, wagon, cart or trolley in the Wye Valley. Timber, planks, poles, bark, boards and trenails were sent to the 'Ship Yard' at Brockweir, Chepstow and Bristol on barges from Mordiford, Sink Green at Dinedor, Hereford, Canon Bridge, Clifford and Moccas together with 'Timber from Hay'. The *Charles, Mayflower, Eliza, John and Mary* and *James* were the barges regularly used by the company for cargoes of timber products.

During the 1840s, the wine and spirit business of W. & John Pulling of St. Owen Street, Hereford, was shipping wines, spirits and cider, as well as bark and slates, to and from Bristol. In 1846 Captain Prout at Chepstow was 'taking the Bark on board to carry from the Warehouse', probably shipped for Messrs. Pulling on the *Trevor* mastered by Prout. Other shipments of chopped bark between 1846 and 1850 were carried by Charles Wheatstone on the *Ann* for the Pullings.[26]

> In 1827, 154 journeys were made by the barges *Ann, Charles, Eliza, Hereford Sloop, Hereford Trader, James, John and Mary, Mayflower* and *Wellington* on behalf of the Liverpool & Bristol Company transporting corks, soap, tallow, nails, sugar, vinegar, wine, spirits, boxes, hoops, malt, hops and timber to many places between Bristol and Hay. The *John and Mary*, a 48-ton barge, was built in Hereford by John Easton in 1826, and the *Ann* of 30 tons was built at Llandogo in 1812. She was later used to convey bark to Chepstow for William Pulling in 1849 and 1850.

Lime, Pantiles, Stone and Bricks

Over the centuries lime had been in demand for tanning, building and agriculture, as well as making medicinal products. On the limestone hills of the Wye Valley the overgrown quarries and tumbling limekilns are a reminder of the good quality lime that was produced in the past. Once the limestone had been cut from the nearby quarries, the lime burner's job was to place layers of limestone and fuel into the charge hole at the top of the kiln, and fire the furnace from below. This produced clinker which fell into the draw hole at the bottom, where, if slaked with water, it produced a fine powder of lime. The clinkers were loaded into baskets, barrels or bags, transported by packhorses and carts to the barges and shipped up or down river from the late 18th century to be discharged at many wharf sites. At Mordiford coal and lime-coal for the local kilns was 'put out' (unloaded) and 'measured' (weighed) into baskets and dozens before delivery or transhipment. The lime was sold in baskets or dozens, the barge accounts suggesting that 30 baskets equated to a dozen, which itself weighed about 36 lbs.

'Lime was listed amongst the significant downstream cargoes on the River Severn in 1786' whilst in 1787, 21 lime kilns were recorded in the Forest of Dean.[27] One company quoted the following prices from their lime kiln in the lower Wye, the price reflecting the distance the lime had to be shipped: 'at Hereford 25s three months Credit, at Sugwas 28s discharging, at Hoarwithy 18s, at Wilton 15s or 6d a Basket'.

Quantities of pantiles, stone and bricks were shipped up and down the Wye for building works from the late 18th century. Walter Hill was a Ross lawyer and owner of the Rope Walk, the Thrushes Nest and the whole of the Hill Bank overlooking the Wye, where he established a 'Shrubbery or Pleasure ground' after moving the ruinous and inconveniently placed Pye's Almshouses. In 1795 he took delivery of a large amount of lime and '600 Pantiles & 2 doz. creese [ridged tiles] £3 3s 3d, 650 Pantiles £2 15s 3d'. The following year another delivery of lime and pantiles was made to him, probably used to build his gothic summer house, terracing and curved paths leading down to the meadow and riverside below.[28]

At the turn of the 18th century lime and brat (a form of limestone probably used for road repairs) was transported either by barges or wagons to Old Forge, Mainoaks in Goodrich, and freighted from Wilton to Bristol, to Weir End in Bridstow, to Dock Pitch in Ross, to Sir Hungerford Hoskyns at Harewood and to Hereford.[29] In 1810 and 1811 lime was shipped downstream from Hereford to Ingestone, Carey, How Caple and Wilton, together with 100 tons of stone to Wilton for £10, and 12 tons to Bristol for £15. Loads of lime were also discharged at Belmont, and produce from the lime kiln at Knapp Green in Little Dewchurch was sold by the 'dozens' and freighted to unrecorded destinations. Tons of slate tiles came from Bristol to Chepstow, then were transhipped at Brockweir and freighted to Wilton and Hereford. There is only one notable cargo of bricks, that being 1,000 shipped from Monmouth to Hoarwithy.[30]

In 1824 lime from the Vention kilns at Lydbrook was sold at 5s per dozen and by the barge load for a price that varied according to the distance. It was 7s to Old Forge, 8s 3d

Lime kilns at Ganarew, from where lime would have been taken to the Wye for shipment

Three barges and a pleasure boat on the Wye below Goodrich
as sketched by James Wathen in the 1790s

to Glewstone, 9s to Ross, 12s to Hoarwithy, 13s to Carey, 15s 3d to Holme Lacy, 17s to Hereford and £1 to Sugwas. Shortly after this date the lime trade in Herefordshire and the Wye Valley began to decline due to competition from the large scale Radnorshire lime-works which eventually superseded the local lime industry.[31]

Agricultural Products
The Wye provided a convenient and accessible highway for agricultural products to be transported either to the local neighbourhood or to more distant towns and cities. From the 18th century it was used to convey wheat and flour to Bristol. More specifically, from 1795 William Porter of Wilton was shipping a range of agricultural products from the Ross area, including '2 Bush. Rye grass', 'Kidney Potatoes', 'Turnip Seed', '5 Sacks Wheat', '11 Sacks Barley', '8 lb Trefoil', '2 Bush. Oats' and '1 Dutch Clover'. (In July 1797 he overpaid his bargemen by 10s.) From 1800 large amounts of seeds, oats, rye grass, clover and barley were shipped from the large estates at Pengethley, How Caple, Ingestone and Caradoc. In 1802 '17 Sacks of Barley' were shipped from Wilton to Bristol for Mr. Vaughan of that city. In 1805 Daniel Platt from Monmouth transported 15 sacks of peas from Wilton to Monmouth for 15s, together with 15 sacks of wheat for the same price, and four bushels of rye grass for £1 8s.[32]

In the early 1800s sacks of malt were freighted to Bristol and some even to Newport. Mrs. Wiltshire from Wilton was engaged in shipping both malt and hops, while Mr. Powles from Hoarwithy was sending '5 Bales of Hemp' and '6 Sacks Flax' to Bristol. Hemp was used for rope making and flax for making sacks, sails and linen goods.[33]

Throughout the first quarter of the 19th century peas, vetches (used as animal feed), beans, oats, seeds, barley, wheat and rye were regular consignments to Bristol from the towns and villages of Herefordshire. The barge accounts show it cost £3 8s to ship 24 sacks of wheat from Hollington in Holme Lacy to Bristol, £3 for 24 sacks of barley from Dinedor to Bristol, and £2 17s for 19 sacks of barley from Hereford to Bristol. From Wilton, William Porter, William Bonnor, Henry Platt and Charles Prosser were shipping large quantities of wheat and barley to Monmouth, Brockweir and Bristol, and during the 1820s The Liverpool & Bristol Company was transporting oats, beans, barley, malt and vetches on barges called the *James*, *Charles*, *Ann*, and *John and Mary* or delivered by 'The Evans's Cart' or 'William's Carriage'.[34]

Cider, Wine and Spirits

Holme Lacy was renowned for good quality cider as recorded by Thomas Baskerville in 1682: 'Hom-lacy, where my honoured uncle, the Lord Scudamore, now defunct, did live, a person to which the whole country is obliged for his worth, he being the man that brought the now so much famed redstreak cyder to perfection'. By improving the quality of cider

Unloading cider from a barge at Hereford c.1800

Lord Scudamore made it a fashionable drink in the cities of London, Oxford and Bristol. Before the Wye became navigable the Scudamores were supplying Ross and Gloucester with 'Corn & Cider', but the 'Carriage of Cyder for Mr. Jones of Hereford' in 1698 may have been by barge when cider and corn were first shipped to Bristol from Kings Caple.[35] In 1727 Ross was 'famous for good cyder, a great manufacture of iron ware, and a good trade on the River Wye'.

Cider soon became an important export from Hereford where it was 'collected from small wharves along the Wye and stored in warehouses for export down the river on barges. The warehouses were often of considerable size, and some at Pearce's Wharf ... were capable of holding two to three hundred hogsheads of cider.' An 18th-century hogshead generally contained 64 gallons, but the Herefordshire hogshead held almost double that amount. From Hereford the cider was shipped to Bristol, Bridgewater and ports along the Welsh coast. As with the shipping of other goods, the trade depended on the state of the river; if too low or in flood the barges were unable to sail. When a great flood swept away three bridges in 1795, the cider was lost from the warehouses in Hereford.[36]

An account of Perkins from How Caple dated 1795 records '2 Apr To Freight 18 Hhds. Cider £4 11s', '21 Dec To Freight 5 Hhds Cider 5s' and the following year '11 May To Ft. 15 empty Hhds 15s' and a further consignment of 31 hogsheads of cider for £11 15s 6d. In 1802 John Crumpton was delivering '2 Pipes, 1 Cask of Cider to Monmouth 7s 6d' and '4 Hhds Cider from Wilton to Monmouth 16s'. From Woolhope, Huntsham and Caple, cider in hogsheads or casks was destined for Bristol, as was a cider mill shipped from Walford in 1812 for £5 5s. During the 1820s Pullings of Hereford were shipping cider on the *Trader* in pipes, barrels, casks and kilderkins, and in 1847 an order for '1 Puncheon, 5 Hogshead, 6 Quarter casks £6 17s 6d' had been paid to 'the Owners of the Schooner *Friends*'. A pipe held 100 gallons or more, a barrel 36 gallons and a kilderkin 18 gallons.[37]

A barge on the Canal du Midi in southern France with a cargo of wine c.1930

From the 12th century wine was imported from France to Chepstow which enjoyed a long association with the wine trade, and from the 15th century French, German and Portuguese wines were shipped in casks from Bristol along the Severn, and on the Wye to Chepstow. In 1753 a levy was paid at Chepstow for '1,242 pipes, 19 butts, 114 hogsheads and 14 quarter casks, or about 165,000 gallons'. Ships arrived at Chepstow with cargoes of wines and port including the *Venus* in 1755 'with Wines' and in 1771 Captain Burton from Oporto arrived on the *Elizabeth* 'laden with wine for Mr. Fydell' who was followed by a succession of wine importers at Chepstow.[38]

In the 18th century Taylor of Carmarthen imported 'Old Red and White Port Wines of the best quality' from Portugal to Bristol, and Gardner in Gloucester dealt in wine, port, madeira, claret and champagne from France, Portugal and South Africa as well as rum from the West Indies. George Buckle's business founded in 1789 at Chepstow expanded within 50 years to include warehousing that held 500 pipes and 100 hogsheads of wine and spirits, and in bond '9,783 gallons of Portugal wine, 8,496 gallons of Spanish white wine, 387 gallons of Pontac [claret], 342 gallons of Bronti [marsala], 1,710 of brandy and 2,240 of rum, as well as whisky and gin not under bond'.[39]

From 1771 Nathaniel Purchas, a brewer, bark and wine and spirit merchant dealt in brandy, rum and other liquors. The alcoholic beverages were shipped from Chepstow in his barges the *Jupiter* and *John* or by other companies' vessels to his brew-house in Fownhope, from where they were sold.

Cases, individual bottles, barrels and hogsheads of wine were shipped on the *Eliza*, the *James* and the *Hereford* from Brockweir during the 1820s mainly to Messrs. Pulling in Hereford.[40]

From at least the 1830s Pullings were taking large deliveries of rum, whisky and brandy from a warehouse in Bristol, as well as from William Jameson in Dublin. Jameson also supplied Pontiac (claret), using either the *George and Francis*, a schooner of 59 tons that was owned and mastered by John Prout, or the *Trevor*, a 100-ton schooner also mastered by John Prout, who also shipped bark to Chepstow for Pullings in 1846.[41]

Provisions, Commodities and Miscellaneous Items

Perishable goods such as fish, meat, cheese and butter were seldom shipped on the Wye because of the unreliability of the river with its shallows in summer and floods in winter. Nevertheless, the Wye was used to transport a wide range of other goods in mixed cargoes, though the Lugg much less so. In 1795 William Prosser of Wilton carried sugar and cheese, and the same year cheeses and apples were shipped from Ingestone. In 1798 William Porter carried salmon from Hoarwithy to Wilton, and in 1800 Charles Cumberland from Aramstone in Kings Caple had two chests of oranges delivered together with his liquors from Wilton at the same date that '2 Sacks flour, 8 sacks potatoes' were freighted from Wilton to Mr. Vaughan at Bristol. Between 1825 and 1827 most of these goods were being carried by the Liverpool & Bristol Company together with some perishable goods including butter, herrings, flour, bacon and vinegar.

Larger and bulky items included church bells from St. Nicholas in Hereford shipped down the Wye to Chepstow in 1718, from Eaton Bishop in 1725 and from All Saints in

Hereford in 1769. At Chepstow it is understood that the bells were taken up the Severn to Rudhalls' bell foundry in Gloucester for recasting, and then returned along the same waterways. In Wales it is 'commonly believed, though so far without confirmation, that the bell for Hay church produced or recast at the Evans foundry in Chepstow in 1740 was transported by water; certainly this seems to have been the case with that for Llywel cast from the same foundry in 1739'. In 1756 William Evans at Chepstow also recast the bells from Leominster Priory, which were sent down the Lugg and the Wye.[42]

An unusual cargo was forced on Luke Hughes in 1740. Three troops of Horse Guards were marching from Gloucester through Ross to Hereford in November that year, when the constable at Ross was ordered by the justice of the peace to impress wagons to carry the troops' baggage. The constable could not find sufficient wagons and was also concerned about using the roads as they were 'very deep and founderous'. So the constable hit on another plan, and Luke Hughes was ordered to 'unload a barge he then had near the Town of Ross to undertake the Carriage of these Baggages by Water to Hereford'. He was paid the 'usual rate', but was dissatisfied with the amount and petitioned Hereford Quarter Sessions for an extra allowance for his trouble.[43]

From 1744 items such as candles and tallow were also shipped, oakum and cloth in 1795 and one box of soap and a malt mill in 1796. The accounts also show entries such as 'To Freight Household Furniture, 18 Packages £3 10s' for Captain Roe in 1800, a ladder in 1801 and alabaster in 1806 for 'His Grace the Duke of Beaufort'.

Occasionally letters and passengers were taken on board, including in one instance a group of men and women convicts conveyed on Thomas Prosser's barge from Hereford Gaol to Bristol, from where they were transported to America in 1740.[44] A letter was sent by 'Biss' trow' to Edward Woodhouse in 1785 regarding his order of '3 Puncheons Rum, well coopered' and informing him that his 'young man passenger' must be there on the day of sailing. Other letters were sent by barge, as indicated by the entries in the accounts of 'To postage of a letter 8d' and 'To money sent £2 5s 2d' in 1810.[45]

The junk (old ropes) and rags that were sometimes shipped up river to the papermills made the return journey as quires of paper. An unusual delivery in 1811 was from Sir Hungerford Hoskyns of Harewood, who shipped half a ton of hair and '1 bundle of Ropage' paying one shilling to 'the porter taking the bag for ye hair', and on another occasion sending 12 bags of hair to Hereford. Throughout the 1820s there were shipments of paper, soap, leather, lumber, one or two traps, a hat box, boxes of glasses, grates, barrels of pitch and bags of nails to Hay, Canon Bridge, Sink Green, Hereford, Mordiford, Whitchurch, Redbrook, Monmouth, Brockweir, Chepstow and Bristol.

From 1830 to 1850 bark, timber, apples, barley, fleece, meat, lamb's wool and potatoes were either delivered by wagon or shipped on barges from Wilton to Hoarwithy, Glewstone Boat, Monmouth and Hereford. On 9 August 1852 an order of 42 sacks of corn was 'delivered this day to a barge at Wilton' with a final entry in one ledger on 9 May 1854 for '20 sacks of white wheat to Monmouth'. Names such as Porter, Biss and Dowle were associated with these cargoes on the Wye from Wilton.[46]

5   BOAT BUILDING AND ASSOCIATED TRADES

The craft of boat building existed from early times when man first utilised rivers for travel and transport. The boats would have been constructed on the river bank at a convenient place where the raw materials were available. The earliest craft used on the river were known as truckles or coracles, which Charles Heath well described in 1828 as 'a basket shaped like the half of a walnut shell, but shallower in proportion, and covered on the outside with a horse's hide or canvas. It has a bench in the middle, and will just hold one person; and is so light, that the countrymen will hang it on their heads like a hood, and so travel with a small paddle (which serves for a stick), till they come to the river, and then they launch it, and step in.'[1] Coracles were associated with fishing rather than with transporting goods, although occasionally they were used for feats of daring like the journey made by Luke Hughes to the Isle of Lundy in the Bristol Channel, again described by Charles Heath.

Coracles at Ross in the 1870s

Hughes undertook the journey for a frolic. It took him two weeks, or a touch over, and fortunately the weather was 'serene'. He also took precautions, keeping within close distance of a vessel all the way to Bristol in case of accident.[2]

By the time that shipwrights on the Wye were constructing barges, experience had been gained building barges and seagoing vessels at Chepstow. As mentioned in chapter 2, the *Scudamore* galley was built at Chepstow in the 1720s by a ship's carpenter and his men assisted by rope makers, sail makers and others working on the rigging. Large quantities of ropes and cables were also bought from a Mary Knight in Bristol.[3]

During the first half of the 18th century a huge amount of timber was conveyed on barges or floated down the Wye from

An illustration of 19th-century boat-building

Holme Lacy, Fownhope, Chase and Penyard Hills near Ross to Chepstow. On the Lugg, timber from Hampton Court and the Scudamores' land bordering the river was also shipped downstream to Chepstow. Some of the timber was used for making hoops, laths and trenails for the shipbuilding industry, but most was transhipped to Plymouth to be used for building ships for the Navy. In the 1770s timber was conveyed down the Wye from Whitney and Hardwick and anchors and chains forged at Tidnor on the Lugg were in demand by the naval shipyards during the Napoleonic Wars.[4]

Some of the timber, however, was retained for building ships locally, and constructing a ship on the banks of the Wye would have followed a fairly standard procedure. The frame of the ship would be laid out and assembled in a dock or on a wharf where the vessel could be supported 'on the stocks' whilst being built by the shipwright. Sawpits would be constructed nearby where the timber could be sawn into the requisite planks. The ships' hulls were built of oak, and the masts of fir or pine, being lighter and straighter. Once the planks of the hull had been nailed and pinned together, the ship was caulked by driving oakum – made from picking apart old ropes – into the seams to prevent leaking. The oakum was then covered with hot melted pitch or resin to prevent it from rotting, and the hull coated with coal tar.[5] The building of a trow on the Severn during the 18th century took three to six months, and the cost of producing a 60-ton trow then would have been about £300.[6]

An early boat builder at Chepstow was George Evans, a ship's carpenter mentioned in 1718. He owned a sloop called the *George* which he probably built to carry timber from Chepstow to Plymouth for William Rea. In 1727 another ship's carpenter employed by Rea was James Hopkins of Brockweir who repaired 'a large barge called the *James* used and worked on the lower Wye and made chiefly for carrying the timber bought in partnership down the river to Chepstow and thence to be carried to Plymouth for the use of his majesty's navy'.[7]

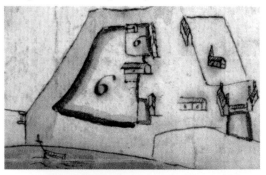
Part of a map dating from 1721 showing the ferry boat at Fawley

'Bark stripping and charcoal burning consumed far more oak trees than ship building ever did' and as the timber for ship building yards was sourced over a wider area, the Wye Valley only supplied a small percentage. It appears that around 58 trees were required to build an 80-gun naval ship, while to build a 60-ton trow or barge in the 18th century it is estimated that at least four oaks of 120 years of age and weighing some 35 tons each were required. There would have been a large amount of wastage which ended up as payment in kind to the ship builders and was often used in houses or to make other timber products.[8]

Along the banks of the upper Wye local boat builders and carpenters made the ferries and horse boats used at the various river crossings. Ferry boats carrying people, horses, carts and livestock provided an important link between river and road transport. At Kings Caple, William Hudson was paid £4 10s for 'building a new horse boat' and £1 5s for 'a new small boat' to be used at Hoarwithy Passage. The materials for both boats included oak planks, pitch and tar which cost £25 0s 2d in 1772, but 20 years later the boat needed replacing so a person was sought 'for Building a Boat for the use of Hoarwithy Passage and to officiate as Boatman'.[9] At Goodrich in 1783 Thomas Hudson proposed to 'make build & completely finish a good substantial & workmanlike manner a ferry Boat' to be made of 'good sound & well seasoned Oak Timber except so much of the Bottom thereof as is usually made of Elm' for 'the Sum of one & thirty pounds & ten shillings'.[10]

The first known barge built on the upper Wye was around 1780 at Rhydspence in the parish of Brilley on the Herefordshire/Radnorshire border. It was a 40-ton vessel, over 56 feet in length and over 12 feet broad with one mast and named *Sally*. Although the builder is not mentioned, it was owned in 1805 by Thomas Hughes, a merchant from Monmouth. The boatyard would have been at the ferry site where there was access to the Wye with 'plank and navy timber' available from Mr. Stallard's timberyard at Whitney and Hardwick. The river crossing at Rhydspence was on a well known route, its name being derived from the Welsh 'rhyd' meaning ford.[11]

In 1787 the *William*, a 43-ton barge, was built at Hereford by Richard Lewis who also built the 44-ton barge the *Molly* in 1795. Lewis has proved an elusive boat builder, possibly a member of the Lewis family of Monmouth, but as Richard Crompton acquired the *William*, it is likely that the barge was built at Crompton's Wharf in Pipe Lane in Hereford. From 1814 the *Molly* went downstream and was acquired by Robert Thompson, Philip Vaughan and James Hall, ironmasters at Tintern and Redbrook. The *Valiant* was a 43-ton barge built at Hereford during this period, and was one of Daniel Pearce's four barges at his wharf near Wye Bridge.[12] If the same *Valiant*, it had been for sale in 1808 as a 'complete and well-built Barge' and advertised as 'well worth the attention of Timber Merchants'.[13]

Between 1799 and 1801 Thomas Maund built another *William*, a 42-ton barge, and the *Kitty*, a 38-ton barge, at Hereford. As the *Kitty* was owned by Jonathan Crompton in 1808, it was probably built at Crompton's yard. By 1812 Thomas Maund was at Wilton and in 1819 he was living with his son in 'part of the Great House' (Wilton Court) 'at per year £9 9s 0d', opposite the quay and wharf where John Thomas had built his 17-ton barge called the *Rival* in 1804. Three years later at a boatyard 'which may have been near the old gasworks' in Hay, a 39-ton barge was built by Thomas Thomas. It was named *Penelope* and was later used by James Biss, a corn factor in Monmouth.[14]

Date	Name	Place	Type	Builder	Tons
1780	*Sally*	Rhydspence	barge	unknown	40
1787	*William*	Hereford	barge	Lewis, Richard	43
1790	*Valiant*	Hereford	barge	unknown	43
1795	*Molly*	Hereford	barge	Lewis, Richard	44
1799	*William*	Hereford	barge	Maund, Thomas	43
1801	*Kitty*	Hereford	barge	Maund, Thomas	38
1803	*Peggy*	Hereford	barge	unknown	23
1804	*Rival*	Wilton	barge	Thomas, John	17
1807	*Penelope*	Hay	barge	Thomas, Thomas	41
1807	*Eliza*	Lydbrook	barge	Morse, George	41
1808	*Betsey*	New Weir	barge	Maund, William	37
1812	*Ann*	Hereford	barge	Crompton, George	32
1812	*George*	Hereford	barge	Crompton, George	32
1814	*Thomas & Mary*	Hereford	barge	Mann, Thomas	41
1815	*Rhoda*	Hereford	barge	Woore, Philip	39
1815	*William*	Fownhope	barge	Wheatstone, R	40
1816	*Happy Returns*	New Weir	barge	Woore, Philip	35
1818	unnamed	Ross	steam	Teague?	
1820	*Prudence*	Lydbrook	barge	Woore, Charles	42
1822	*Hereford*	Hereford	sloop	Hopkins, Evan	54
1822	*Hereford*	Hereford	sloop	Easton, John	60
1823	*Pomona*	Hereford	snow	Hopkins, Evan	108
1824	*Martha*	Holme Lacy	barge	Thomas, Joseph	38
1824	*Helen*	Hereford	snow	Easton, John	122
1824	*Liberty*	Hay	barge	Prout, Capt. James	32
1824	*Herefordshire*	Hereford	schooner	Hopkins, Evan	90
1825	*Champion*	Hereford	snow	Easton, John	124
1825	*Mary*	Hereford	snow	Easton, John	130
1825	*Thomas*	Wilton	trow	unknown	37
1826	*John & Mary*	Hereford	trow	Easton, John	48
1826	*Betsey*	Lydbrook	trow	Woore, Charles	48
1827	*Paul Pry*	Hereford	steam	Radford, William	31
1827	*Earl of Hopetown*	Hereford	steam	Easton, John	140
1828	*Mary & Elizabeth*	Bullingham	barge	Thomas, Joseph	46
1831	*Jane*	Bishopswood	barge	Woore, Esias	17
1832	*Collinque*	Hereford	schooner	Easton, John	140
1834	*Water Witch*	Hereford	steam	Radford, William	24
1837	*Bee*	Hereford	trow	Swift, Thomas	18
1854	*Ann & Peggy*	Fownhope	trow	Wheatstone?	13
1854	*Lady Alma*	Fownhope	trow	Wheatstone?	12
1856	*Monmouth Trader*	New Weir	trow	unknown	24
1902	*Wilton Castle*	Ross	steam	Dowell, Thomas H.	

A table showing the boats built on the Wye between Symonds Yat and Glasbury

George Morse, a barge owner at Lydbrook, was in joint occupation of 'Two wharfs adjoining each other on the River Wye' which must have formed his boatyard where he built a 41-ton barge called the *Eliza* in 1807. The following year William Maund built a 37-ton barge at New Weir. It was known as *Betsey* and was owned by Henry Pewtner, who lived in a house adjoining the New Weir ironworks at Symonds Yat in Whitchurch. An illustration of 1811 depicts the boat building materials at a wharf at New Weir, where another barge called the *Happy Returns* was built by Philip Woore a few years later.[15] The shipbuilding family 'headed by John Woore built boats not only in Monmouth but at other riverside places on the Wye'.[16]

At Hereford in 1812 the *George*, a 32-ton barge, was built by George Crompton, possibly for the lime trade as used by Jonathan Crompton in 1813 and subsequently purchased by William Jones of Mordiford, a place associated with the lime burning industry. Two more barges were built at Hereford in 1814 and 1815, the *Thomas and Mary* by Thomas Mann, and the *Rhoda* by Philip Woore. Previously Mann had been trading in timber, elm boards and large quantities of coal from Wilton. In 1815 the first barge at Fownhope was built by Richard Wheatstone, the 40-ton *William*, and in 1818 an enterprising boat builder at Ross was constructing a 'Steam Barge intended to carry Coal, and navigate the Wye to the City', the 'inventor' being 'the spirited proprietor of the Lidbrook and Deep Level Colliery, in the Forest of Dean'.[17]

At least 14 barges, trows, snows, sloops, schooners and steam boats were built on the banks of the Wye between New Weir at Symonds Yat and Hay during the 1820s. The *Prudence*, a 42-ton barge, was built by Charles Woore at one of the Lydbrook wharfs in 1820 for James Ward who operated from Bishopswood. At Hereford a snow or sloop of 54 tons, appropriately called the *Hereford*, was built by Evan Hopkins on 'a meadow nearly opposite Castle Green'. When she was launched in February 1822 the *Hereford* 'majestically glided into the Wye to the gratification of nearly 3,000 persons, whom the ceremony had attracted to the spot'. She was decorated with the City Arms and tastefully painted for her owner John Easton, a timber merchant.[18]

Joseph Thomas of Lower Bullingham was described as a barge builder who built the *Martha*, a 38-ton barge, at Holme Lacy in 1824. The boatyard is not known but may have been at Shipley at Holme Lacy where a boat house and a piece of land known as the Boat Piece belonged to the Scudamores.[19] The same year the *Helen*, a large snow of 122 tons and over 69 feet long with a breadth of 20 feet, was registered at Chepstow. She had been built the previous year by John Easton and, according to the *Hereford Journal*, 'was launched from the timber yard nearly opposite the Castle Green. She descended to the bosom of the Wye in fine style, and the launch afforded great satisfaction to a very large concourse of persons, who had assembled to witness it. The brig is a remarkable fine vessel, combining elegance of form and strength of structure; she is generally admired by the naval officers resident in the city, and allowed to be highly creditable to the workmen employed on her.'[20]

The same year the *Liberty*, a 32-ton barge, was built at Hay by Captain James Prout, and the *Herefordshire*, a schooner built by Evan Hopkins, was launched in Hereford and taken to Bristol for rigging. This was followed in 1825 with a 24-ton brig called the *Champion*, a launch again lauded by the *Hereford Journal*: 'built by Mr. Easton, in his yard opposite the College garden, [the brig] was launched, and descended from the stocks to the bosom of the Wye in fine style. The early hour at which the launch took place was owing to the water having attained the proper height necessary to facilitate the operation: the ease with which the vessel glided into her element was highly creditable to those who conducted the arrangements, and gratifying to several who had assembled to witness the launch.'[21] In 1825 two more vessels were completed, the *Mary*, a 130-ton snow built by John Easton at Hereford and 'launched from his yard opposite the Castle Green' before being taken to Chepstow for rigging, and the *Thomas*, a trow of 37 tons built at Wilton, probably on the wharf but by an unknown shipwright or carpenter.[22]

In 1826 John Easton in Hereford built a 48-ton trow called the *John and Mary* which was purchased by John Milward. The same year another trow named the *Betsey* was built at Lydbrook by Charles Woore. This 48-ton trow was co-owned by John Trotter of Lydney and James Ward of Bishopswood. The later was involved in the Lydney Trading Society 'established as a goods and passenger service from the Severn to the Wye' on their horse-drawn tramway. The following year the most inventive and enterprising vessel was made at Hereford – a steam-boat of 31 tons named the *Paul Pry* built by William Radford, her keel 'laid in Mr. Easton's yard, opposite the Bishop's Palace'.

The launch of the *Paul Pry* drew considerable attention in November 1827 when '6 to 7,000 persons assembled in the building yard and in the Castle Green, and other spots where a view could be obtained on the banks opposite to the place where the fine boat rested on a cradle destined to carry her to the element on which she was so shortly to float. At twelve precisely, a beautiful barge, built on nearly the same spot by Mr. Easton, was sent as an avant courier to her more majestic sister, and glided into the Wye amidst the shouts of those present.' After the successful launch attributed to Captain Radford and the workmen 'she was taken above the bridge, where her machinery will be immediately placed: in about 14 days it is almost certain she will be ready to work. She is a beautiful boat about 64 tons admeasurement [presumably when laden], and the engine is fourteen-horse power.' It was considered that a 'steam tug boat would be able to work loaded barges on the Wye in 3 ft of water day or night and in 2 ft in day only'.

The *Paul Pry* was owned by the Wye Steam Boat Company and by 15 December 1827 she was 'equipped and fit for Work' and ready for the 'Transport of Goods or Merchandise to or from Chepstow to any parts of the Rivers Wye and Severn'. On her first voyage upstream in 1828 'She left Chepstow on Wednesday, and reached Monmouth the same day towing a barge after

WYE STEAM BOAT COMPANY.

THE Company's STEAM TOW-BOAT the PAUL PRY, being now equipped and fit for Work, they are ready to receive TENDERS from any one willing to Contract for the Transport of Goods or Merchandise to or from Chepstow to any part of the Rivers Wye and Severn.

For further particulars and information apply (if by letter, post-paid,) to the Agent of the said Company, at Mr. Lucy's, Dry-bridge House, Hereford.

An advertisement for the services of the Paul Pry *placed on 15 December 1827*

her. On Friday she proceeded from Monmouth to Lydbrook, which she left the next day, towing a barge as far as the Kerne Bridge and arrived at Wilton' but did not reach Hereford until Monday evening.[23] As she was in fact not found suitable for trading on the Wye, the gentlemen who owned her sent the boat to Liverpool, from where Joseph Kelly, the shipwright employed in building her, had hailed, and where she was used as a sea-going vessel. She was later used by the Saint George's Steam Packet Company.

In 1828 the *Mary and Elizabeth*, a 46-ton barge, was built by Joseph Thomas at Bullingham, maybe on one of the fields adjacent to the horse towing-path.[24] John Easton built the 261-ton *Hereford* and the 400-ton *Liverpool*, both sea-going vessels, in 1829 at his yard at Brockweir.[25]

At Bishopswood another member of the Woore family built a small 17-ton barge in 1831. It was named the *Jane* and may have been in response to an advertisement placed by 'the Wye Horse Towing Path Company, desirous to receive Tenders for the Building of Two Horse Ferry Boats, according to Specifications to be seen on application to Mr. James Ward, at Bishop's Wood'. James Ward was a coal merchant and in 1834 he applied 'for land near Lydney Basin on which to install a smith's shop and saw-pit in order to build boats and barges', but the land was let to a prior applicant. The following year 'a fine substantially built schooner, named the *Collinque*, of 140 tons burthen' was launched from John Easton's yard in Hereford.[26]

At Hereford on 26 April 1834 'a steam vessel, the *Water Witch*, built by Captain Radford, was launched with 60 persons on board, being the largest vessel yet built above the bridge. It drew 17 inches of water as launched, and 34 inches when loaded with engines etc. The length was 80 feet, width 23 feet with a fine figure of a water witch holding a book. It was to ply on one of the English rivers and to be fitted out at Chepstow. It went down the Wye on 21st July, on its way to Liverpool, where it was expected a customer would be found.' Captain Radford RN had founded the Wye Steam Boat Company 'to put steam boats on

The Water Witch *built at Hereford in 1834*

the river for the purpose of towing barges', but the venture turned out to be unsuccessful on the Wye.[27]

It is not known where the 'Steam Boat called *The Man of Ross*' was built, but certain clues suggest Ross or Chepstow. In June 1836 the 'Safe, Commodious and Elegantly Fitted' steam boat made her first voyage and it was announced she 'will continue to Ply to and from Ross and Chepstow, Twice a Week, during the Summer Season'. The pleasure boat left Ross at 10am and reached Monmouth at 4pm, refreshments were served on board 'on moderate terms' and the fare for adults was 5s from the Dock Pitch, Ross.[28]

One of the last vessels to be built on the upper Wye before navigation ceased was the 18-ton trow called the *Bee* built by Thomas Swift at Hereford. As a timber merchant in Monmouth he would have supplied the materials. The last three trows were all built when the Hereford, Ross and Gloucester Railway was being constructed and after the railway opened. At Fownhope the Wheatstones built the 13-ton *Ann and Peggy* in 1854 and the 12-ton *Lady Alma* in 1855 on their site at Lucksall. At New Weir, on the deserted site of the ironworks at Symonds Yat, the *Monmouth Trader*, a 24-ton trow, was built probably by one of the Woore family and purchased by Charles Prosser, a Monmouth timber merchant.

After a flirtation with steam during the 1820s and 1830s it was at Ross that the *Wilton Castle*, a stern wheel steamer, was built and successfully

TOUR OF THE
RIVER WYE,

From Ross to Goodrich Court and Castle, Symond's Yat, Whitchurch, New Weir, Monmouth, Tintern Abbey, and Chepstow.

THE admirers of the beautiful and romantic Scenery of the River Wye will now have an opportunity of making the deservedly celebrated Tour of the River from ROSS to CHEPSTOW, in ONE DAY; and at the same time be afforded AMPLE TIME for an attentive survey of the numerous attractions its Banks present; by the Establishment of a Safe, Commodious, and Elegantly Fitted up

STEAM BOAT,
CALLED
"THE MAN OF ROSS,"

which made her first Trip on Monday last, the 27th of June, 1836, and will continue to Ply to and from ROSS and CHEPSTOW, TWICE A WEEK, during the Summer Season.

The times of Starting during the present and ensuing Months, are as follow :—

ROSS TO MONMOUTH.	MONMOUTH TO CHEPSTOW.
Monday July 4 10 morn.	Monday July 4 4 after.
Thursday .. 7 5 morn.	Thursday .. 7 11 morn
Monday .. 11 8 morn.	Monday .. 11 2 after.
Thursday .. 14 10 morn.	Thursday .. 14 4 after.
Monday .. 18 10 morn.	Monday .. 18 4 after.
Thursday .. 21 10 morn.	Thurs. 21 not sail from Mon.
Monday .. 25 7 morn.	Monday .. 25 2 after.
Thursday .. 28 10 morn.	Thursday .. 28 4 after.

CHEPSTOW TO MONMOUTH.	MONMOUTH TO ROSS.
Tuesday .. 5 8 morn.	Wednesday .. 6 8 morn.
Friday .. 8 10 morn.	Saturday .. 9 8 morn.
Tuesday .. 12 1 after.	Wednesday .. 13 8 morn.
Friday .. 15 5 morn.	Friday .. 15 12 noon.
Tuesday .. 19 6 morn.	Wednesday .. 20 7 morn.
Friday 22 not sail from Chep.	Friday .. 22 8 morn.
Tuesday .. 26 2 after.	Wednesday .. 27 8 morn.
Friday .. 29 5 morn.	Friday .. 29 11½ morn.

FARES:

Ross to Chepstow 10s. Ross to Monmouth 5s. Monmouth to Chepstow 5s. Chepstow to Ross 10s. Chepstow to Monmouth 5s. Monmouth to Ross 5s. Children under twelve years of age half-price. Dogs 1s. each.

A considerable allowance will be made in the Fares to Families and large Parties. Persons returning within a week to either place will then be charged half-price.

Refreshments may be had on board, on moderate terms, and every attention will be paid to the comfort and convenience of the Passengers.

Any further information may be obtained by applying at the King's Head Hotel, Ross; Packet Office, Dock Pitch, Ross; Ship and Castle on the Quay, Monmouth; and Steam Packet Office, Chestow.

An advertisement of 2 July 1836 for the services of the Man of Ross

The Wilton Castle

launched in 1902. She was designed as a pleasure boat 'by owner and skipper Thomas Henry Dowell, save for the engine which came from Gloucester. With room for roughly 100 persons she was the pride of the Wye.' The *Wilton Castle* was flat-bottomed, 65 feet long, 10 feet in breadth and travelled at 8mph, but due to lack of passengers was laid up around 1912. 'In sad retirement she spent many years tied to the river bank and there like the barges before her, she rotted slowly away.'[29]

Associated Trades

Adjacent to the boat building sites were saw pits where the timber was prepared for the shipwrights. It has been estimated that 'for an 18th century trow of 60 tons, which would actually carry about 70 tons of timber, over 150 tons of timber would be required'. Working in the saw pit was hard and laborious, with a sawyer above and an apprentice below who would be covered in sawdust. The trenails, required for fastening the timber, had to be made from good quality wood as shown in the 1720s when 'the timber from Hom Park was not sufficient to answer the contract ... and that some better sort of young wood or tough for trenail pins' was required.[30]

The accessories of a barge included her masts, sails and anchor, together with ropes, tarpaulins, oars and shafts – poles for pushing the barge off shoals and shallows. Although most barges went to Chepstow or Bristol for rigging, some earlier and smaller vessels may have been rigged on the wharves and boatyards along the Wye. Sails made from flax are known to have been made at Littledean in the Forest and in 1793 at Hereford, where a temporary building was erected 'for the purpose of carrying on the sail cloth manufactory'. There was a sailmaker at Chepstow in 1810, and in 1815 there was a 'poor traveller passing through Bartestree, a sailmaker'.[31]

CITY OF HEREFORD.

THOMAS BARRETT,
FLAX-DRESSER,

MOST respectfully acquaints his Friends and the Public, That he has opened a Shop, next door to the Sun Tavern, High-Town; where he carries on the Flax-dressing Business, in all its various Branches, wholesale and retail.

T. Barrett has constructed a Rope Walk, for the purpose of making all sorts of Tar Ropes for Barges, and Lines and Twines of every description.

Orders punctually executed, and on the very lowest terms.

An advertisement offering the services of a flax-dresser in Hereford in 1796

Another essential item on the barges were the anchors made in the forges along the Wye during the 18th century. It was a skilled operation 'since, unlike almost all other end-products of the iron industry of this period, an anchor could not be made from a single bar of iron'. Until 1705 anvils were manufactured at Lydbrook, where anchors may have also been made and 'in common with other forges, Tintern cast a small quantity of Miscellaneous goods' which may have included anchors. At Tidnor on the Lugg in 1790, the forge was apparently producing anchors and chains.[32]

Flax was grown in several parishes around the Ross area including the Flaxridge on the boundary of Ross and Weston under Penyard. Here a spring of water flows into a muddy pool which was probably used for retting the flax, a method used to rot away the pithy core. In 1796 Thomas Barrett, a flax-dresser and ropemaker in Hereford, 'constructed a Rope Walk, for the purpose of making all sorts of Tar Ropes for barges', while in Ross the Newton family and Joseph Hardwick were flax-dressers from the 18th century. In the 1800s flax and hemp from Hoarwithy was freighted to Bristol when 'one stone of flax' was priced at 10s 6d.[33]

Ropes were made at Hereford, Ross, Monmouth and Chepstow. At Hereford in 1775, Thomas Morris informed the public that he had 'laid in a fresh stock of the best Hemp, and engaged some of the best hands from Bristol, in order to carry on the business of Rope and Sack-making to the greatest perfection in all its branches, hoping for a continuance of the public support'. In 1774 William Walker, a ropemaker from Gloucester, was flax dressing at Capuchin Lane in Hereford, and at Ross in 1779 John Newton, a rope-maker, had a Rope House, a length of 300 yards known as the Rope Walk and a workhouse where his utensils and stock were valued at £150.[34] The Book of Trades for 1811 describes a rope walk as follows: 'At the upper-end of the rope walk, is a spinning-wheel, which is turned round by a person, who sits on a stool or bench for the purpose; the man who forms the

Barge accounts for 1800 and 1805 for freighting flax and hemp to and from Bristol and Hoarwithy on the Wye

rope or string, has a bundle of dressed hemp round his waist. From this he draws out two or more ends, and fixes them to a hook; the wheel is now turned for which the threads are twisted, and as the spinner walks backward, the rope, or more properly the rope yarn, is lengthened.'

Tarpaulins were used to cover the open hold to protect the cargo from the weather, and one of 1794 measured 34 feet by 2 feet 9 inches. In 1796 tarpaulins were made from heavy duty flax and supplied by Harvey Wason & Co. in Bristol for barges on the Wye.

Other essentials on board were the baskets, sacks, casks, hampers and bags for carrying the cargoes of lime, coal, seeds, wheat, flour, potatoes, wine, spirits and hops that were

Hereford, November 8, 1775.

THOMAS MORRIS, Rope-maker, without Bye-ftreet Gate, returns his moft fincere thanks to his Friends and the Public for the favours he has already received, and begs leave to inform them, that he has laid in a frefh ftock of the beft Hemp, and engaged fome of the beft hands from Briftol, in order to carry the bufinefs of Rope and Sack-making to the greateft perfection, in all its branches, hoping for a continuance of the public fupport. —He likewife makes and fells all forts of Twine, Whip-cord, Jack-lines, Safh-lines and Hair-lines; alfo Curled Hair, Ran-thread and Shop-thread, with many other articles, wholefale and retail, on the moft reafonable terms.

An advertisement by a rope-maker in Hereford in 1775

usually packed in 'pockets'.[35] Baskets and hampers were made from the branches of willow trees grown in withy beds to a certain length and known as osiers. Osiers were cut in the early spring, before the sap rose, and then peeled and boiled so as to obtain a finished component for the basket maker, who 'by skilfully combing, weaving, knotting and plaiting produced the finished basket'. There were withybeds at Wilton and Brampton Abbotts, with John Newton and Joseph Evans making baskets in Ross from the late 18th century. In 1801 'Bundles Twigs from Backney' were delivered to 'Mr. Evans Basket maker, Ross'.[36] In 1822 there were at least three basket makers in Hereford situated in Eign Street, and others down the Wye at Monmouth and Chepstow.[37]

6   WHARVES – SYMONDS YAT TO WEIREND

Wharves, quays, slipways or docks were the names given to any 'tying up places' or 'landing stages' conveniently sited along the banks of the River Wye where barges were loaded and unloaded. It was traditionally known that every Wyeside village had its wharf and barge, a fact confirmed by the numerous sites revealed by barge accounts, maps, surveys, newspapers, journals, deeds, documents and investigations of the river by foot and canoe. The official meaning of a wharf is a 'fixed platform, commonly on pilings, roughly parallel to and alongside navigable water, where ships are loaded and unloaded'.[1] The wharf sites along the Wye vary from purpose-built stone quays to soft grassy banks and coal and timber yards.

Adjacent to some town and village wharf sites were warehouses, inns, bark ricks, timber and boat yards, coal wharfs and the occasional 'locking stock' where goods could be stored to await collection by barge.

At Monmouth there was a busy quay and 'commodious Wharf, to which a flight of spacious stone steps adjoins'. Only slightly further up the Wye is Dixton church, located so near to the river that it has been frequently flooded. The parish is divided by the Wye into

Monmouth Quay

69

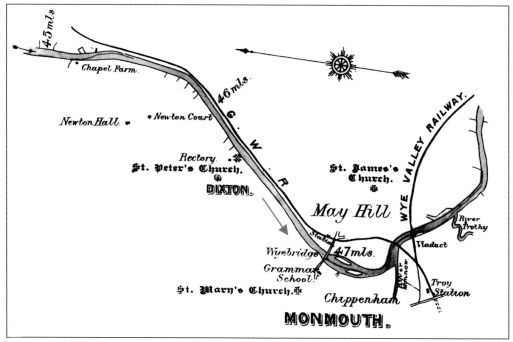

Stooke's map of the Wye at Monmouth and Dixton

Dixton Newton and Dixton Hadnock on the left bank, where in 1845 the Commissioners of Woods and Forests used the Boathouse Meadow as a wharf. By 1860 this had become known as the Crown Timber Wharf.[2] In Hadnock Woods the 'Coling of coles and brays' (cooling of charcoal and its fragments called brays) took place in 1745, and in 1806 the Duke of Beaufort paid for 'halling and freight' from Hadnock.[3] At the boundary between Monmouthshire and Herefordshire the barges were hauled across the river at the Chapel House Roving to follow the towing path.[4]

Upstream above the roving the Wye barges entered Herefordshire at Ganarew on the right bank, where the house and outbuildings known as Wyastone Leys occupy a site that was documented in 1645 as the Lay. It was purchased by Mr. Atley from London who built a house in the late 18th century in this delightful valley. In 1820 Richard Blakemore, an ironmaster and Member of Parliament,

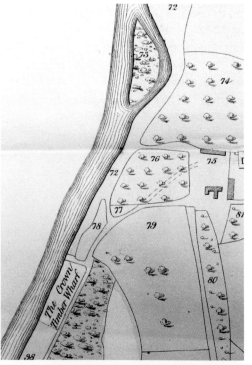

A map of 1863 showing the Crown Timber Wharf at Dixton

purchased the property and rebuilt the mansion with materials ferried across the Wye from the remains of Hadnock House, which was being demolished. He improved the estate by pulling down cottages, constructing new roads and establishing a deer park stocked with a herd of deer from Glamorgan. In 1855 Blakemore died at the age of 81, and the estate passed to his nephew. After his death in 1858 the property was sold to John Bannerman of Manchester, who rebuilt the house in Jacobean style with towers and turrets, and changed its name to Wyastone Leys in 1862.[5]

Symonds Yat

The gorge at Symonds Yat provided the 'grand scenery' that so excited the Wye tourists seeking the Picturesque, who left vivid descriptions of New Weir and Symonds Yat in their prose, poetry and paintings of the 18th and 19th centuries. William Gilpin wrote: 'On the right side of the river, the bank forms an amphitheatre, following the course of the stream round the promontory. Its lower skirts are adorned with a hamlet; in the midst of which, volumes of thick smoke, thrown up at intervals, from an iron-forge, as its fires receive fresh fuel, add double grandeur to the scene.' The 'serpentine winding of the river' attracted Samuel Ireland who wrote that 'the Wye increases in width, and its current is so strong, that it is with extraordinary labour and difficulty the barges are towed up. I have seen eight or ten men throwing themselves on the earth on every pull.'[6]

The Wye at Symonds Yat makes a three mile loop around the towering promontory known as Yat Rock, which became a tedious journey for the bargees and hauliers to cover a distance of only half a mile in a straight line. The Wye tourists avoided this meander by

An illustration of New Weir by Samuel Ireland in 1797

Map of the New Weir Works dated 1758 showing the buildings, roads and a barge on the Wye

New Weir in 2009

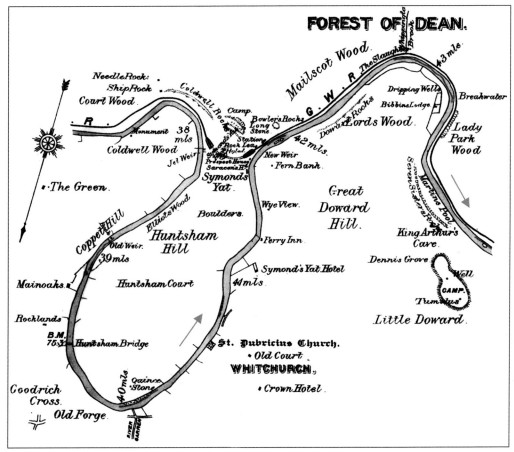

Stooke's map of the Wye in the vicinity of Symonds Yat

allowing their boatman to land them at the riverbank to enable them to ascend the steep climb and admire the famous view before descending to continue their journey. For the tourists, bargemen, iron workers and those crossing the ferries, a number of inns, cider and beer houses were established. At New Weir there was the Old Public or Miners Rest, and at Symonds Yat there was the New Inn at the lower ferry and the Ferry Inn at the upper ferry.[7]

At New Weir the original forge was built by the Earl of Shrewsbury around 1570, but was threatened over the years with destruction by rioting, weather conditions, floods and legal disputes.[8] In 1758 a plan details the iron-working site run by John Partridge, but a wharf or dock was not shown – although it has been considered that 'the leat and forge pond appear to have been the access by boat'.[9] Most of the evidence for wharves and barges at New Weir is from writings, paintings and prints, an early account entry of 1590 recording a payment 'towards mending of Boats for carrying of Old Timber and Slate from the Wayre'. A few years later it was possible to 'carry iron from Whitchurch in small boats' to Monmouth, and in 1753 pig iron was conveyed from Tintern to New Weir when a lease included a sale of stock including 'boats and fishing equipment'.[10]

A barge moored at Whitchurch in 1890

Due to the importance of iron-making at New Weir in Whitchurch, the weir and lock were allowed to remain providing the structures were maintained. At the lock, Charles Heath noted in 1803 that 'the barges trading on the Wye received great assistance from a Capstan, in towing them in and out of the Lock' and 'in passing through the Lock, afford some amusement to the minds of those who are not in the habit of witnessing such scenes. On opening the gates, after the vessel is lowered to the level of the river, the current sets into the lock, in opposition to the stream. In order therefore to bring her into the tide, some force is necessary. No sooner is the signal made for assistance, then young and old, boys and girls, fly to the rope, and, with a zeal most hearty, soon deliver the vessel from her otherwise stationary situation, to the active current of the river.'[11]

As the forge first declined and then ceased working during the early 19th century the site, occupied by a number of 'workmen' in 1811, was used for boat building and the delivery of goods brought by river, including herrings and casks.[12] On the opposite bank it is known that 'trading barges' were 'tied up in the deep water' where the Royal Hotel now stands, and that after the opening of the Ross to Monmouth railway there was a siding where 'iron ore brought on barges or down from the hills was loaded'.[13] On the right bank of the Wye at English Bicknor in Gloucestershire the inhabitants in 1851 'were earning a living from trade on the Wye'.[14] Despite the opening of the Ross to Monmouth railway in 1873, photographic evidence suggests that barges still plied the river downstream from Whitchurch until the end of the 19th century.

At Symonds Yat West in the parish of Whitchurch, four former wharves have been identified. There was the Alpine Wharf, 'a small area of the west bank of the River Wye

Remnants of winch gear at Gumries Shore Wharf

near the Saracen's Head Ferry'; a public landing at Ye Old Ferrie Inn, 'a strip about 20 yards long by the west bank of the River Wye'; and the Gumries Shore Wharf, 'a small area, being about 50 yards of the west bank of the River Wye, a short distance north of Ye Old Ferrie Inn'.[15]

The fourth wharf along this stretch of the river was Lane End Wharf, 'being a small area on the west bank of the River Wye near Whitchurch Parish Church'. This would have been

Lane End Wharf in 2009

in use in 1783 when a property known as Brook House Farm was advertised as a potential tannery with a large malthouse 'within a few hundred yards of the navigable River Wye, by means of which an extensive trade may be carried on to Hereford, Monmouth, Chepstow and Bristol'. The name is retained in the name of Old Wharf Lane which leads to the site, later used as a coal wharf.[16]

Goodrich

From Symonds Yat the Wye forms a large horse-shoe bend around Huntsham Hill in Goodrich. At the northern tip of the bend is Old Forge, where a wharf dates from at least 1797 when Mrs. Powell was shipping lime to Bristol and other places; in 1811 Mrs. Moore was transporting flour, wheat and oats to Bristol. In 1818 the two women were each operating a wharf at Old Forge from a grassy bank just over the parish boundary, and Mrs. Powell was still trading in 1827. By the 1840s the two wharf sites were owned by Thomas Powell and a warehouse had been built on land belonging to Osborne Yates. The warehouse was converted into a home and called the Barge House in 2011.[17]

At Huntsham there was a ferry known as Hunsomes Boat in 1684 and Hunson's Rope in the 1790s. Lime was shipped from Huntsham during the 1790s, and in 1838 Osborne Yates occupied the Ferry House, the Barn and Yard, Windlass Meadow and other adjoining land along the riverside. From Huntsham 'the river takes a fine course, gliding through a long reach of hills, whose sloping sides are covered with large lumpish detached stones, which seem, in a course of years, to have rolled from a girdle of rocks'. Further upstream at Mainoaks there is evidence of a wharf dating from 1795, and during the 1790s lime was freighted from below the lofty crags of the Coldwell Rocks.[18]

Accounts from Old Forge at the Huntsham bend in 1797

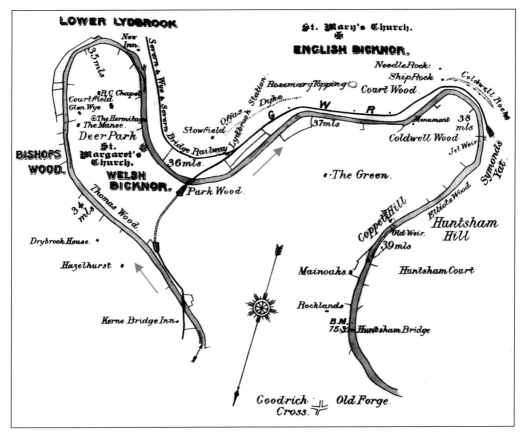

Stooke's map of the Wye between Huntsham and Bishopswood

Lydbrook

Before reaching Lydbrook the Wye flows between Welsh Bicknor and English Bicknor to Stowfield, where in the 1790s lime coal was loaded from a wharf onto barges for delivery to the lime kilns along the river. In the Forest of Dean between Stowfield and Lower Lydbrook there was a Wyeside quay where coal was delivered by Teague's horse-drawn tramway in 1802. The same year it was recorded that 'the coal company in Hereford have within a few weeks past purchased, or got on lease, every wharf and landing-place on the Wye at Lydbrook'.[19]

At Lower Lydbrook there was plenty of riverside activity associated with Lydbrook Forge, with entries in the barge accounts for 'fire cole for ye use of Lidbrook Forge' in 1744, and 'carriage of Charcole as of Redbrook & Lidbrook' in 1745. By 1770 there was 'a large wharf, where coals are shipped for Hereford, and other places. Here the scene is new, and pleasing. All has thus far been grandeur and tranquillity. It is now life, and bustle. A road runs diagonally along the bank; and horses, and carts appear passing to the small vessels, which lie against the wharf, to receive their burdens.'[20]

In 1797 the wharf at Lydbrook was 'very large and extensive'; from there 'a considerable commerce in coals' was carried on to Ross, Hereford and other places. Around this date

The remains of Teague's Wharf at Lydbrook in 2008. James Teague was a Free Miner born in Ruardean in 1750. Unable to read or write, he nevertheless joined in a business venture with the owners of the Perch Hill Mine in 1796 to construct a tramway from the mine down to his quay on the Wye at Lydbrook. The tramway operated for a few years but soon fell out of use and the track was lifted for use elsewhere in 1815.

Mr. Thompson, George Morse and James Teague were shipping coal, lime and seeds from the Lydbrook wharves. In 1808 the Lydbrook ironworks were for sale, together with four wharves occupied by George Morse and John Gage, James Pearce, Richard Bennett and John Williams.[21] Further upstream a site formerly occupied by the Wheatstone family 'used as a wharf or laying down Coal and other Things and opposite to a Meadow lying on the other side of the said River called the Boat Meadow' was leased to John Mason in 1803 and John Harrison in 1806, probably on the site occupied by the former Quay Row at Waterscross. From 1824 this wharf was busy loading lime from the Vention lime kilns, sold 'By the Barge Load' to places both down the Wye and upstream as far as Sugwas beyond Hereford.[22]

Below the Vention lime kilns a beer house was established in the early 19th century by the Harrison family. They were

The Vention Lime

IS really possessed of truly superior Qualifications for the purposes of Manure, Mortar, and Water Cement. Its pungent and highly caustic properties recommend it to the consideration of Skinners, Tanners, and Soap-boilers.

PRICE PER DOZ.

At the VENTION LIME-KILNS, near Lidbrook, Five Shillings.

PRICE DELIVERED, AS FOLLOWS :—

By the Barge Load.	£.	s.	d.	By the Barge Load	£.	s.	d.
At Old Forge, per doz.	0	7	0	At Glowson Stenders,			
Goodrich Ferry, do..	.0	8	0	per doz.	0	8	3
Wear-End,....... do.	...0	8	6	Wilton and Ross,do.	...0	9	0
Backney,.........do.	...0	10	0	Linedor,.......do.	...0	11	0
Cobler's-Point, do.	...0	11	6	Hoarwithy,.......do.	...0	12	0
Carey, ... do.	...0	13	0	Hancocks,.........do.	...0	14	0
Ox-ford,.......... do.	..0,15		3	Bullingham,.......do.	...0	17	0
Hereford,.........do.	...0	17	0	Sugwas,... ....do...	1	0	0

Apply to Mr. WILLIAM WHITE, Wye-Bridge Wharf, Hereford, who has on hand a choice assortment of BEST FOREST COAL, COKES, LIME-COAL, & FIRE-BRICKS. Orders will also be thankfully received by JOHN WALKINSHAW, Lidbrook, near Ross.

An 1824 advertisement for supplying, and shipping by the barge load, lime from the Vention kilns

The Vention lime kilns at Lydbrook

succeeded by John Wheatstone who named it the Royal Springs. Nearby was the New Inn of 1773, in use when the tramway opened in 1812 and run successively by those associated with the river trade during the 19th century before being demolished. At Lower Lydbrook another New Inn emerged in 1837, owned by the Vaughan family of Courtfield; the inn later became the Courtfield Arms. The Anchor Inn of 1698 suggests a connection with the river trade but it stands almost a mile from the Wye.[23]

From Waterscross a field path through riverside meadows led to an enclosure in Ruardean called Wyelands, where a wharf was established in 1821 by the Lydney Trading Society who 'established a goods and passenger service from the Severn to the Wye', aiming to reduce the transport costs of iron, tin-plate, sand, flour, grain and groceries. There are scanty remains of the tramway that had been extended to this wharf from Lydbrook after an Act of 1810, and no evidence remains of the wharf which closed shortly after 1840 – or of the small inn reputed to have offered hospitality to travellers and traders.[24]

Bishopswood

The horse-drawn tramway from Mierystock terminated at Bishopswood in 1814, with one fork crossing the Walford road to reach an existing wharf known as Burtons or Bishopswood Wharf, and a second fork heading to the right to the forge of John Partridge's ironworks, and then left under the road through an arched tunnel to Cinderhill Wharf. The use of the tramway was short-lived, and around 1830 the branch to Cinderhill Wharf was discontinued. Burtons or Bishopswood Wharf dates from at least 1783 when a dispute over ownership occurred between the Vaughans of Ruardean and the Clarkes of Hill Court

79

in Walford. In 1789 Mr. Holder was paying '£2-2-0 being one yrs rent for the wharf at Bishopswood, formerly Rented by Mr. Watkins & afterwards taken to by Mr. Partridge & held by him for one year ending Lady day 1788'.[25]

At Bishopswood the bargemen would have been excited to see the smoke and activity at the 'Bishop's Wood Iron works, and Coal-wharf; behind which is Bishop's Wood house, belonging to John Partridge esq. and occupied by Mrs. Ives the mother of his lady. The brook that runs into the Wye, called Bishop's brook, parts the counties of Hereford and Gloucester, and the parishes of Walford and Ruardean. The latter, called Ruardean has much scenery, eminently picturesque', as described by Thomas Fosbroke.[26] From 1823 James Ward was shipping coal and other goods from the coal wharf on his vessels the *Prudence*, a 42-ton barge, the *Mary*, a 130-ton snow, the *Betsy*, a 48-ton trow and the *William*, a 43-ton barge.[27]

Walford

The handsome Kerne Bridge was built over the Wye after an Act of 1825. It was originally a toll bridge with a table of payments ranging from one penny to nine pence, and was intended to improve communications by road between the Forest of Dean and Hereford, and provide a link with the horse tramway from Bishopswood. The arches were wide and high enough for barges to pass under, but no known evidence suggests any wharfs or tying

Samuel Ireland's depiction of the Goodrich Ferry in 1797

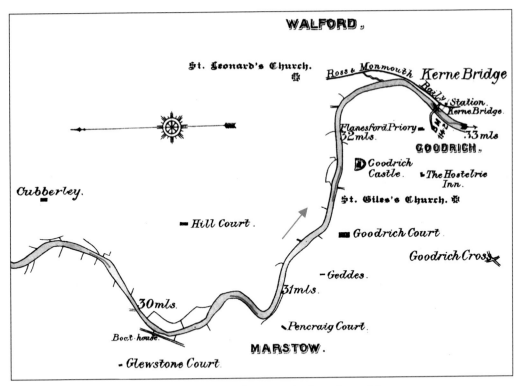

Stooke's map of the Wye from Goodrich and past Marstow

up places at this site. The wharfs were situated further upstream on both sides of the Wye at Goodrich Boat, where an ancient route from Ross to Monmouth crossed the river.

The road from Ross to Goodrich Boat was turnpiked by the Ross Trust in 1749, the way following the line of the present minor route to Hom Green. The toll road passed between the elegant 17th-century Hill Court and the picturesque Old Hill Court, and led ahead to the riverside. At this delightful setting, below the rugged ruins of Goodrich Castle, were the remains of an inn and a boat house and a half-buried milestone, originally inscribed '3 miles to Ross, 1 mile to Cross Keys'.[28]

On the Walford bank the Boat Meadow was used as a 'landing and standing' for the ferry and the barges and trows loading and unloading. However, according to writings and illustrations of the 18th and 19th centuries, it was the 'Wharf, Tow Path and Bowling Green' with its Boat Inn on the Goodrich side that was more frequently used. This was a scene of 'bustling life and an incessant passing to and fro beneath the half green half frowning ramparts, very pleasant to behold. Here were both a ford and a ferry with its ever amusing incidents and not unfrequent, alas! loss of life, and a ferry. A large rope was stretched across the stream, between two lofty poles, and the ferry-boat securely slung, was drawn from side to side with its motley freight – horses, gigs, market women in scarlet cloaks, white faced Herefords, and tourists. The confusion being generally heightened at the critical moment by the passage of a fleet of barges laden with timber, or piled high with bark.'[29]

Joseph Clarke of Hill Court,
1680-1738

During the 18th century, Hill Court in Walford was occupied by the Clarke family, who owned land and property on both sides of the Wye including the Boat Meadow. In 1738 Joseph Clarke's executors were settling the accounts on the sale of some cider. They paid bills for 'Landing 48 hhd, & 22 casks', 'cranige, halling and gauging', 'a man for filling up', 'Boatmen for taking it' and 'a man for selling, turning and Halling' for a total of £6 10d, producing a profit of £ 56 3s from the sale. Deliveries of hampers and bottles were made 'to the Hill' by the boatman, John Hughes, in 1750 to Stephen Clarke, and in 1753 to John Clarke. During the 1780s and 1790s 'loads of coal' were hauled to the Hill and divided amongst the tenants including putting a delivery of coal on the riverbank for a Mr. Jones.[30]

Probably also from the Boat Meadow, Mr. Elton shipped '3 Hhds Cyder' and '3 Empties from Bristol' in 1795, Mr. George Watkins conveyed '4 bush. of flower @ 18/6' in 1810, and Kingsmill Evans Esq. of the Hill received '3 Crates of potage from Bristol' and several bushels of oats in 1811. From Goodrich Rope on the opposite bank, lime was shipped by Mr. Davis the ferryman, who kept the Boat Inn and offered 'a clean room and frugal fare' to those using the ferry and working the barges in the late 18th century.[31] In 1838 the Ross Turnpike Trust advertised for 'raising and hauling stone' to be delivered to Goodrich Boat for road mending.[32]

Glewstone

The original route of the main road from Ross towards Monmouth closely followed the Wye, passing an ideal wharf site known in 1749 as Glewstone Stenders or Tenders. In 1809 lime, casks, bottles and barley were freighted by 'Trow' and 'Barge' for Mr. John Griffiths, and in 1814 turnips and swedes were transported from Glewstone for Mr. Addis at Glewstone Court, 'pleasantly situated within a short distance of the much admired River Wye, and

HEREFORDSHIRE.

TO BE SOLD BY AUCTION,

BY WILLIAM MERRICK,

At the Callow Inn, on Tuesday, the Fourth day of December next, between the hours of Three and Four o'clock in the afternoon, subject to such Conditions of Sale as shall be then produced,

NINETY ELM TIMBER TREES, fit for Plank or other Navy purposes, marked and numbered with white lead, standing on certain Lands at Trewaugh Farm, in the parish of Langarren, within six miles of Monmouth, five miles of Rofs, and four miles of the river Wye, at Glowston.

Mrs. Peak, at Trewaugh, will appoint a person to shew the Timber; and for further particulars apply to the Auctioneer.

An advertisement for sales of timber 4 miles from the
Wye 'at Glowston' (Glewstone) in November 1798

The Wye at Glewstone Stenders or Tenders

near the Turnpike-road from Ross to Monmouth'. During the 1840s 'barges loaded and unloaded timber and stone', and the nearby cottage served bargees and travellers as the 'Glewstone Boat Beer House', where James Price was the victualler and the proprietor of a pleasure boat.[33]

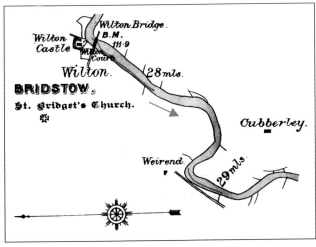

Stooke's map of the Wye near Weirend

Weirend

The Wye makes a sweeping and swift meander at Weirend, a name that is a reminder of the former weir, mills and fishery that were recorded in 1697 when the stone weir was 'six feet high with a hedge upon part of it'. The mills were rented for less than £10 a year and were situated half a mile below Wilton Bridge, but shortly after this date went out of use. When William Llewellyn acquired a cottage with a garden and small parcel of land 'near the Weare End', he may have taken advantage of this site at the start of an unhindered navigation on the Wye.[34]

By 1754 William Llewellyn had left the Wear End cottage and established himself at Wilton where he built a 'storehouse built on ye Waste by Wilton Bridge and on which he has made a Wharf'. Although Llewellyn had moved upstream, Weirend provided a convenient place to load and unload lime and brat from the Lime Kiln Field. Brat was probably a name given to a form of limestone, and may have been used for road making and repairs.[35] From 1795 Rev. Jones from Weirend was trading in lime and brat, between 1800 and 1809 John Addis was trading in lime, pantiles, swedes and turnips, and in 1811 Benjamin Mabe at Lower Wear End paid £1 10s for '2 dozen lime'.[36]

7   WHARVES – WILTON QUAY & ROSS DOCK

From Weirend the bargees would have negotiated a meander of the Wye to reach a pleasing sight at Wilton with its two riverside inns, coal wharf, warehouses, quay and wharves on each side of the river. Having negotiated the handsome stone-arched bridge a view of Ross would have come into sight with barges along the wharves at Ross Dock. From the mid 18th century the dock situated below the town became 'enriched with pleasure boats constantly in motion, in their passage to and from Chepstow, giving life and beauty to the scene. These boats are lightly constructed and navigated by three men either with or without a sail.'[1] At the dock the Wye tourists boarded the pleasure boats fully laden with provisions and were taken down the Wye by boatmen. Passengers seeking 'the Picturesque' were thus fully equipped to capture the untamed beauty of the Wye in paintings, poetry and prose.

Wilton Quay and Wharves

Wilton in Bridstow parish was considered to be the 'quay or wharf to Ross by furnishing a convenient accommodation for the shipping and landing of goods sent up and down the river'. As soon as the Wye was cleared of weirs and became navigable after the 1695 Act, an enterprising young man called Luke Hughes became 'the first proprietor of any barge on the river at this place established for trading purposes' and in 1701 was admitted and sworn as a Freeman of the City of Hereford as one of the first 'bargemen' on the Wye.[2] He and his family were responsible for establishing the New Bear Inn (later renamed the King's

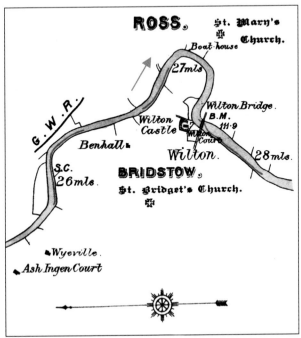

Stooke's map of the Wye at Wilton and Ross

Head) and developing the quay and wharves at Wilton on the waste of the manor. Others soon followed and, known as the 'men of the river', they began to trade on the Wye from this small hamlet.

In 1735 Luke Hughes leased 'All that house or Building then lately erected upon a piece of Waste Land in the Lordship of Wilton upon Wye at a place called the Vineyard [on the corner of Wilton Lane] for Lodging and storing goods to pass by the Barges and Boats upon ye River to Bristol'. The lessors were later listed as Luke Hughes aged 58 of Wilton, William Hughes aged 22 of Goodrich and John Rideout aged 30 of Bridstow, and the tenant as William Llewellyn. The same year William Barrow leased the 'White

In the background is the King's Head Inn, formerly the New Bear

Lyon' and two years later Thomas Barrow rented a parcel of waste ground '12 or 13 yards in Length and about 12 or 13 in breadth & Bounded by the Bridge on the North and in part on the West end by the End of the piers or Buttress or Butment of the said Bridge and then open to the River Wye'.[3]

By 1738 Luke Hughes borrowed enough funds to expand his use of the riverside by leasing Pidgeon House Close where he erected a messuage and other dwellings later known as Wye Bank.[4] By 1754 another wharf was established by John Mason Vaughan, a Wye boatman who lived in Ross. He erected a shed to be used as a warehouse on each side of the bridge next to the river. The same year William Llewellyn leased 'a Storehouse built on ye Waste by Wilton bridge on which he has since made a Wharf', and occupied another wharf made 'on ye west side of the Wilton bridge on the waste of the manor without any licence granted for that purpose or any rent paid for the same', which had been 'made by one Edward Tamplin'. Elizabeth, William Llewellyn's widow, was brought before the court in 1774 'for not removing her Old Barge lying in the Road leading from Wilton to the Vineyard'.[5]

By 1776 another wharf site had been added opposite the Great House (Wilton Court) 'between the highway on the west and the river Wye on the east and extending north to stable and land of the [Guy's] Hospital'.[6] (Guy's Hospital had acquired the Herefordshire estates of James Brydges, Duke of Chandos, in 1731-2 as an investment. Only a small proportion of the estates came into their immediate

WILTON-UPON-WYE, HEREFORDSHIRE.
TO BE LET,
WITH IMMEDIATE POSSESSION.

ALL that spacious and newly erected MALT-HOUSE, and WAREHOUSE, with a Horse-Mill, Chark-House, Cellar, Yard, and Garden, standing in the Village of Wilton, in the Parish of Bridstow, and late in the Occupation of Mr. Wm. Porter, deceased.

These Premises will be found desirable for a Maltster, and Corntactor, being in an excellent situation for Business, and capable of making Four Thousand Bushels of Malt annually.

For a View and other Particulars apply to Mrs. Norton, Wilton, or to Mr. Tristram, Ross.

The Malthouse and warehouse advertised to be let in 1815

86

The Malthouse and barges sketched through an arch of
Wilton Bridge by James Wathen in 1800

possession, for much was held in reversion for the duke's daughter-in-law – his son having died a few years earlier – for her life. Only when she died in 1754 did Guy's Hospital obtain full possession.)

William Porter, a carpenter, became involved in the river trade as a maltster and corn factor who operated a 'regular trow from Ross and Wilton to Bristol for a few years', and may have assisted in the building of two barges. His business was based at the Malthouse, which had formerly belonged to Thomas Prosser when it had been partly used as a 'Meeting House for Protestant Dissenters'.[7] From 1777 Porter carried out major repairs for Amos Jones at the 'Old Malt House' and the Great House where Elizabeth Llewellyn and her two daughters lived. He also constructed a 'Coal Wharf', built 'two Bark Houses', made repairs to the 'Lower Warehouse', and for the price of £97 1s 1d erected a stone and timber quay.[8]

In 1780 the 'Quay or landing-place on the river Wye' was leased to Thomas Wood, a Ross apothecary, whose under-tenant Charles James was at liberty 'to use the doorway from the warehouse to the quay' which measured '81 ft in length and 20 ft in breadth'.[9] James also leased the 'messuage or Inn called the White Lyon with garden, stable, slaughter house and wharf' with an agreement that a room was to be 'used as a gaol for the manor of Wilton, with liberty of passage, free mooring on the wharf of such ferry boats as they think fit'.[10] By 1807 William Porter had finished repairs at the Great House and Malthouse and made a request to James Woodhouse, the agent of Guy's Hospital, to take over the lease as 'well calculated for the business of a cornfactor and barge owner' as no other premises in the village were suitable for his large family of six children.[11]

James Woodhouse was from a family of lawyers and property owners who were related to the family at Aramstone in Kings Caple. James followed in the footsteps of his uncle as an agent to the Hospital Governors. It was not until after his death in 1809 that they discovered his dishonesty and incompetence over sales and exchanges.[12] Between 1805 and 1809 Woodhouse and Porter were trading fish, cheese, bark and slate with receipts for rents paid 'for landing on the waste', 'Lower Warehouse', 'on Dock Meadow' and for 'faling and stripping Bark'.[13]

Another property owner involved with the river trade at Wilton was William Wiltshire who followed his father as a corn factor. He died in 1803 and was buried in the same tomb as his father, who had died in 1785, in Bridstow churchyard. William Wiltshire's daughter Mary married Henry Platt and they continued in the river trade until their deaths, which are recorded on a memorial window in Bridstow church.[14]

The Biss family of Hereford also owned property at Wilton, and after

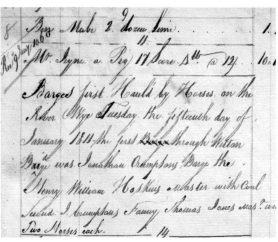

A record in the barge accounts of the first use of horses hauling barges through Wilton Bridge on 15 January 1811

The tomb of William Wiltshire at Bridstow Church

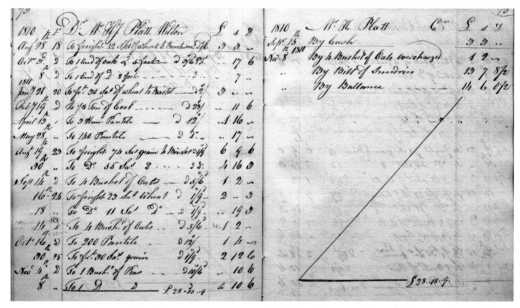

Accounts of Henry Platt showing amounts paid for freighting goods including coal, pantiles, wheat, oats, grain and peas

James Biss died in 1812 his wife Susannah 'continued to carry on the business of Coal-merchant and barge owner in the same way her husband had done for the space of three years or thereabouts. She was assisted by her son Mr. Charles Biss and it was carried on with the consent and approbation of all the residuary of her Husband's Will and particularly with that of Mr. William Pulling Jun. who married a daughter of the late Mr. Biss.' Although she carried out the management according to her husband's will, and was assisted by her son with the consent of her son-in-law, she claimed it was due to 'injurious competition between Persons in the trade that ... she sustained a considerable loss'. Her stock had to be sold which led to 'an unfortunate dispute' between the two families.[15]

Accounts of the Biss family from 1801 recording the shipping of flour, wheat and baskets of lime – as well as replacing a spar on one of their barges

In 1817 James Hughes, a descendant of the legendary Luke Hughes, died. James had held certain rights to the White Lion Inn, the Bear Inn, a blacksmiths shop, a warehouse and the quay alongside the 'Towing Path', but there were doubts about his rights which were not resolved until 1821 when his son Thomas, who occupied the 'Bear Inn and warehouse in Wilton', raised a mortgage of £720. This amount probably went towards refurbishing the Bear Inn, which was renamed as the Kings Head. He later sold the inn to become a baker in Gloucester, ending the family's long connection with Wilton.[16]

The wharves at Wilton were used for boat building in the early 19th century. In 1804 John Thomas built a 17-ton barge named the *Rival* for its owner in Monmouth, and in 1825 the *Thomas*, a 37-ton trow, was built by an unnamed shipwright or carpenter. William Porter part owned a sloop of 65 tons called the *Wilton*, which between 1787 and 1801 'sailed regularly to Bristol from Wilton and Ross' and from 'Abbey Tintern and Brockweir'. Porter shipped bags of clover seed, sacks of wheat, peas, hop pockets, 'Paper Parcels', deal, hogsheads, barrels and even salmon. As his business expanded, delivering coal and freighting wheat and barley from Hereford, Fownhope, Ballingham, Hoarwithy and Fawley, Porter was able to became the sole owner of a 147-ton coastal brig called the *Lively* in 1803.[17]

Those involved at Wilton during the early 19th century were William Wiltshire, James Hughes, Charles Prosser, William Bonner, Henry Platt and Mary Platt, who were shipping 'Sacks of wheat to Bristol', 'Hard Coal', '2 stone Flax', 'Baskets of lime', 'Oats from Monmouth', 'Hops to Bristol', 'Sacks of Wheat to Brockwear', '200 Pantiles', 'Seeds from Bristol' and '11 Sacks from Wilton to Bristol'. Although based at Hereford, James Biss was the owner of two trows whose cargoes included 18 sacks of flour from Wilton to Bristol and 28 sacks of wheat from Wilton to Brockweir.[18]

By 1839 James Thomas & Co. occupied the Great House, the Coal Yard and the Warehouse at Wilton, whilst George Webb kept the White Lion and occupied the remaining buildings on the Vineyard. Charles Biss owned Wilton House which was let to John Stevens, Charles Prosser owned and occupied the 'House, Malthouse and Garden' and Mary Platt was living at Wye Bank (now Bridge House) and owned several cottages, meadows and farm buildings at Hall's Barn (Orles Barn) and a malthouse in Wilton.[19] In 1852 Elizabeth Prosser was living at Wilton when the last known barge shipment was recorded in the Wilton ledger, destined for Edward Phillips, a corn dealer in Monmouth. The cargo consisted of 53 sacks of 'wheat' and 43 sacks of 'white wheat'.[20]

Wilton Bridge

With an increase in travel and transport during the Elizabethan period the local citizens began to petition for a bridge to replace the 'dangerous and unreliable crossing in floods or during low water,' where numerous accidents and loss of life occurred due to the overloading of boats crossing the 'furious and dangerous river'. The Wilton-upon-Wye Bridge Act was passed in 1597 to replace the ferry and to compensate Charles Brydges at Wilton Castle for the loss of his income from the ferry. The handsome six-arched structure was built of local sandstone and completed by 1600 as a toll bridge. The tolls continued to be collected until 1612 when they were bought out under the terms of Thomas Webbe's will.[21] (This Ross benefactor bequeathed £200 to buy out the tolls and purchase 'of Charles bridges esquire his heirs and assigns the ten pounds which is due and payable yearly to the said Charles to his heirs and assigns out of the pontage of Wilton Bridge'.)

When approaching Wilton Bridge the bargees would have faced a challenge negotiating their barges under the arches against a strong current. The hauliers followed the path to the bridge, walked to the top of it, and then crossed the road with the long tow rope still attached to the top of the mast, the rope scoring into the stonework of the bridge's parapet. When the barge reached the bridge the mast was lowered, the master releasing the tow rope. Those on the bridge hauled it in and swiftly dropped to the crew on the barge

to be refastened once the vessel reached the opposite side of the bridge and the hauliers could continue their strenuous journey upstream.[22] At a meeting of the Rivers Wye and Lugg Navigation and Horse-Towing Path Company in 1832, the Ross Turnpike Commissioners were concerned over the danger to road users and questioned the 'means of obviating the passing of the Towing-ropes across the Road at Wilton Bridge'.[23]

In 1884 Henry Tweed wrote about the deeply cut grooves on the coping-stones of the bridge, noting that they were the 'marks left by the once busy traffic which used to ply up and down the now almost boatless river in days before railroads were thought of, when the Wye was the main outlet for the trade of the country and a navigable river. They were cut by the barge ropes. Below the bridge may be seen the wharves now choked with mud, at which the barges loaded and unloaded their cargoes, and driven into the masonry across the road are

A barge shown passing under Wilton Bridge in 1839,
and a photograph showing the bridge parapet scored by the bow ropes

Two illustrations of barges passing Wilton Castle. The upper one is from an estate map of 1755 and the lower one is by Samuel Ireland in 1797

iron fastenings to which the vessels were secured. For the river traffic then was the life of Wilton.'[24] Once under Wilton Bridge some barges would have sailed on to Ross, whilst others loaded or unloaded on the upstream side of the bridge where the wharf, buildings and meadows around Wye Bank were occupied by the Wiltshire and Platt families. They had good access onto the horse towing-path, Wilton Bridge and the turnpike roads to Ross, Hereford and Monmouth.

Before reaching Ross the barges passed the ruins of Wilton Castle, which had been built to defend an ancient river crossing. Initially constructed as a motte and bailey, with later remains dating from the 13th century, during the Civil War the castle was burnt by the Royalists and left as a charred ruin which was sold to the Governors of Guy's Hospital in 1731. A dwelling house was built partly within the walls of the great tower and by 1796 was described as a 'desirable residence' when let to Revd. William George. He took delivery of pantiles and lime in 1803, and the next tenant, Guy Hill, received loads of lime, tiles, tar and slates which were 'hauled' and 'freighted' for a total of £3 14s in 1811 and 1812. These building materials were probably unloaded at the Platt's wharf, unless the castle had a suitable landing stage.[25]

Ross Dock

In 1727 Ross was noted as 'a good old town, famous for good cyder, a great manufacture of iron ware, and a good trade on the River Wye'. The barges were hauled to an area known as the Dock, reached from the town by crossing Dock Meadow situated beside the river

Looking at Wilton Bridge and wharf from the meadows below Ross
by W. Radclyffe in 1840

An engraving of Ross in 1838 shows barges being propelled by sail and oars, hauled by two horses and towed by two men

below the town or by 'a flight of spacious stone steps' that led from the top of Dock Pitch (Wye Street).[26] The first known mention of the Dock was in 1747, a few years before the Rector John Egerton started to entertain his influential guests with a boat trip down the river, which developed into the Wye Tour.[27] From the mid 18th century the Dock area was alive with boatmen, bargees and tourists mingling with local craftsmen making rope, weaving baskets and dressing flax.

Because of the force of the river water during heavy rain, the floodplain on the edge of Ross was constantly subjected to the cutting of new water channels. It seems likely that these multiple channels in the past caused the former Bridstow parish boundary to be on the then Ross side of the Wye.[28] This meant that all the wharfs and meadows below Ross in Bridstow parish were under the ownership of the Governors of Guy's Hospital. The Dock Meadow was 'the meadow near Ross' where Thomas Griffiths 'built a Storehouse and lands goods, it lying close under the town of Ross on the River Wye'. The rent was paid to Guy's Hospital in 1754 by John Puckmore, who 'reserved to himself a liberty of laying pipes in the meadow thro' which he serves the town of Ross with water'.[29]

Ross in the 1790s was described as a town 'abstracted from its elevated and delightful situation, has little to render it worthy attention; the prospect from the churchyard a spot to which the traveller is generally conducted on his arrival displays a very extensive and enchanting landscape both above and below the town',[30] scenery that attracted those seeking the Picturesque. From the Prospect the Wye tourists enjoyed a splendid view of the river and the dock where a variety of goods were unloaded from the barges: tiles and deals (planks of wood) shipped from Chepstow and Bristol, '11 Bags ashes from Hoarwithy', '13 Tons Tiles from Brockweir', '4 Hampers Bottles from Bristol', and bundles of twigs for basket-making. Amongst goods being loaded were oats, barley, wheat, flour, coal, lime,

A barge moored at Ross in the 1850s

timber, '25 Packs Wool to Chepstow', '2 Boxes Soap to Chepstow', '1 Cask Butter to Bristol', '28 Bundles of Hoops to Bristol' and '7 Sacks Peas to Bristol'.[31]

The Jones family of Ross traded on the Wye from 1786 when John Jones, described as a merchant, was co-owner of the *Wilton*, a 65-ton sloop, and of the *Fanny*, a 125-ton brigantine. There was Amos Jones, a grocer, who had use of a wharf at Wilton from 1797, and during the early 19th century Charles and Philip Jones of the Cleeve were shipping lime, tiles, flour, barley and wheat from their wharves on the Ross side of Wilton Bridge. It was probably the same Amos Jones of Tudorville who received deliveries by barge of hampers, boxes and '12 chairs from Bristol' in 1808 and '9 Doz of lime' in 1811.

By 1823 the water works had been taken over by John Tovey, who occupied the Dock together with John Tristram. William Newton had 'His own Dock' and Joseph Newton was at 'His own flax House' and had use of the 'Ropewalk', all situated near and around the Dock and adjacent to warehouses and malthouses along 'the street leading from the market hall to Wilton Bridge'.[32] In 1827 Ross Dock was kept busy with the 'numerous and important' exports of the district – 'Great quantities of cider, hops, oak-bark, wood, wheat and timber' were sent down to Brockweir where they were shipped to London, Bristol, Ireland and other places. The imports were slate, deals, and heavy goods sold by shopkeepers, although these were 'few and of little consequence'. Coal was 'brought from the Forest of Dean in Gloucestershire, partly by river, and partly by mules, and sold at a reasonable price'.[33]

At the Dock a small licensed house kept by Stephen Lane blossomed into the Hope and Anchor Inn where beer and cider was served to the thirsty bargemen, and no doubt

*These days Ross Dock
is mainly used by canoeists*

to the Wye tourists if they had not already been adequately provided at the larger and more comfortable coaching inns. Alternatively a climb up the steps led to the Lamb Inn, where accommodation as well as refreshment was available in the 'Bar, Parlour, capacious Dining-room, six bedchambers, two kitchens, three cellars and Brewhouse'. That was before the land agent John Morgan sold and closed the 'well-accustomed inn' in 1830 and later sold the 'One Mill', 'Water Works' and four cottages at the Dock in 1847.[34]

A few years later the river trade ceased, leaving one solitary barge moored at Ross Dock and 'as the nineteenth century progressed the barge traffic settled into a steady decline, a decline that was rapidly accelerated by the opening of the Hereford, Ross and Gloucester Railway in 1855. After this date, with the exception of a few timber barges that went up as far as Hoarwithy and possibly Fownhope there was precious little of the hey-days left, a fact that was abundantly clear by the number of old barges and trows that were abandoned at the river's edge slowly rotting away.' One such vessel that had sunk into the bank near the Hope and Anchor was still visible at the beginning of the 20th century.[35]

8   WHARVES – BRIDSTOW TO HOLME LACY

Whilst the Wye above Ross has been less used for navigation than the stretch of river below the town, there is still plenty of evidence for wharves, barges, cargoes and those involved in the river trade, especially at Hoarwithy, Fownhope, Mordiford and Hereford. Between Bridstow and Holme Lacy the bargees glided around the large meanders of the Wye 'along the midst of a fine valley, screened on each side by broken banks and fine woody hills, which in autumn, by the variety of shades they present, add an ornamental lustre to the gaieties of nature, till, descending the swift current at some small distance the view varies, and the vanished prospect is succeeded by one of superior beauty; for winding round some woods, it opens to a large and more variegated scene'.[1]

Due to the way the river meandered between Bridstow and Holme Lacy there were a large number of ford and ferry crossings, but by the early 18th century many of the fords were either redundant or had been replaced by ferries, which meant the shallows of the fords could be deepened to allow a channel for the barge traffic. The Commissioners of the Rivers Wye and Lugg Navigation were responsible for 'cleansing and opening of the said rivers', and it is understood that, as was the case on the Severn, 'informal measures were taken by those who used the river to keep the channel clear'.[2]

Bridstow, Backney and Brampton

Below Ashe Ingen in Bridstow there was a wharf in the Wye Meadows where Samuel Morris was paying £2 14 6d for 'Dealer & Freight' for 'lime' and 'deals from Bristol' between 1795 and 1800, and during 1810 William Workman from Ashe was shipping oats, vetches and coal. Further upstream near two isolated cottages an enclosed lane led to the riverside, a piece of waste ground and a common at Backney where the Chepstow firm of Messrs. Bowsher, Hodges & Watkins had arranged a loading place during 1809 and 1810. The company shipped large quantities of bark, timber and poles from Backney to Chepstow and Bristol, and paid 9s for 'Loading at Difficult Places', 10s to 'men Roling the timber to the bank' and 5s 'for hauling'.[3]

In 1824 lime from Lydbrook was delivered to Backney at 10s per dozen 'By the Barge Load', and gravel was extracted from the wide and shallow bed of the river. Although the gravel was mainly carted away, some may have been loaded onto barges. At a later date the Hereford, Ross and Gloucester Railway constructed a bridge across the Wye where the

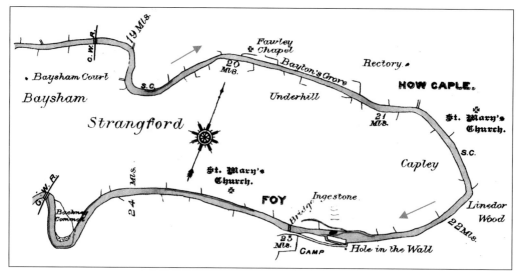

Stooke's map of the great loop of the Wye through Foy and How Caple and then west towards Sellack

river has formed an island as it sweeps around the common and flows between Backney and Brampton Abbotts. From Monks Grove, in Brampton Abbotts, dozens of hurdles were shipped to Bristol in 1810 by Bowsher, Hodges & Watkins, and John Newton shipped 'twigs' from the withy beds for his basket-making business in Ross.[4]

Foy

The winding Wye divides the parish of Foy into Foy East and Foy West, where wharves or landing places were sited on each bank. Before reaching the quaintly named Hole-in-the-Wall on the east bank, a riverside meadow called Cam Meadow was used by Bowsher, Hodges & Co. to ship '18 tons timber' and '3 tons timber' to Chepstow in 1810. Those hauling, steering and sailing the barges were pleased to reach the two beer houses at Hole-in-the-Wall: the Anchor and Can and The Gatehouse, the latter housing 'an alehouse, the Boatman's

The Anchor and Can at Hole in the Wall

The Gatehouse at Hole in the Wall

98

*A sketch of Foy in 1846
shows the masts of barges passing by*

Rest, that catered not only for the bargees passing between Hereford and Monmouth, but also to those crossing the ford below it to West Foy', and also served as 'stabling for the barge horses and a wharf'.

During the 1790s barges shipped hogsheads from Bristol – '6 Hhds of Tours le Bris',[7] '4 Hhds from Bristol' – for Mr. Lovell at Hill of Eaton. 'Elm Boards' were freighted from Foy to Chepstow for Bowsher, Hodges & Watkins, lime coal was delivered to Foy and in 1791 coal was 'measured for Mr. Winneat at the hole' for his lime kilns. On the west side of Foy, Mr. Collins at Ingestone and Mr. Rideout at Carthage paid for goods shipped on the river, which included apples, lime and bottles in 1795, cases of wine and rum, casks, bottles, hampers and hurdles in 1797, timber and Stourbridge bricks in 1801, plus an extra payment for 'Hauling' and 'Landing'.[8]

An atmospheric description of this part of the river is given in 1844. During one dark night a passer-by hurried past 'the pot house called the Hole in the Wall and passed the ferry where the horse-boat was moored to the shore, and had almost reached the wood when the storm came'. The only sound he heard was 'the awful imprecations of a blaspheming bargeman from a barge with a 'red light sailing down the broad stream'. The place was lonely on the road between the river and the wood, where on most nights he 'would have seen or heard some of the labourers of the surrounding farms coming from their toil, or an errand-woman returning from a neighbouring market, or a farmer on horseback jogging from a friend's home'.[9]

Further upstream at Lyndor, a former wharf belonging to the Perrystone estate had probably been used from at least 1752 when the Scudamores from Holme Lacy owned the woodlands. The timber was sold and shipped from 'Lyndor Wood' to the Commissioners of the Navy at Plymouth Yard.[10] In 1802 lime coal was unloaded off the barges *Sally* and *Henry*, and measured for the local lime kilns, and in 1804 Mrs. Clifford from Perrystone shipped an empty 'large cask to Bristol'. Although lime was available in the locality, the Vention lime kiln at Lydbrook was advertising deliveries of lime to Lyndor in 1824 at 11s a dozen for a 'Barge Load'.[11]

How Caple and Fawley
Within a short distance of Lyndor the barges reached a long riverside meadow known as Lord's Meadow lying below How Caple Court and church. This was where 'tiles and coal were imported and oak and timber exported on barges in the 1790s', and was the site of the How Caple wharf of 1799. In 1802. Mr. Perkins from How Caple was shipping hogsheads and barrels of cider and perry to Bristol, which were returned empty. A few years later in 1809, tons of poles and lathes were shipped from How Caple on the account of Joseph Trupp.

James Wathen's sketch of a barge on the Wye at How Caple in 1802

Continuing around the large Foy loop of the river the bargees either pulled in at or sailed past Much Fawley, traditionally known as a ferry and wharf site 'for loading barges with farm produce for transit down the Wye'. Apart from the hoops, oats, potatoes and clover shipped from Fawley between 1795 and 1803, goods imported included '5 tons Tiles from Chep[stow], 3 dozen lime, 6 cwt Seed from Bris[tol]', '4 Hhds from Bris, 1 Hamper liquor fr Bris, 1 Chest fr Bris', and bottles and bags for Mr. Jones and Mr. Seaborne.[12]

A curious custom is recorded in a lease of 1687 of a right of passage for the occupiers of Much Fawley and 'their servant's horses and carriages at all seasonable times between ye boat on ye river Wye at Much Fawley over and through Strangworth meadows and grounds ye Direct way by Strangworth house for ye carrying of lime and cole in their wains and carts from Howle or ye parts adjacent unto ye devised premises and for their market horses to and from Monmouth in such sort as Mr. Rodagon Oswald widdow mother of Elizabeth formerly used the same'.[13] This route across the Wye to transport lime, used to improve the land, from Howle Hill in Walford, and to carry goods on horses to Monmouth market was clearly an ancient right enjoyed by those at Much Fawley. A similar right existed at certain farms on the Guy's Hospital Estate in 1735.[14]

Sellack and Kings Caple

Strangworth, also known as Strangford, in Sellack was originally in Fownhope before parish boundary changes. Although there was a suitable landing place, little evidence suggests any wharves. Further upstream at Baysham, in 1745 the tenant Amos Jones was permitted 'to go through the Meadow lying by the River Wye at the Broken Bank in the parish of Sellack aforesaid with his teams to carry his Corn & Cyder to and from the said River when he shall have Occasion'.[15] One of his successors in 1810 was paying for unusual items freighted on the river, including '1000 of pantiles' and '3 Cwt of Iron weights'. In 1795

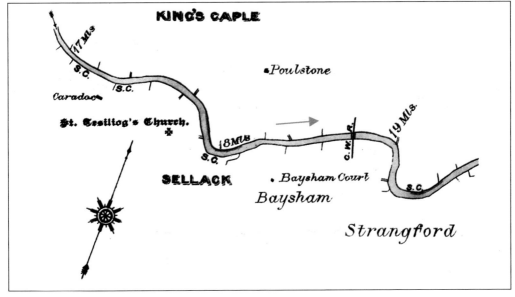

Stooke's map of the Wye through Sellack and past Kings Caple

Rev. James from 'Craddock' enjoyed his 'bottles' and 'oatmeal' shipped from Bristol, as did Mr. Dew from 'Craddock'.

The last known wharf in Sellack was on the parish boundary with Hentland, and belonged to the Kynaston estate in Hentland. The 'Valuable Freehold estate called Kinnaston' in 1799 was 'within a quarter of a mile of the River, by which means Grains and all other produce, maybe conveyed to Bristol, at a small expense'. The wharf was in 'Little Well Meadow' at Shepponhill, and even after the navigation of the Wye had ceased the estate offered the public 'a right of Wharfage for Timber over No 30, paying a Toll of 1s per Ton'. It was probably from this wharf site that timber was shipped and sold from 'Rig's Wood' in 1802.[16]

HEREFORDSHIRE.

TIMBER AND COPPICE WOOD.

TO BE SOLD BY AUCTION,
BY T. TRISTRAM,
At the King's-Head Inn, in the town of Rofs, On Thurfday, the Eleventh day of March, 1802, (and not on Thurfday, the Fourth, as advertifed in a former Paper), between the hours of Three and Six o'clock,

THREE Hundred MAIDEN OAK TIMBER TREES, in Rig's Wood, in the parifh of Sellack, together with all the Store Poles, Saplings, Coppice Wood, &c. now ftanding on 72A. 3R. 18P. divided in Lots.

The Timber is particularly calculated for Navy, Plank, and Cleft, of all defcriptions.

Richard Wood, the Woodward of Pig's-Crofs, will fhew the Timber, &c.; and further particulars may be had of the Auctioneer, Rofs.

N. B. The Coppice is fituate within a quarter of a mile of the River Wye.

An advertisement of 1802 for a sale in Ross of timber from 'Rig's Wood' in Sellack, noting how close the wood where the timber is to be felled is to the Wye

The site of 'Kerry's Lockstock Boat Place' in Kings Caple in 2011

Fortunately for the thirsty bargemen, a forward-thinking John Harris at Sellack Boat in Kings Caple opened his newly built home as the Old Boar Inn to coincide with the opening of the Wye as a navigable river after the Navigation Act of 1695. With the extra trade he added outhouses, a cider mill and storage for hogsheads and other containers, and persuaded Daniel Kerry, a friend of the family, to allow him the use of a piece of land alongside the river as a 'tying up place' or wharf where barges could safely load and unload. At this wharf, which became known as 'Kerry's Lockstock Boat Place', barges were loaded with local hogsheads of cider and sacks of corn to be conveyed downstream and sold in Bristol for a better price, while items such as seeds, hops and bark were shipped up and down stream. The Old Boar (now a house called Shieldbrook) also provided a convenient place for farmers to rest and refresh themselves while waiting for their cargoes, and for travellers crossing the ford and ferry at Sellack Boat.[17]

Mr. Stillingfleet, who lived at Aramstone in 1795, accounted for '5 Ton Fire Coal at 16s, £5 12s, paid discharging and allow Men for drink 5s', and '5 Ton Coal £4 5s'. A few years later Charles Cumberland from the same mansion took delivery of '8 ton House goods', '4 ton Coale', '1 crate 1 cask Vinegar', 'Liquors from Wilton' and '2 chest oranges'. Between 1809 and 1811 large quantities of wheat, oats, barley, peas and ryegrass were shipped to Bristol by Arthur Frere, John Cook and John Wainwright of Kings Caple, and several tons of coal were unloaded at Kings Caple.[18]

John Woodhouse was from a family of lawyers, property owners and merchants who inherited the Aramstone estate after his father's death in 1783. His cousin James was the agent of the Guy's Hospital Estate and was followed by his nephew James from 1780. The family also served as stewards of the Manor of Wilton. It is assumed that through this connection several documents relating to the river trade have passed to their descendants. Aramstone House was burnt down in 1680, rebuilt by the Woodhouse family and demolished c.1954.
The picture shows the house in 1788

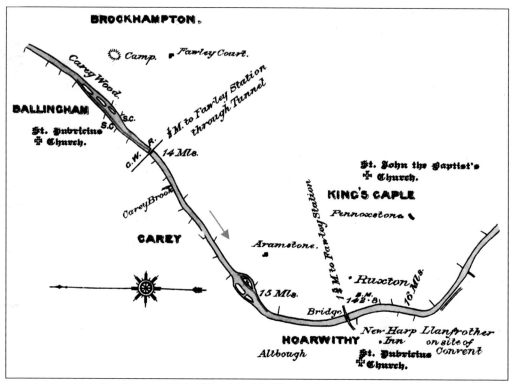

Stooke's map of the Wye through Hoarwithy and Ballingham

Hoarwithy

Hoarwithy developed around an ancient ford crossing the Wye at a wide and shallow part of the river. By 1581 the ferry known as 'ye great passage Boote of Horewethie' was in use with a 'small boat' which were both maintained by John Fidoe of Kings Caple in the late 18th century. Hoarwithy with its sloping banks and proximity to the turnpike road attracted wharf sites for produce from the nearby farms, malthouses, cider mills and the corn, paper and grist mills lying along the Wriggles Brook. About the same period as the Old Boar opened at Kings Caple, the Anchor Inn (now a house called Upper Orchard) opened at Hoarwithy to cater for the road and river trade.

With an increase of trade and transport on the Wye, bargemen found difficulty in mooring at Hoarwithy and moored their craft wherever they could, causing two local farmers in 1779 to notify them that action would be taken 'against every person who hereafter be found mooring barges on either of our lands'. It appears that after this date five wharf sites were established, at Red Rail, the Bark House, the lower and upper Timber Yard and at Hoarwithy Boat.[19] Barges heading upstream first reached Red Rail where an enclosed piece of land on both banks served as a wharf, and next was the wharf and bark ricks at the Bark House used from 1799 by Bowsher, Hodges & Watkins of the Chepstow Bark Company.

The bark company proposed to use a 'Barn near the river at Hoarwithy not yet finished' which belonged to Sir Hungerford Hoskyns of Harewood. The company were to 'cover this

HEREFORDSHIRE.
C Y D E R.

TO be peremptorily Sold, on Friday the 11th day of this inſtant April, at Lanfrother, near Roſs, in this county, about Eighty Hogſheads of Prime Cyder, made of the beſt fruits, Six Hogſheads whereof are Old Cyder, of an excellent quality, and fit for bottleing. The ſale will begin at eleven of the clock in the forenoon.

Cider advertised for sale in the Hereford Journal *for April 1777. Llanfrother being perched above the Wye near Hoarwithy, the hogsheads may subsequently have been transported by barge*

The Hoarwithy Boat Wharf in 2011

Building with Straw or Pantiles' so that the barn could be used to chop six or seven tons of bark over a four year period with 'wharfing for any bark' that the company left there.[20] In 1799 Bowsher, Hodges & Watkins transported '11 tons from Hoarwithy' followed by further quantities in 1800. Timber and 'Elm Boards from Hoarwithy' may have been loaded from the wharf known as the Timber Yard belonging to the Llanfrother estate, where hogsheads of 'Prime Cyder' and 'Old Cyder' were sold in 1777 and possibly shipped from their wharf.[21]

Below the bridge built to replace the Hoarwithy ferry, a wharf was used from 1795 to land 'Junk 4 Tons', '8 Tons Junk', and '3 bags Raggs', all of which was carted to the paper mill at Tressack and returned as paper shipped to Brockweir or Bristol. Lime and coal were unloaded at Hoarwithy, and barley, wheat, flax and hoops were sent downstream by Richard Smith of the Anchor Inn and Mr. Powles, with the paper transported by Edward Williams. Above the bridge a level meadow served as the upper Timber Yard where hurdles, wheat, barley and peas were shipped by Hungerford Hoskyns of Harewood and George Bennett from Altbough.[22]

Ballingham and Brockhampton

From Hoarwithy the Wye flows past a series of former islands at Bibletts, where the horse towing-path company intended the tow path to cross the Wye from Kings Caple to the Ballingham side of the river. Under the terms of the 1809 Act the 'Company of Proprietors shall and may keep a Ferry-Boat at or near the places called Putteston Watering Place, and Bullingham Road, and also at or near Hoarwithy Passage and How Caple'. They were also to 'erect and build any House or Houses, Stable or Stables, or other Building, on the Banks of or near to the said River Wye, for the purpose of collecting the Tolls hereby granted, and for the Use of the Ferries'. Instead of crossing the river at Bibletts, the draft horses, barges and men crossed further upstream at Careyboat, where a house was built by the Wye River Towing Path Co. on the Kings Caple side of the river.[23]

Carey Islands

From the Bibletts the bargees progressed slowly through a delightful valley sheltered by Carey Woods, where timber of between '20 or 30 years growth' was for sale in 1774, and after felling would have been sent downstream. From 1795 goods were conveyed from Carey in Ballingham, including '5 Bags peas to Bristol', 'Bdles. hoops to Bristol', 'Poles to Bristol' and '12 Sks Wheat to Bristol' shipped by Mr. Elliott and Thomas James of Knapp Green, who also took a delivery of coal in 1809. The wharf was probably at Boat Meadow in Carey from where 'Grain from Carey' was transported to Hereford on a barge called the *Charles* in 1827.[24]

At Carey Islands the bargemen needed to battle against a strong current flowing between the remains of Carey Mills and weir, a natural site for a corn mill established there by the 13th century and either rebuilt or converted into an iron forge which had gone out of production by 1697. The barges steered across to the bank at Brockhampton below the wooded slopes of Capler and from where, during the 1780s and 1790s, barley was sent to Brockweir and 'limecole' was delivered and measured for the surrounding lime kilns.[23] At this date the Dean and Chapter Quarry presented a busy sight as stone was being cut for the rebuilding of the cathedral's west face which had collapsed in 1786. Although an effort was made to seek suitable barges to carry the stone to Hereford, it was land carriage that was used.[26]

In 1799 lime coal was 'measured out at Capla for Mr. Pritchard, the *Henry* 12 cwt 30 lbs; measured out of the *Industry* 12 cwt 30 lbs; measured out of the *Henry* 12 cwt 6 lbs; measured out of the *Industry* 9 cwt 21 lbs; measured out of the *Fly* 12 cwt 27 lbs'. In 1843 the Dean and Chapter cut more stone from the Capler quarry which was used for

A barge below Capler Hill depicted by James Wathen in 1793

the cathedral tower. Maybe the quarrymen had cut too much stone as some was for sale in 1845 when 'every convenience for loading' was constructed at Capler.[27] Further stone was needed for the cathedral choir in 1847, when the contractor supplied carriage along the eight mile road route to Hereford.[28]

A barge in the Fownhope area depicted by James Wathen

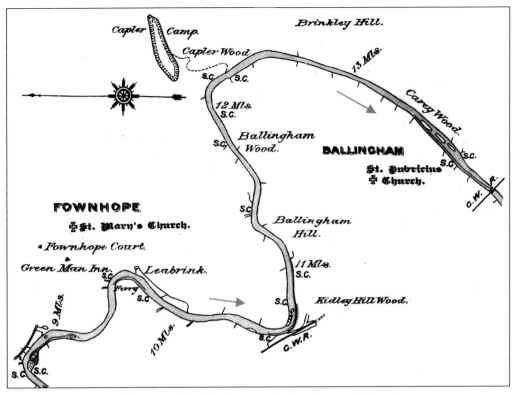

Stooke's map of the Wye between Ballingham and Fownhope

Fownhope and Bolstone

Upstream from Capler the Wye flows below Ballingham Hill and over the rocky remains of Hancock's Weir between the parishes of Fownhope and Bolstone. It was probably at Blackwell's Ditch near Shepherd's Rough on the west bank that timber, hoops, spokes, trenails and 'Cooper's Stuff' were shipped during 1796 and 'Wheat to Bristol' in 1811, with an extra payment made for hauling. The east side of the Wye at this point is dominated by the large parish of Fownhope where many wharf sites were established from the early 18th century for the shipping of timber, lime, bark, beer, wine and spirits. Coal was unloaded at the Coal Wharf for the lime trade, and during the first half of the 19th century the 40-ton *William*, the 13-ton *Ann and Peggy* and the 12-ton *Lady Alma* were built at Fownhope.

During the 18th and into the 19th century, cargoes were loaded on to barges from at least six wharf sites at Fownhope. It is not known which was used to load the timber from the Rudge Wood that belonged to the Dean and Chapter, from the coppices and woods of Martha Lechmere, or from James Kidley's woods in 1719 when it was 'sent down the Wye'. Some of the timber may have been converted into cordwood for the Foley and Rea partnership and 'delivered either to Newent furnace, Bishop's Wood furnace or Lydbrook Forge works'.[29]

Coal barges were unloaded at the Locking-stock, a riverside meadow at the end of Ferry Lane where 'a Wharf may be had for Landing the Coal'.[30] Lime coal was 'put out' during the 1790s at Fownhope Mill and 'bages of whete' were shipped to Brockweir and Chepstow. Bark was dried and stored at the Bark House on the banks of the river at Lechmere Ley in Fownhope, and conveyed on barges which freighted 20 to 25 tons of bark at a time to the tanneries in the Wye Valley. Some bark would have been used by the Fownhope tanner who received a delivery of coal in 1796.

Upstream, the Fownhope brewer, wine and spirit merchant and barge owner Nathaniel Purchas acquired access in 1783 to 'Shiplee [Shipley] boat' (the crossing connecting Fownhope with Holme Lacy) from where he sent tons of bark, pipes of wine, hampers, baskets and empty bottles to Bristol, and due to delays caused by river conditions in 1797 'Pd. five men 1s.6d. p day three days at Chepstow' as an allowance towards their keep whilst waiting for their return journey. His barges returned with pipes and casks of wine

Bryant's map of 1835 showing the wharf at Fownhope and another to the north of the village together with a warehouse, Fownhope Ford and the Ox Ford, and the sites of three ferries

The Bark House at Fownhope

which Purchas supplied as far afield as Kington, Bristol and Chepstow, either by barge or land carriage. In 1793 Squire Thomas Jones of Pencerrig recorded that he sent 'a wagon to Kington to meet a cargo from Purchas of Fownhope, & the next morning they returned with a hogshead of Port wine & 20 gallons of Malt Spirits'.[31]

The last two known wharves that the bargees used at Fownhope were at Lucksall, leased to Nathaniel Purchas in 1775 for his brewery business, and at Even Pits, where a warehouse was tenanted to John Wheatstone in 1774. He was one of the Wheatstone family who were involved in the river trade up and down the Wye. From 1744 they freighted iron, timber, lime and bark until at least 1847, and owned, captained and built barges. During the 1790s lime coal was unloaded at Even Pits for the lime kilns at Fownhope, where it was then measured as shown in the barge accounts: '2 doz. & 32 lb limecole', 'Measured for Mr. Winneot', 'put out of the Henry at Evenpit' and 'Settl.

'Mr. Purchas conducted us through his brewery, and showed us vast depositories of wine; accompanying these attentions with an air of so great good humour, and such a pressing invitation to partake of refreshment, that we took leave of this hospitable gentleman with regret.

We did not leave the neighbourhood, however, without frequently doing honour to the contents of his immediate cellar, which is very deservedly celebrated throughout the whole country.

Wishing to embrace the opportunity of seeing the Duke of Norfolk's house at Hom, we were directed to a ferry, at which a boat is kept for the purpose of conducting passengers over the Wye, but the wind frustrated all our efforts to make ourselves heard, and we were therefore constrained to return by the same road to Mordiford.'

George Lipscomb in *A Journey into South Wales*

With Uncle Whetstone and paid the interest up two that time all that was dew'.[32]

Within a short distance from the river were a number of inns and beer and cider houses, the oldest being the Green Man (formerly the Naked Boy) which served as a coaching inn and also a magistrate's court. There was the King's Arms with its cider mill, and at Even Pits was the Anchor, originally used as storage for wines and spirits by Nathaniel Purchas in 1800 and taken over by Richard Wheatstone, a barge owner. Standing opposite was the Luck's All, a beer house in 1855 'used as a public house in the occupation of Charles Wheatstone'.[33]

Holme Lacy

The river flows between Fownhope and Holme Lacy where 'the course of the Wye may be traced for some miles; and where it hides itself, either by the bendings of its current, or among the woods that decorate its banks, it is only to deceive the eye for a moment, and that it may re-appear in, perhaps, a different direction, or with a broader stream, among the meadows'.[34] The barges sailed past the great mansion of Holme Lacy House, seat of the Scudamore family who owned most of the parish and land, farms and woods in Ballingham and Bolstone.

From 1717 quantities of timber were purchased for the navy from 'My Lady Scudamore' of Holme Lacy. Bargemen such as William Morgan of Monmouth were employed in 1719 'to carry timber down the river Wye from Hom Park to Chepstow' for the Foley and Rea partnership, and William Smith of Bewdley was required to procure men skilled in creating rafts of timber and floating them down river to Chepstow. He provided ten such men 'from the river Severn who were so employed for about three years and in that time brought very great quantities of timber down the river Wye from Hom Park to Chepstow'.

The site of Shipley Wharf in 2007

The remnants of Holme Lacy Wharf in 2007

The timber rafts were formed at the edge of meadow used for pasturing 'horses and other cattle necessarily used and employed in hauling the timber out of the Park to the side of the river Wye'.[35]

From 1745 there were deliveries of 'Coals & Brays from Homlacey to Lidbrook', and a few goods were conveyed to Holme Lacy for Hollington and Bower farms during the 1790s. Sacks of wheat and bags

A barge passing Holme Lacy House in 1806

of barley were transported from Holme Lacy to Bristol between 1809 and 1810. The wharf near the church, adjoining the 'Withy Plantation', and the wharf at Shipley were the places where the barges pulled in to collect the agricultural produce from the local farms. Barges piled with lime from Lydbrook negotiated a further two miles around a serpentine bend to Ox Ford below Folly Farm. At this site a barge load of lime was available at 15s 3d per dozen from the Vention lime kiln in 1824.[36]

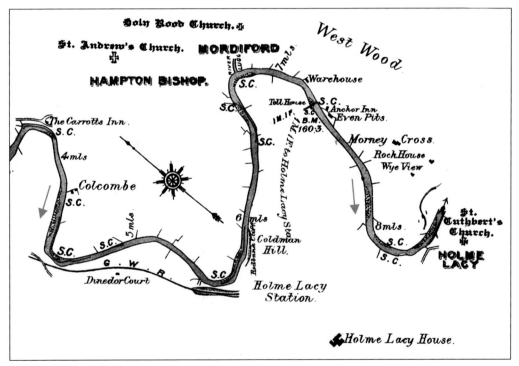

Stooke's map of the Wye from Holme Lacy past Mordiford and Hampton Bishop towards the edge of Hereford

9 WHARVES – MORDIFORD TO LEOMINSTER AND TO ROTHERWAS

Mordiford has always been threatened by flooding due to its vulnerable position at the junction of the Wye and its tributary the Lugg. The worst recorded flood was caused by the Pantaloe Brook in May 1811 when 'the village of Mordiford was visited by a tremendous storm of thunder, lightning, wind, and rain, by which the little river Pantaloe was swollen in some places to an extent of 180 feet in width, with a depth of 20 feet. In passing the village it swept away a large barn and cider mill, and a cottage adjoining, when William Husbands, miller, Ann Evans, his niece, Elizabeth Greenly, widow, and her infant child, Jemima, were drowned just above the said village, on the road leading to Woolhope. Many hundred tons of rocks were blown up and carried through the said village, by which several houses of the inhabitants were much injured, and gardens nearly destroyed.'[1]

Mordiford

At Mordiford the Lugg is crossed by a long and narrow stone bridge and causeway said to have been built in the 14th century and repaired in the 16th century. The 1697 Survey of the Rivers Wye and Lugg reported that the 'shallow below the bridge needs narrowing, and one arch of the bridge raising so as to allow vessels to pass in times of flood. Vessels of 12 to 14 tons can pass here over most of the summer period.' An arch was therefore raised to facilitate the passage of boats. No mention was made in the

James Wathen's depiction of barges at Mordiford in 1795

The confluence of the Lugg (on the left) and the Wye

Survey of any locks, and these were constructed at a later date and present by 1786 when Mordiford began to emerge as a busy place associated with the river trade.[2] It was here that cargoes were measured and transhipped onto smaller barges for deliveries up the Lugg. Below the bridge there was a pound lock where the navigation channel rejoined the river before its confluence with the Wye, where another lock was sited in the 18th century.

Visitors to the Hereford family at Sufton in 1796 passed 'through Mordiford, and joining the Wye, sail down its clear and winding current' to alight from the boat at the Wye meadows and walk to Holme Lacy, then occupied by the Duke of Norfolk.[3]

The barges that sailed into Mordiford during the 1790s were the *Fly, Dick, Henry*, the *Industry* of 57 tons and *Sally* of 40 tons all transporting lime coal from Stowfield in Lydbrook to Mrs. Cole of the 'Lime Works near Mordiford'. The coal was 'taken out' of the barges and measured in dozens and pounds on the banks of the Lugg.

The Liverpool & Bristol Company barges that pulled in at Mordiford

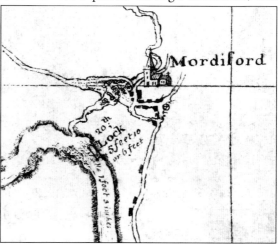

Taylor's map of 1763 showing the confluence of the Lugg and the Wye

during the 1820s were the *Wellington*, the *James*, the *Trader* of 16 tons built at Chepstow, and the *Ann* of 30 tons built at Llandogo. The 'Goods' of bottles, bales of leather, hampers and hoops on the *Trader* were transhipped here onto the *James* and *Ann* which then headed for Bristol, with some items 'left at Mordiford for Mr. Wheatstone', a carrier from Hereford and probably a member of the barge owning family. On another occasion cider, leather, barley, wheat and flour were 'put out' from the *Wellington* and loaded onto the *Trader* and *James*, and in 1829 chests of soap, bags and hogsheads were taken 'out of Barge at Mordiford'. If the river conditions were not suitable, the cargoes from the barges were unloaded onto trolleys, wagons and carts.[4]

The trolley was a horse-drawn vehicle similar to a small dray with a flat loading platform without sides. It was a low-slung two-wheeled vehicle used in conjunction with other transport at docksides and canal wharfs. The trolley from Mordiford transported casks, pipes and hogsheads presumably of wine, port and cider, chests of soap and vinegar to 'eastern' parts of Herefordshire. From the *Wellington* the men transhipped bottles, bales of leather, bags and baskets onto a trolley destined for Hereford, and in 1829 agricultural products of cheese, oats, beans and maize were transported to Mordiford by trolley for transhipment. A carrier service continued into the mid-19th century, when Halford from Fownhope and Jones from Woolhope were listed as carriers 'passing through' Mordiford.[5]

The bargees measuring, transhipping and loading, the hauliers towing the barges on the Wye and Lugg, and the drivers of the trolleys, carts and wagons at Mordiford must have welcomed the warmth and comfort of the Moon Inn where beer and cider were served from at least 1813. A short distance away, on the banks of the Wye, was another inn – the Carrots (now Bunch of Carrots) at Hampton Bishop. This was named after a carrot-shaped piece of sandstone seen in the bed of the Wye where the Stank ferry conveyed passengers across the river. A tradition exists that an upturned boat was kept in the orchard and occupied by a tenant who called it Noah's Ark.[6]

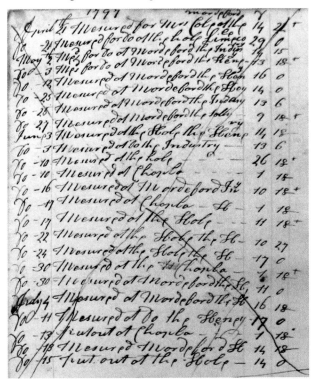

A record of the measuring of coal at Mordiford in 1797

A third inn, or beerhouse, operated for a while near the bridge itself. In 1834 William Jones of Mordiford was the owner of the *George*, a 32-ton trow that had been built by George Crompton in Hereford. The master of the barge was Francis Goodman, a coal dealer at Even Pits in Fownhope who had been previously busy shipping goods on the *Ann*, the *Trader* and the *Wellington* from Hereford and Mordiford in the 1820s. Goodman in 1836 became master of the *Nelson* at a time when William Jones was running a beerhouse at Mordiford Bridge.

Hampton Bishop

In 1802 a traveller from Mordiford noted he 'Crossed the Lug by a long and narrow bridge, under which that river flows with great rapidity. The meadows on each side are very flat, and often under water, as is also the road, for more than two miles. This has occasioned a vast number of graduated posts, four feet high, to be placed by the way-side, which serve at once to inform the curious of the depth of the water in flood-time, and to caution the timid against the dangers they are likely to meet with.' Since the early 18th century a high earthen bank known as a stank was constructed along the banks of the Wye and the Lugg at Hampton Bishop in an effort to prevent flooding. The stank and constant flooding would have made it difficult for barges to land, but in January 1797 coal was unloaded for Mr. Lane, Mr. Norman, Mr. Potter and Mr. Davis at Hampton, though whether from the Lugg or from the Wye is unknown.[7]

The Lugg

The Survey of the Lugg in 1697 described in detail the obstructions along the river – a mixture of low bridges, weirs up to nine feet in height and floodgates – which if removed would allow 'free passage for boats of 20 tons'. With improvements made to the navigation after 1714 'a few barges navigated as far as Leominster', a distance of 25 miles.[8] Although these improvements proved to be somewhat ineffective due to the engineer who, instead of building proper locks, instead erected lock gates where he found bridges crossing the river. Nevertheless, a basin and wharf were made at Eaton Bridge on the edge of Leominster, and 'barges were made and conveyed goods to and from the town'. After the town's church bells were successfully sent to Chepstow for recasting and returned by barge in 1756, no further attempts were made to improve the Lugg navigation until 1777. This was the start of a scheme to link the Lugg by canal to Stourport, but despite receiving approval and support it failed to achieve the transportation of the 'cheapest of coals' and 'a variety of other Articles, such as Grain of all sorts, Merchandise of every denomination, Timber, Vessels.

'The river Lug rises in Radnorshire, and entering Herefordshire on the north-west border near Stapleton-castle in the hundred of Wigmore, is almost immediately augmented by a stream called the Wadel; when taking a direction nearly east, it receives the Pinsley at Leominster. Inclining afterwards towards the south, it is aided by the more considerable stream of the Arrow, between Eaton and Stoke, in the hundred of Wolphy, and of the Frome, between Lugwardine and Mordiford. The whole is after received by the Wye, immediately below the pleasant village of Mordiford, after passing a fine and fertile part of the county, about 30 miles in extent, without calcu-lating the circumflexions in its course.'   John Duncumb, 1805

Charcoal, bark, Cider, Malt, Hops, Wool, Leather. Lime and Lime-stone, Iron in Pigs and Bars and various other Articles', which had been the hoped for outcome.[9]

In 1805 the Lugg was considered to be 'too narrow and too much sunk between its banks to be an object of beauty; in some respects it resembles the Wye, being impatient of control and liable to sudden overflow, not solely from causes common to most rivers, but also from being dammed up or driven back by the higher current of the Wye, at the point of their junction. A similar inconvenience, with respect to navigation, is experienced when the Lug is swelled by partial rains, which have not equally affected the Wye; a rapidity and force are then given to the Lug in its discharge into the Wye, which it will probably be ever difficult to restrain or correct.' The final Wye and Lugg Navigation Act of 1809 'for making a Horse Towing-path on certain Parts of the Banks of the said River' only empowered work along the Wye and not the Lugg.[10]

The Lugg was just as dangerous as the Wye, with several reports of drowning. In 1789 the body of a missing person believed to have fallen into the river was not found until a month later 'when it was accidentally discovered by a man fishing'. In 1808 a girl fell into the river near Tidnor Forge 'in stepping from it to the bank, [and] no assistance being near, was drowned'. In 1812 W. Howells, 'a servant of Mr. Prince, was found on Sunday morning, drowned in the Lock of the Mill Pond', and in 1854 at Leominster a man had a narrow escape from drowning when he fell from a bridge that was 'nothing more than a narrow plank', even though he was used to crossing it.[11]

Lugwardine

From Mordiford barges made their way up the Lugg and under the heightened arch of Hampton Bridge before reaching Tidnor Mill in Lugwardine, one of three mills in the village. It was originally a corn mill, but by 1776 had been converted to an iron forge. There was 'a spacious and convenient wharf with three flights of steps' used for landing the pig iron, charcoal and coal transported by barge from the Forest of Dean.[12] Further upstream the barges were hauled under Lugwardine Bridge, which had been rebuilt in 1740 to accommodate the river trade, and widened and improved in 1824 for road traffic. Nearby was the Anchor Inn of 1807 where timber sales were held, and which became the Crown and Anchor in 1813.[13]

Between 1791 and 1805 barges were delivering coal to Lugwardine from John Harrison, George Morse and James Ward from Lydbrook and Bishopswood. The barges probably moored and unloaded just above Lugwardine Bridge where there was easy road access. On 7 March 1795 a barge delivered a total of between 12 and 13 tons of coal, allocated to a number of tradesmen and residents, comprising: '2 ton for Mr. Powell', '1 ton for Mr. Cowban', '1 ton for Miss Trehurn', '2 ton for Mr. Bowler, '10 cwt

*The plaque on the parapet
of the bridge at Lugwardine*

The Lugg Bridge Mills at Lugwardine

for Joncey Butcher', '10 cwt for William James', '1 ton for Thomas Probert', '1 ton for Mr. Bainhom', '1 ton for Mr. South', '2 - 3 ton for Young Mr. Prece', who owed 10s 6d from a previous delivery. Apart from these deliveries there were a few made for Mr. Morgan and Mr. Gould at Longworth during 1798 and 1799.[14]

It was another mile upstream before barges carrying coal, corn and timber reached Lugg Bridge Mills where 'there was a convenient wharf for the barges that came up the river from the Forest of Dean ... On the west side of the river was a lock, to enable small barges to pass on their way to Leominster'. In 1811 Richard Prince, a miller, grain dealer and coal merchant, rebuilt the mills with spacious warehouses and stabling for eight horses.[15] Seven years later the mills were 'To be let' and advertised as 'on the Banks of the Navigable River Lugg within two miles of the Navigable River Wye'.[16]

Withington to Wellington

From Lugg Mill Bridge fewer barges made the journey upstream along the course of the sinuous Lugg flowing through and between the parishes of Withington, Sutton St Nicholas, Moreton-on-Lugg and Marden, under the bridges of Wergins, Moreton and Laystone and over a shallow ford at the Vern. This crossing led to the wooded slopes of Dinmore Hill, where wood was coppiced regularly to supply oak bark to the tannery at Leominster. Near this fording place the bark may have been loaded on to barges destined for the tannery. In 1749 the locks and floodgates erected on the bridges of the Lugg were 'a nuisance and to be removed' and the bridge arches raised to allow the passage of barges upstream to Wellington and beyond. In the 1790s coal was unloaded at Wellington, possibly at Laystone Bridge, and carted along Hay Way Lane to people living in the village and at Wellington Marsh. Over 20 tons of coal and a grindstone were transported to Wellington on 20 December 1794.[17]

Bodenham, Hope under Dinmore and Stoke Prior

The barges had a long and circuitous stretch of the Lugg to navigate from Wellington to Bodenham, with few places open to offer beer or cider until reaching the New Inn, which was accessible from the banks of the Lugg at Bodenham. Because of the meandering Lugg two crossings half a mile apart were established at Bodenham. Below the church the ancient ford was replaced with a wooden footbridge by 1722, while Bodenham Bridge weakened by a raised arch, was continually in need of repair and 'out of repair from 1747'. Standing beside the bridge and on the banks of the Lugg was a warehouse built and used for a limited period to store goods transported on the barges.[18]

From Bodenham Bridge the bargemen and hauliers towed the barges upstream around a large loop of the river passing Hampton Court and from 1810 slid under the estate's Lawn Bridge. Much earlier, passing Hampton Court in 1699, was a 'large barge with sails down', 'hauled up the river by six men while another with sail up' was coming downstream, a scene that was captured by an artist. At this date Hampton Bridge did not have a raised arch because the water level was lowered by means of a lock, but in 1749 it was ordered that these 'locks and floodgates' on the bridge be removed. The bridge was replaced and subsequently often reported as needing repair, and a new bridge was built in 1826. From a nearby wharf, cordwood was shipped downstream from the Hampton Court estate, where a short walk led the bargemen to the Oak Inn close to the church at Hope-under-Dinmore.

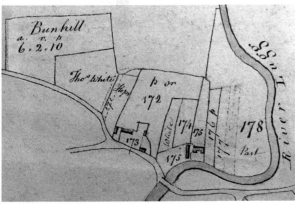

A plan of and reference to the Warehouse built and used for a while to store goods transported on the Lugg

At Ford, a bridge recorded by Leyland was 'in decay' by 1702 and repaired in 1736 'without regard to the navigation', suggesting that few boats were using this stretch of the Lugg. Coal was delivered in 1799 to an unknown wharf site in Stoke

Volca Bridge

Prior, and because of dangerous river conditions the men were 'housed' for a payment of 2s 6d. The following year deliveries of coal were again shipped to Stoke Prior, probably unloaded at Volca Bridge and carted along a lane to Wheelbarrow Castle and into the village, where the Lamb and the Swan inns were situated.[19]

Eaton Hall Bridge

Leominster

The bridge at Eaton Hall was constructed high enough to allow the passage of barges before reaching their final destination at wharves situated above Eaton Bridge in Leominster. The tired and weary men reaching Leominster were grateful for a short step to the Old Iron Boat Inn, possibly named after an iron boat used on the Lugg. A slightly longer walk led to the aptly named Anchor, a name associated with the river trade.[20] The cargoes that reached Leominster by barge included goods ordered by Edward Woodhouse of Leominster between the 1760s and 1780s. At this period the Woodhouse family were trading as ironmongers and seeds-men, also shipping hops and cheese to Chepstow in 1766.[21]

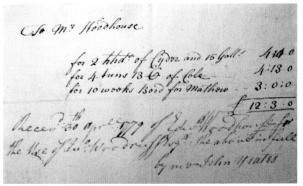

1779 receipt for cider and coal delivered to Edward Woodhouse

In 1769 ironware, hoops, nails and vinegar were amongst the goods ordered and shipped to Edward Woodhouse, and the coal and cider receipts of 1779 suggest the transportation of these goods by river. In 1782 James Biss was paid to freight 'Hops to Bristol', and in 1784 3s was paid for 'halling Hops & Clover' to Chepstow. In 1785 Woodhouse ordered '3 Puncheons of Rum, well Coopered & Cased' from Bush Elton & Bush in Bristol, one for himself, one for James Woodhouse of Aramstone and another for Francis Havard of Hereford to be carried by 'Biss's Trow' with £87 5s 4d paid for 'Custom Duty & Freight'.[22] During the 1820s fragile goods such as bottles and glass were shipped upstream on the Wye on the *Ann* to Hereford and then presumably taken overland to Bodenham, Hampton and Leominster.[23]

As schemes for improving the Lugg navigation including plans to construct 'navigable cuts' had failed, it was not until after 1791

LEOMINSTER CANAL

Being now completely Navigable
From that Borough to MAMBLE WHARF,

NOTICE is hereby given, to all Freeholders, Farmers, Hop-Dealers, &c. &c. that, on the first of June, a communication will be opened between that Navigation and the River Severn, at Bewdley, and consequently with all the Northern Counties; from whence Goods will be brought to Leominster every Thursday morning, and will arrive at Hereford the same evening.—From the latter place, the conveyance will be continued to Leominster every Wednesday morning, and thence along the line of the Canal, at the rate of 15s. per ton cheaper than by the present mode.—Wool sent from Hereford will be delivered at Stourport, at 5s. 6d. per pack; and, from the latter place, Hops will be conveyed to Worcester at 8½d. per bag, all charges included.

For further particulars, enquire of PHILIP HARRIS, Eign-street, Hereford; of JACOB WYLES, Canal Office, Leominster; or at COTTERELL'S Wharf, Bewdley.

May 15, 1797.

A notice of 1797 indicating that the proposed canal had reached Mamble Wharf

121

that a start was made for 'a canal to extend to Kington, from Leominster and Stourport'. The cost from Kington to Leominster was estimated at £37,000, between Leominster and Stourport at £83,000. Duncumb noted that 'a part of the latter extent was completed in the year 1796, and has effected some reduction in the price of coal, without reaching so far as Stourport. A miscalculation of expenses ... has stopped, for the present at least, all further progress.'[24]

Dinedor, Bullingham and Tupsley

Dinedor, on the west bank of the Wye, was a parish dominated by the Bodenhams who resided at Rotherwas in a 'modern and elegant' property with grounds 'stretching towards the banks of the river, plain and very fertile, crowned towards the south by some gradual ascents, on which are the beautiful woods of Rotherwas: towards the south-west, the view is terminated by the lofty object of Dyndor Camp, from the summit of which are a great variety of prospects of the surrounding country'.[25] Before reaching Rotherwas, the barges passed Dinedor Court with its Boat Meadow and the farm at Sink Green, where sacks of barley, wheat, peas and 'timber from Sink Green' were shipped to Bristol in 1810, a year

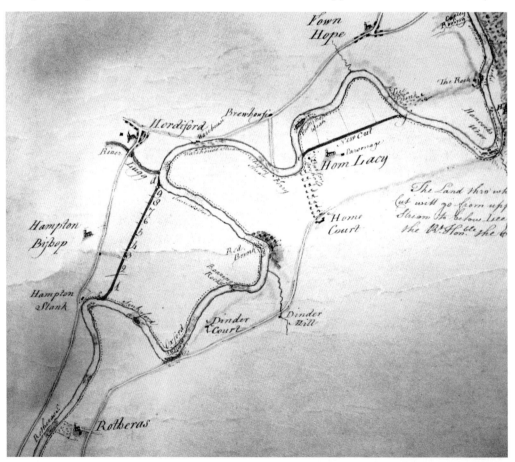

A map of 1779 showing the Wye in detail between Holme Lacy and Rotherwas

when coal and lime was delivered on the upstream journey. This trade continued into the 1820s on the *Eliza* captained by William Hoskins, the *Mayflower* and the *John and Mary*, the timber from Sink Green being delivered to Messrs. Watkins in Chepstow.[26]

There were no inns or beer houses in Dinedor after 1667 when an alehouse was suppressed by the Quarter Sessions.

During the late 18th century Charles Bodenham resided at Rotherwas, which had been rebuilt by his grandfather. Charles, as an appointed proprietor of the Horse Towing Path Company, allowed a section through his land in 1805.[27] Below the house a wharf existed where bushels of seeds were unloaded for 'Charles Bodenham

A broken bridge on the towpath at Bullinghope in 1882

A barge passing Rotherwas House

A photograph taken by Alfred Watkins of the Whalebone Inn

Esq.' between 1797 and 1801. Then in 1810 'The Fallage of the greater part of that valuable Coppice called Rotherwas Coppice (Tithe Free), situate in the parish of Dinedor' was auctioned at 'the Hotel' in Hereford, and may have been transported down-river by barge.[28]

Before reaching Hereford the barges passed a wharf at Bullingham where John Knill was shipping sacks of wheat, barley, vetches and ryegrass to Bristol, and Richard Prince was importing coal and lime and exporting '15 Sks of Wheat to Bristol, 14 Sks Barley ditto, 32 Bushel of Oats ditto' in 1810. On the banks of the Wye near the towpath, Joseph Thomas built the *Mary and Elizabeth*, a 46-ton barge, in 1828. A few years later widow Ann Crompton was residing at Bullingham and sold the *William*, a barge of 43 tons, to James Ward of Bishopswood in 1833. For the bargees and hauliers, masters and men there was the Nag's Head for drink and shelter kept by Mrs. Rosser.[29]

On the north bank of the Wye opposite Bullingham is Tupsley on the outskirts of Hereford. From the early 1700s the Woodhouse family of merchants had an association with this area. Barge-loads of coal were discharged at Tupsley between 1797 and 1801, either at the Lower Boat field or at a wharf over the boundary in St. Owen's parish.[30] Both river and road travellers in 1802 would have passed 'a public-house, with a sign so singular in its appearance, that it would be difficult to understand how it could be denominated, if an inscription had not been affixed, signifying that this is the real blade bone of a whale'. The inn was named after this curious bone, which may have been brought by 'one of the boatmen, coming upstream with a barge from Chepstow'.[31]

10 WHARVES – HEREFORD CITY

Although a wharf was recorded at Hereford Castle in 1256 it was probably used for transporting goods across the river, as it was unlikely that any boats would have reached Hereford until after the passing of the 1695 Navigation Act which made provision 'for the building of warehouses or storehouses' on the site of Hereford Castle.[1] By the late 1690s it appears that the Wye and Lugg still had major difficulties for those wishing to navigate the river above Lydbrook, although accounts exist of pig iron being transported from Redbrook to Hereford in 1692.[2] To improve the navigation between 1696 and 1700 a certain amount of work was carried out by William Williams 'bringing the barge to

A barge approaching Hereford in the early 19th century

Hereford Wear for drawing the stakes'. He appears as the first known bargeman from Hereford followed by Luke Hughes and William Welch, who were admitted as Freemen of the City in 1701, Thomas Wells, a waterman in 1702 and Thomas Hall, a bargeman in 1707.[3] These names suggest that some rudimentary wharves were in existence before another was built at Hereford in 1725 by Philip Symonds.[4]

From the Hereford wharves quantities of timber, bark, lime, cider and grain were exported downstream, with 26 tons of cider freighted to Bristol in 1777. The main import was coal, transported upriver from Lydbrook and the Forest of Dean. It had been estimated that Hereford required 3,650 tons of coal per year and that water transport was the cheapest method. Although it was acknowledged that 'Hereford is not favourably situated for manufactures or commerce, it is ill supplied with fuel, and that not good, but the uncertain state of the river, from its shoals and great rapidity, prevents that constant and uniform navigation which can only support a regular and extensive trade'.[5]

At the time the Wye was navigable the situation of Hereford was described as 'delight-fully placed nearly in the centre of the county' where 'the Wye bends its course round a point of land for a distance of near two miles, when we are brought almost as near to the town, as when we quitted it. The river as we passed down, still continued its circuitous windings, but with a more placid surface, seldom meeting any obstructions in its course ... The general face of the country is rich in verdure, and the cattle grazing on the banks of the river or lazing in its stream, are objects that perpetually contribute to enliven the scene.' In the 1790s the river was 'frequently covered with boats and other small vessels' but during dry seasons barges 'were laying at Hereford for upwards of four months, for want of water to carry them down'.[6]

After a meeting in 1790, an Act was passed in 1791 enabling a canal to be constructed between Hereford and Gloucester. In 1829 the horse-drawn tramway opened and enabled the transportation of coal from south Wales which could be sold at a cheaper rate than the coal conveyed on barges from the Forest of Dean. The canal did not provide a threat to the river trade at Hereford until it eventually reached Hereford in 1845 at a cost of £131,436.

A bill for conveying stone required by the Dean & Chapter of Hereford Cathedral from Brockweir to Hereford in 1793

As the growth of trade on the canal rose, there was a decrease in the river trade which finally ceased in the 1850s after the construction of the Hereford to Shrewsbury Railway, the Newport, Abergavenny and Hereford Railway and the Hereford, Ross and Gloucester Railway, which took over the carrying and transportation of goods.[7]

Eign and Putson

It may have been due to lack of water at the wharves near Wye Bridge, that a wharf began to operate from 1790 at Eign on the edge of the city. The wharf was sited on the north bank at a sharp bend of the river where up to eleven men were hired for hauling the *Fly*, *Dick* and *Industry* barges during the autumn of 1790. On 19 January 1792 one ton of coal arrived for John Powell of Eign, and 2s 6d was paid to the men for drink. Later in the year further amounts of coal were delivered to Eign for Mr. Powell, Mr. Thomas and Mr. Gwatkin. Lime was also unloaded at Eign between 1802 and 1812 for Mr. Watkins and James Jones.[8]

The Eign wharf was accessible from the road and by 1843 was occupied by a bone mill and timber yard just a few years before the building of the Hereford, Ross and Gloucester Railway disturbed the site.[9] To the east of the Eign Brook, a lane led to a landing stage used by the ferry as well as the wharf. It is understood that the brook was canalised up to Eign Mill so that Wye barges could reach the corn mill. For the weary hauliers and bargemen there was the opportunity of a drink of cider or beer from the Whalebone Inn at Eign, before continuing upstream to Putson on the opposite bank.[10]

In 1792 David Davies was in possession of Panson Cottage at Putson – the 'customary messuage with garden and orchard' – where coal 'was put out for Jn Cook'. The cottage was later occupied by the Bird family, who were probably responsible for transforming the building into one of 'whimsy and caprice', which in 1804 passed to the 'Company of the Proprietors of the Rivers Wye and Lugg Navigation and Horse Towing path'. The

Panson Cottage was transformed at the end of the 1700s into a home of 'whimsy and caprice' featuring 'a round dovecote-like structure with a central chimney and an adjoining wing'. This painting of it by James Wathen in the 1790s also shows a barge.

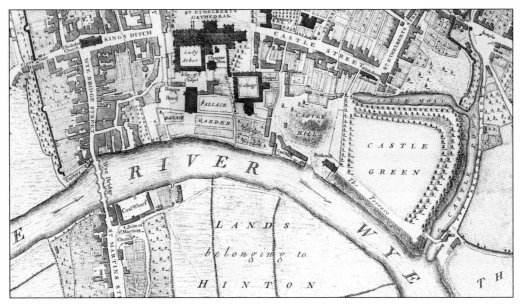

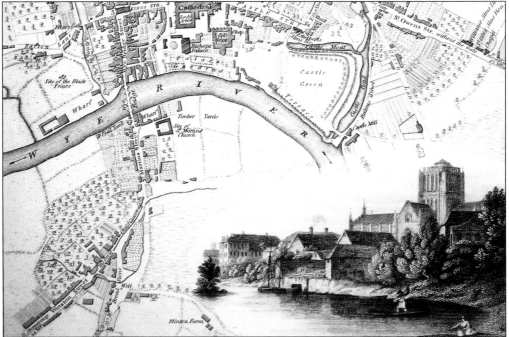

Top: Part of Hereford as depicted on Taylor's map of 1757. It shows the castle mill in the east, a wharf below the Castle Mill and a wharf on the south side of the river adjoining the bridge. Opposite was the piece of land known as Tenters (see p.136).

Lower: The same part of Hereford shown on Cole and Roper's map of 1806. The Castle Mill is still there, the wharf below Castle Hill is shown but not named, the coal wharf on the south bank now has adjoining timber yards, and a coal wharf is sited on the west of Wye Bridge opposite a wharf on the north bank. The decorative drawing shows craft on the river.

agreement to purchase the cottage and land was finalised in 1809 when the towpath was created through Putson, past Panson Cottage and two traditional 'Watering Places'. Under the terms of the 1809 Rivers Wye and Lugg Navigation Act the 'Company of Proprietors shall and may keep a Ferry-Boat or Ferry-Boats at or near the Places called Putteston Watering Place, and Bullingham Road ... for the Purpose of conveying the Horses or other Beasts, and the Men attending them, across the said River Wye'.[11]

Timber Wharf (south bank)

Further upstream from Putson the barges unloaded their cargoes at various timber yards and coal wharfs situated on both sides of the river. The bargees created a busy scene as they moored their vessels, unloaded, loaded and secured their cargoes, chatted with fellow bargemen and waited for suitable river conditions. Opposite Castle Green there was an area known as the Timber Yard in St. Martin's parish where wharves were leased in 1805 by Thomas Bird to George Buckle, Thomas Pearce, William Watkins and William James. Thomas Bird kept one wharf for himself and Jonathan Crompton leased one from William Downes. Several of these traders and merchants also leased wharves on the north bank.[12]

From the 1820s the timber yard became a boat building site where Evan Hopkins built a sloop of 54 tons named the *Hereford* for John Easton, a Hereford timber merchant. In 1823 John Easton built the *Helen*, a snow of 122 tons, and the following year Hopkins built and launched a schooner called the *Herefordshire*. Easton constructed two more vessels in 1825, the *Champion*, a brig of 24 tons, and the *Mary*, a 130-ton snow. In 1827 the keel of the *Paul Pry*, a steam vessel, was 'laid in Mr. Easton's yard, opposite the Bishop's Palace'. The last two boats constructed at the timber yard were the *Collinque*, a schooner of 140 tons built by John Easton in 1835, and the *Bee*, an 18-ton trow built by Thomas Swift in 1837.[13]

East Side Wye Bridge Wharf (south bank)

A little further upstream on the south bank was the site of one of the earliest Hereford wharfs 'near and unto Wye Bridge', where Richard Moore traded in 1733 and George Barrow in 1740. Before 1789 the site was occupied by James Packwood who was a barge owner and related to a family employed as corn factors, skinners and bargemen.[14] In 1783 George Packwood was paid £17 2s 3d for pebbles collected and sold to the Hereford Paving Commissioners.

HEREFORD.
WAREHOUSES TO LET.

TO be LET, and Entered on immediately, at PEARCE's Wharf, near *Wye bridge*,—TWO large and commodious WAREHOUSES, capable of holding between two and three hundred hogsheads of cyder.

☞ For particulars apply to Mr. Bird, in Hereford.

Nov. 11, 1788.

An advertisement for the letting of warehouses at 'Pearce's Wharf' in 1788

Daniel, the most prominent member of the Pearce family, married into the Symonds family in 1786, and his wharf – shared with George Buckle and William Price 'late in occupation of James Packwood' with 'newly erected Tenement and Dwelling House' – was on the south side of the river near Wye Bridge. In 1788 Pearce was letting 'two commodious Warehouses, capable of holding between two and three hundred hogsheads of cyder', and in 1798 advertised his barges for sale at the Saracen's Head, the wharfside inn. The *Valiant* was a barge of 30 tons, draught 2 feet 9 inches, and the *Dan and Ann* of 25 tons, draught 2 feet 5 inches, which were both 'in complete repair, and fit for the Severn Trade'. In 1800 James Packwood, the Cromptons and James Biss added their names to a public notice advising an increase in the 'price of freight' for the conveyance of goods on the River Wye.[15] In 1801 from 'Mr. Buckle's Wharf, in Hereford',

HEREFORD.

TO BE SOLD BY AUCTION,

BY WILLIAM MERRICK,

At Mr. Buckle's Wharf, in Hereford, on Friday, the Twenty-third of October instant, in Lots,

SIXTEEN large CASKS, of 200 Gallons each; and upwards of 150 PUNCHEONS, and other CASKS, in good condition; together with a great number of Coopers' Tools, Tubs, Funnels, Racking Cans, Cocks, Oak Sleepers, &c. The whole well worth the attention of Cider Dealers, and the Public in general.

To be viewed as above, on the Twentieth and Twenty first instant, by applying to William Price, at the Wharf.

October 3, 1801.

casks and puncheons, cooper's tools and utensils were for sale 'worth the attention of Cider Dealers', and in 1824 William White of Wye-Bridge Wharf offered an assortment of 'Best Forest Coal, Cokes, Lime-Coal, & Fire-Bricks', with lime from the Vention lime kiln in Lydbrook delivered at 17s a barge-load.[16]

Barges at the coal wharf on the south bank of the river. This scene was painted by James Wathen in September 1794. (The rounded stone structure at the end of the bridge was probably associated with the bridge gate, the ruins of which were demolished in the 1780s.)

On the wharf a warehouse, used by the trustees of the Wye Navigation for storing goods, was accessed 'by steps from the river and a comparatively narrow door through which dockers passed when transhipping from the Wye. On the Wye Street side, a flat-arched double door gave access to the warehouse where goods were transferred onto carts by a hoist'. In 1829 William Cooke was distributing salt from Droitwich 'on considerable lower Terms than they have ever been supplied' and offered 'a constant Supply of Best Forest Coal, at a Reduced Price' from his 'Commercial Yard, East Side Wye Bridge'. The building was later associated with the slate trade and used as the Dorset Ale Stores.[17]

Wharf on the west side of Wye Bridge (south bank)
On the upstream side of Wye Bridge a coal wharf was established before James Packwood moved there in 1801, when he 'disposed of' a 'Quantity of American Flour' to the poorer inhabitants of the city and adjoining districts from the 'Coal Company's Wharf, Wye-bridge'. At this date the company was seeking bargemen 'of good character, acquainted with the Navigation of the Wye' as barge masters. In 1806 this wharf was occupied by Thomas Prothero, where a yard 'lately used by Mr. Bird, near Wye Bridge, re-opened for Sale of Coal' at 25s per ton ordered from James Packwood in St. Martin's Street.[18] In 1808 William Davis and David Jones took over this Hereford Coal Wharf with its 'driving-way, weighing machine and Clerks Office', built on a site where 'two tenements formerly stood'.[19]

> ## COAL.
> THE Public are respectfully informed, that the YARD lately used by Mr. BIRD, near Wye Bridge, is re-opened for SALE of COAL.
> Orders sent to James Packwood, St. Martin-street, will be immediately attended to.
> Coal of the best quality, 25s per Ton.
> Hereford, Dec. 31, 1805.

From 1815 the Hereford Coal Wharf continued to be leased to David Jones, who went into partnership with Richard Thompson. The use of the wharf and its premises passed from Ann Thompson, widow, and Henry Cooke to the proprietors of the Hereford and Abergavenny Tram Road. Although there had been opposition to the horse-drawn tram road from barge owners, it finally opened in 1829, transporting coal from the south Wales collieries in competition with barges carrying coal from the Forest of Dean. For the tram road company the premises were adequately provided with a dwelling house, counting house, tram house, stables, weighing machine, workshop, yard and coal wharf.[20]

Castle Quay and Corporation Wharf (north bank)
From Eign the barges negotiated a long meander of the Wye before reaching Castle Quay and Corporation Wharf, where steps eased the loading and unloading of goods. Castle Quay was probably established before 1725 when Philip Symonds, mercer, leased a piece of ground from Hereford Corporation, who had a right to 'dig for gravel'. It was 'inclosed into a wharf and several buildings' and was 'bounded by the way next to Castle Hill leading to the Castle Green on the North and the way from Castle Street to Baminghams on the East [side of Castle Green], the River Wye on the south side and certain outhouses belonging to the Vicars Choral of the Cathedral Church of Hereford on the West'. Adjoining the

This picture by James Wathen of August 1794 shows a barge unloading at Castle Wharf on the right, close to a warehouse containing bark

wharf Symonds leased a 'Warehouse and Stables' measuring 39 feet in length and 22 feet in breadth from the Vicars Choral.[21]

From 1728 Joseph Trumper, a glover, was one of the joint partners 'of owners and proprietors of Trows, Boats, Barges and other Vessels for mutual benefit, profit and advantage', and took over the lease in 1748. It remained with the family until 1800 when it was assigned to James Biss who had moved from a 'warehouse, granary and wharf adjoining the river Wye, situate in Pipe Lane' at Wye Bridge. Biss died in 1812 and bequeathed all

The access to the site of Castle Wharf from Quay Street

his messuages, tenements and personal estates to his 'good friend Warren Jane of the town of Chepstow' and included 'if my son Charles shall be minded or desirous to purchase any part of my said freehold or leasehold messuages lands tenements or hereditments situate in the parish of St John Baptist aforesaid or at Lidbrook in the County of Gloucester for the purpose of carrying on the trade or business of a Coal Merchant Wharfinger and Trow and Barge owner that he shall have the preference'.[22]

Warren Jane from Chepstow was an apothecary and barge owner, one of the many merchants and barge owners from the lower Wye who were associated with the river trade in Hereford. He had a snow of 119 tons built and named after him in 1783, and although a senior partner of a firm of surgeons he enjoyed 'a world wide trade in timber and bark' from his warehouse near the Wye at Chepstow. Others not based in but involved at Hereford included William Hartnell in Bristol, George Buckle and Swift & Co. from Chepstow, Owner Browne from Brockweir, George Morse and John Harrison from Lydbrook and William Porter from Wilton.[23]

After the death of James Biss in 1812, his wife Susannah continued leasing 'All those two stables with the appurtenances situate on the Backside of the College aforesaid in the county of Hereford having the said College Garden on the South and West and the said College stables on the North and Also all that their piece of ground whereon a Warehouse and Stable is erected and built'. Susannah later moved to Wilton and her son Charles, 'of Wilton Castle', continued the business.[24] Her daughter Elizabeth married William Pulling, son of a cider merchant from Devon, and they established themselves in Hereford from 1813 as wine merchants and distillers. William Pulling the elder took over this lease of premises adjacent to a 'warehouse belonging to the Castle Quay' in 1815 for one year, while a family dispute was being settled.[25]

William Pulling dealt in wines, spirits, cider, bark and slate from Castle Wharf adjacent to his premises at Castle Hill, St John Street and later in East Street. From at least 1822 he shipped his 'Up and Down' cargoes to and from Chepstow and Bristol at the same period

A busy river scene painted by James Wathen, with several barges moored at the Castle Wharf on the right, a barge possibly getting underway in the middle of the river, and a small pleasure boat with a roofed seating area

The remains of North Wharf on the left and Castle Wharf in the middle distance

that John Easton, a timber and coal merchant and corn factor, was operating his business as a carrier to Bristol from Castle Quay. A few years later Isaac Price, an auctioneer and valuer of timber, was offering 'Building Materials, at reduced prices, at his Yard, near the Castle Green and Old Bridewell, adjoining the River Wye', which suggested his use of the Corporation Wharf.[26] In 1830 'Conveyance by Water' to Bristol was served by John Easton's barges from the Castle Wharf, and by William Cooke and Swift & Co. from the 'Commercial Wharf', which seems to have been another name for the Corporation Wharf. From 1835 John Easton's business was taken over by William Bunning using his own sloops and barges, and by the 1840s was trading with Pulling and Gibson importing large consignments of rum, brandy, gin and whisky and shipping bark, cider and spirits down river to Chepstow, Gloucester and Bristol.[27]

A view across the Wye to the North Wharf in August 1795 by James Wathen

North Wharf Wye Bridge (north bank)

The North Wharf on the down side of Wye Bridge was used from at least 1721 for mooring barges.[28] Towards the end of the 18th century cider, porter and beer were stored by Jonathan Crompton, barge owner, in warehouses in Pipe Lane near Wye Bridge. In 1798 Crompton wished to 'inform his Friends from whom he has received similar favours in the Bristol Trade, and the Public at large, that he has formed a connection with Owner Browne, of Brockware, who has a new-built Sloop, well calculated for the Trade, with which he will punctually attend every Spring Tide, to take and bring all kind of Goods to and from Bristol, consigned there, or to Hereford, Kington, Hay, Talgarth, Builth, or the intermediate places directed; and that he is prepared with barges well calculated for the undertaking, steady and punctual Masters, and good Warehouses for storing all kinds of Goods'.[29]

Pipe Lane (Gwynne Street)
which led from the river
to the centre of Hereford

By 1805 Jonathan Crompton had pulled down a malthouse with outbuildings and built two brick houses insured by the Sun Fire

The North Wharf in 1870

Office. He continued to trade in porter from a warehouse in Pipe Lane until 1809 when part of his premises were for sale, 'capable of being a complete Brewery, or of carrying on any extensive business ... with a large and spacious Wharf, adjoining the River Wye, of 110 Feet in length, and 64 Feet in width, surrounded with Five large brick-built Warehouses, and Six Granaries over, 139 Feet long, and 23 Feet wide, with two Stables and a long range of Sheds and Compting-Houses'. He moved to another wharf 'over Wye Bridge' where he dealt in coal.[30]

Fryars Wharf (north bank)

Travelling upstream the bargemen negotiated the arches of Wye Bridge and turned fairly sharply to reach Fryars Wharf. In 1757 the area was known as Tenters where 'wooden sheds were used for making curved timbers for ship building, and also for drying skins'. It assumed its name from the tenters who hung out sailcloth on hooks to dry.[31] Prior to 1799 The Fryars belonged to William Moore and consisted of a 'substantial Quadrangular Warehouse or Building, capable of containing a considerable quantity of Cider or other bulky goods on the ground floor, with Lofts or Granaries above', also with sheds, offices, counting house, comfortable habitation and a 'good firm Quay, in a great depth of water' in the tenures of Richard Westwood, James Weaver and Mr. Porter.

There was also a 'capacious Wharf or Landing Place' in 'the tenure and occupation of Mr. William James'. This wharf was 'capable of holding several tons of Timber and Bark, with every convenience for stacking, housing and preparing for the Chepstow and Irish markets, commanding by its situation a very fine woody country, and has been the most frequented deposit for those kind of goods for a number of years. Timber of the greatest dimensions may be shipped from hence, there being a sufficient depth of water at its lowest state to admit

HEREFORD FLOUR COMPANY.

TO BE SOLD BY AUCTION,

On Monday, the Thirteenth of June, 1803, at the New Inn, in the city of Hereford, between the hours of Four and Five in the Afternoon, and subject to such Conditions of Sale as will be then produced (unless disposed of in the mean time by Private Contract),

THOSE desirable FREEHOLD PREMISES, called or known by the name of

THE FRIARS,

In the parish of Saint Nicholas, within the liberties of the said city, adjoining the River Wye, situate most advantageously for carrying on an extensive Manufactory, Brewery, or other mercantile concern, having always sufficient depth of water to admit several Barges, with their sides close to the bank, load at one time, and to be moored, when loaded, in the same situation, as long as may be necessary, with proper driving ways to the same, all which will be sold in the following Lots:

LOT 1. Two Acres of rich PASTURE LAND, of an oblong form, the longest side adjoining the said River, together with a Shed erected on the same.

LOT 2. An extensive CIDER CELLAR, and WAREHOUSES, WHARF, and BUILDINGS, now let to Mr. Westwood, of which possession may be had in October, 1804.

LOT 3. Another BUILDING, adjoining Lot the second, consisting of a Warehouse, and Cellaring, together with large Buildings, nearly complete, intended for a Flour-Mill and Engine-House, upon an extensive scale, with land thereto belonging.

LOT 4. Two BARK-HOUSES and SHEDS, together with a Timber Yard belonging to the same, contiguous to the River.

For a view of the Plan, and further particulars, apply to Mr. John Green, at the New Inn, or Mr. Parker, Builder, in Broad-street.

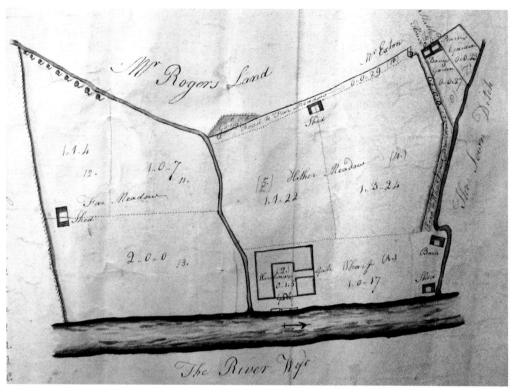

*A plan of Fryars Wharf in 1800
with its warehouse, barn and shed*

*Fryars Wharf sometime before the late 1780s, after the collapse of the cathedral's west front
and when the spire was removed, with barge, landing stage and buildings*

several barges with their sides close to the bank to load at one time, and to lie moored when loaded'. A dwelling house and stables 'parted from the premises by a road-way leading to the Wharf', was leased to Richard Evans, John Pearce and Edward Jones.[32]

This valuable site came up for sale in 1803 with 'an extensive Cider Cellar, and Warehouse, Wharf and Buildings, now let to Mr. Westwood'. There was another warehouse with cellaring, a building nearly completed intended for a flour mill and an engine house, and two bark houses with a timber yard close to the river.[33] From this wharf in 1838 was launched the *Water Witch*, as detailed in chapter 5.

Wharfside inns

Those working and trading at the wharves were well served by local inns and cider houses. The Star or Seven Stars was an ancient inn situated near the river and wharves at Wye Bridge East. The inn, frequented by bargemen, was an ideal place to hold an auction in 1808 of a 'complete and well-built Barge, called the *Valiant*, thirty-two tons Burden, well worth the attention of Timber Merchants, being capable of taking in heavy Timber'. From 1810 the Crompton family of bargemen were associated with running the 'Seven Stars in Pipe Lane' which became known as the Bell. The Saracen's Head was another favourite of the bargees, and two barges owned by Daniel Pearce were auctioned there in 1798 when the inn was kept by William Greenly.[34]

Other licensed premises either conveniently placed or with names reflecting their association with the river trade included the Royal Oak, where a barge was sold in 1778 and where Crompton's premises were auctioned in 1809. There was the Black Lion of 1710 in Bridge Street, the Spread Eagle of 1749 on the east side of Wye Bridge, the Catherine Wheel of 1794, the Ship of 1799 kept by Henry Hawkins, a barge master with a wharf at Wye Bridge, the Dog of 1804 in St. Martin's Street and the Waterman's Arms of 1848.[35] There is a tradition that a building near Castle Wharf once served as an inn near the brewery of 1752 and this may have been the Anchor of 1761 in Little Castle Street.[36]

Hereford imports and exports

These Hereford wharves with their warehouses and tying up places would have provided a bustling scene of men loading and unloading barges of coal, stacking timber, making bark ricks, piling coal, rolling barrels and handling baskets, bags and boxes. Bells from the churches of St. Nicholas and All Saints were shipped from quays in 1718 and 1769 to be recast at Gloucester, and in 1779 hogsheads, gallons of cider, 'tuns of cole' and 'dozens of lime' were delivered by barge for Mr. Woodhouse. During the 1780s and 1790s the Dean and Chapter were receiving Painswick stone from Gloucester, deal, candles and beeswax from Bristol, and large amounts of stone from Hay, Coldwell and Brockweir.[37] James Packwood, Thomas Bird and Jonathan Crompton took deliveries of lime in the earlier 1800s, bricks came from Stourbridge in 1802, slate from Bristol in 1810 and two years later Mr. Price at Hereford was dealing in wines, spirits, hurdles and spokes from his wharf.

A vast range of goods were unloaded at the Hereford wharves and quays during the 1820s. Wines and spirits were brought to Messrs. Pullings; chests, bags, hampers, bottles,

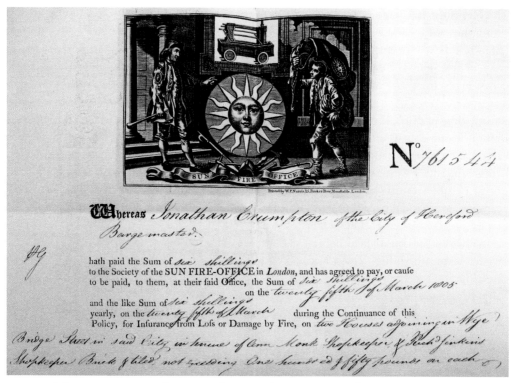

A fire insurance certificate issued to Jonathan Crompton 'bargemaster' in 1805

soap and sugar were carried on the *James*; paper came from Brockweir; hoops and corks from Bristol; and many other items including cheese, glasses and iron bars were conveyed on the *Mayflower, Hereford, Ann, Charles, Mary* and *Eliza* operated by various barge owners and masters including William Hoskins, Francis Goodman, George Peacock, George Pearce and William Moxley who were trading under the name of The Liverpool & Bristol Company. On the return journey oats, wheat, timber, hops, hurdles, hoops, poles and cider went downstream to Wilton, Monmouth, Brockweir, Chepstow and Bristol.[38]

The most important import was coal from the Forest of Dean which was unloaded and weighed at the Hereford coal wharves. One rogue bargeman called Francis Jenkins from Ross was hauled up before the magistrates for selling several tons of coal which 'in weighing the said coal did make use of four half hundred weights one wereof was iron two of them lead and one other of them a great stone'.[39] From the 1790s tons of coal from Stowfield and Lydbrook were shipped to John Crompton and Daniel Pearce, in 1811 Mr. Price was receiving large quantities of coal and lime coal for Mr. Pearce, and in the autumn of 1811 at least 68 tons of coal were sold by Mr. Almond at Hereford. In 1819 the imports into the city consisted 'mostly of coal, deal and slate, for immediate consumption, and heavy goods for the use of the shopkeepers', and the cost of coal was 'at a dear rate; the price seldom being under £1 1s. a ton'.[40] By 1844 the city coal merchants included William Bunning at Castle Quay and Henry Cooke at the Welch Coal Wharf. In 1851 Thomas Lewis was at Eign Wharf competing with merchants trading on the Hereford and Gloucester Canal.[41]

The Hereford Bargemen

From the early 18th century men residing in Hereford were employed as bargemen, barge builders, watermen, rafters, lightermen and barge masters. They were recorded in wills, as freemen, in newspapers, in Quarter Sessions and listed in directories, with some occasionally fined or charged for misbehaviour or wrong-doings. In 1705 Luke Hughes was presented for obstructing the 'Common Shore leading down from Wyebridge Street' during 'time of rain'. The following year Francis Poole owed a 'bad debt' of 32s 6d, whereas Phillip Scandrett was entitled to keep 'one piece of timber floating down the River Wye valued at 5s' which had presumably become loose from a floater. In 1733 Joseph Jones, bargeman, and 'a woman along with him who goes by the name of Ann Jones' (supposed not to be his wife) of St. Owen's had to be removed from their lodgings. The following year Ann Jones 'being very big with child' was beaten, assaulted and abused 'in a violent manner' in the cathedral precincts.

In 1759 William Baker, barge-owner, bequeathed his 'Trow and three Barges together with all the Sails Rigging and Furniture' and his messuages, warehouses and dye house in St. John to his wife Elizabeth, who later also inherited £50 from Edward Cox. Richard Penny in 1770 owed a mercer £2 6s for 'goods sold and delivered', in 1771 Thomas Basset was gaoled for one month for 'refusing to navigate a boat down the river' and in 1776 John Greenway, a barge owner, married a butcher's widow. In 1793 James Biss, Jonathan Crompton and

1759 Will of William Baker, bargeman

Daniel Pearce were all based in Hereford. Despite being a barge master, John Crompton of St. John's parish qualified for a payment of £1 from the Lord Chandos Charity in 1797, a charity that made payments out of the interest on a capital sum of £500 'for the benefit of poor freemen' at St Giles' Hospital who were 'housekeepers, not receiving alms'. In the 19th century records show there was James Packwood, a barge owner, in 1800; John Jones, a bargeman who tragically drowned in 1804; Richard Lewis, a coal barge owner in 1818 of St. Owen's; George Bryder, a barge builder of St. Martin's in 1822; William Cooke, a barge owner in 1829; and John Thomas, barge builder of St. Nicholas in 1838.[42] Since 1844 Robert Vaughan 'had let out boats' and by 1848 had entered into a dispute with Mr. Davies, a coach-builder.[43]

11   BELMONT TO GLASBURY

The majority of barges that reached Hereford emptied their cargoes at the busy quays and wharves and returned downstream with timber, bark, grain and cider. In the 18th century 'the boats and barges on the sides of the river ... please the imagination with an idea of national industry'. It was only a few smaller craft that continued further up the Wye with loads of coal and lime which were delivered at Belmont, Sugwas, Canon Bridge, Bridge Sollers, Byford, Monnington, Moccas, Clifford, Hardwick, Whitney, Hay and Glasbury with a tradition – but no evidence – that 'navigation was possible as far as Aberdw'.[1]

Belmont, Warham and Sugwas
Towards the end of the 18th century Belmont, in the parish of Clehonger, was 'delightful, being placed on a fine ascent, close to the banks of the Wye, which in this part glides by with a broad and pleasing stream, forming a most delightful sweep'. On the opposite bank

A barge being towed past Belmont in 1800

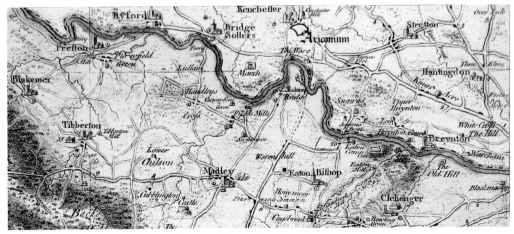

Taylor's map of 1754 showing the Wye between Breinton and Preston-on-Wye

the woods of Breinton and Wareham added 'much to the agreeable scene from Belmont', a house that was built of Bath stone in 1788 for Mr. Matthews where the river 'at this place seems to forget its usual rapidity, and forming itself into a deep and majestic body, glides with a placid stream, through rich and verdant pasture ground'.[2] From April 1810 Mr. Matthews at Belmont was regularly discharging cargoes of lime at his wharf below the house, and on the opposite bank there was a stone wharf below Warham which also served the ferry connecting Warham (in Breinton) to Belmont.[3]

On 16 July 1853 the *Hereford Times* reported that a steam paddleboat measuring 42ft 6ins in length and 8ft to 9ft wide, was built in London for F.R. Wegg-Prosser – for pleasure excursions on the Wye. It steamed from London to Gloucester but because of the narrowness of the locks on the Hereford and Gloucester canal, its paddles had to be removed. Once it had finally arrived at the Hereford wharf of the canal, it was taken to Belmont on a timber carriage drawn by four horses.

Picture of a steamer at Belmont in 1894

Upstream, in the parish of Eaton Bishop, the bargemen struggled over the shallows of the ford and ferry crossing at Lower Eaton, where a 'horse boat for conveying animals and vehicles, and a boat ferry for passengers' crossed the water to Sugwas, passing an island known as the 'gravel bed'. On the opposite bank at Sugwas were the comforts of the Boat Inn kept by Joseph Bevan in 1818, and at Eaton Bishop above the Wye at Ruckhall was the 'Drink-house' kept by James Evans.[4] At Sugwas Boat Wharf, coal was delivered for Mr. Green, Mr. Phillips and Dr. Symonds during the 1790s, and large quantities of lime were unloaded between 1800 and 1813 for Mr. Jones. A few goods including hampers, oats and peas were sent downstream with extra payment made to 'men from Hereford' – bow hauliers – either '10, 12 or 11 men up, 5 down'. In 1824 lime at £1 a barge-load was shipped to Sugwas from the Vention lime works at Lydbrook.[5]

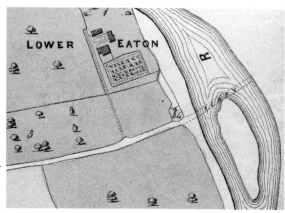

A map of 1854 showing the ford and ferry crossing at Lower Eaton

The former Boat Inn at Sugwas

Old Weir, Canon Bridge and Bridge Sollers

The Wye makes a large and sharp meander at Weir Cliff below Old Weir, where lime was unloaded in 1808. The '13 Men from Hfd to Wear Cliff' were paid £1 12s 6d and 6s 3d was paid to '5 men from W Cliff to Hay'. In December of that year an empty hogshead was 'returned with Perry'.

The bargees were probably not aware that they passed over the course of a Roman road known in 1811 as Stone Street that led south from the Roman town of *Magnis* at Kenchester to Great Brampton. Stone Street connected Chester with Caerleon, passing through two towns which lie within the present county of Herefordshire – Leintwardine and Kenchester. They also passed by Roman remains at New Weir in Kenchester which were possibly 'the supports of an ancient quay, wharf or landing stage'. Local tradition suggests that corn was shipped from New Weir in the 19th century to be milled at Eaton Bishop.[6] On the opposite bank in Madley parish a wharf was in use from 1797 when lime, coal and turnip seeds were delivered for Mr. Pye and Mr. Bennett at Brampton just a few miles south along the Roman road. The line of the Roman road is marked on Taylor's map.

In the 1790s Canon Bridge House in Madley parish was a desirable summer residence 'placed on a beautiful terrace near the banks of the Wye' standing adjacent to a busy timber yard. In 1795 W.S. Symonds of Canon Bridge received a letter regarding 'the carriage of timber and for keeping the road passable at all times' from the Whitehouse Estate in Vowchurch to the 'wharf gate' at Canon Bridge.[7] Tons of timber and planks were sent by Messrs. R. Purchas & Skipp from Canon Bridge to Chepstow between 1810 and 1812 for a total of £132 15s 3d. Further timber was sold in 1813 as 'Navy Timber of prime quality, very great lengths, and extraordinary large dimensions, situated on the Whitehouse Estate 6 miles from Canon Bridge from whence down the navigable River Wye, it may be conveyed to any of the Ports or Yards in the Kingdom'.

These great lengths of timber were lashed together to form rafts that were floated in '10-12 mile stages down the river to Chepstow, and so out into the Bristol Channel. The Napoleonic Wars had created a keen demand for timber of shipbuilding class with a consequent advance in value. But one oak of exceptional length and straightness was transported by road to a point on the coast near Tenby, and erected for fixing a lanthorn at the top to guide mariners out to sea.' Between 1825 and 1827 the Liverpool & Bristol Company conveyed 'timber from Canon Bridge' to Brockweir and Chepstow on barges named *Ann, James, Charles, Mayflower, John and Mary* and *Eliza* operated by Easton, Peacock, Goodman, and Hoskins from Hereford.[8] During the same period the Canon Bridge 'Timber Yard' recorded cargoes and floats of timber, bark and boards on these barges and timber conveyed by Ward from Bishopswood and Powell from Old Forge. In June 1828 the Canon Bridge Timber Yard appears to have ceased operation and was 'given up to Mr. Powell'.[9]

At Bridge Sollers 'the clarity and mountain sprightliness of the

An extract from the Timber Yard Account at Canon Bridge in 1827:	
Aug 22 Geo. Pearce a barge load timber	19s
G P a Float	19s
24 Rosser a barge load of Timr.	19s
Sept 4 Thompson a barge load Timr.	19s
4 *Prudence* a Trow 45 Tons burden Of James Ward's Bishopswood	19s
Oct 27 *Prudence* James Ward's as above A freight of Timber each time	19s
Nov 10 Pit Ash by a boat Mr. Pearce Stretton informed About 1½ Tons Plank for Mr. E James of Hereford	1s 6d
16 18T 26 ft Timber & Planks	19s

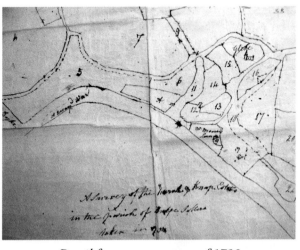

Detail from an estate map of 1730 showing the position of a decayed wharf (on the left) at Bridge Sollers

waters of the river make this a favourite spot for the angler; salmon, trout and grayling are obtainable and coarse fish are plentiful. The sunken road below the main road at Bridge Dingle, terminated at a river wharf similar to that at Byford, and it is said that stone used in the Cathedral was shipped here and brought by barge to Hereford. Here was an ancient ford, with licensed toll ferry used when the river was in flood.' Below the Dingle was the Salmon Inn serving those crossing the river and the bargees.[10] One wharf upstream from the ferry was reported as 'decayed' in 1730, but another on the Madley side of the Wye was probably the one used

The Salmon Inn at Bridge Sollers in 1880

in 1778 for discharging the lime required at Lulham Farm under the terms of a lease which required 'as much Lime as can be bought for five Pounds at the Lime Kilns in the parish of Fownhope'.[11]

Byford, Preston, Monnington and Moccas

The barges faced a number of river crossings between Byford and Moccas. A punt and a wide flat-bottomed boat carried passengers, carriages and animals across to Preston-on-Wye from Byford. A few hundred yards downstream 'the roadway ends at the water's edge in what was known as the wharf in the days of the barges'. During the 1790s coal was delivered at Byford wharf, with an occasional barge-load landed for Mr. Price at Foxley. For this long haulage of coal from the Forest of Dean the barge master and his men were paid an extra amount of 8 shillings, and were able to refresh themselves at the Boat Inn which was also used by those using the ferry, the nearby timber yard and the saw mill. This inn

The way to the site of the Byford ferry in 1922 (left), and in 2012

'stood at the top of the slope in the river bank leading to the dock where these vessels lay'. In 1810 '20 ton 26 feet timber' was shipped from Byford to Chepstow, in 1807 pantiles were delivered on the opposite bank at Preston-on-Wye for Preston Court, and lime was discharged in 1814.[12]

The main hindrance to improving and extending the navigation of the Wye was the obstruction of the river by innumerable weirs that had been constructed to provide power for the medieval mills and forges with fish garths for breeding fish, which were all to be removed under the terms of the 1695 Navigation Act.[13] Clearly the work had been carried out haphazardly on this stretch of the river, for in 1717 the Dean and Chapter of Hereford noted that at Preston 'there was a breach formerly made pursuant to the act of King Wm. But ye breach had been so unfortunately made that it throws the force of water forward upon ye meadow that the same had been very much washed and ye soil taken away by the River', and at Monnington the weir was 'not wholly demolished but only a narrow breach made'.[14]

The original weir at Monnington had been about 8 feet high and made of loose stones and stakes that had probably been constructed at the Monnington Falls, 'a barrier of rocks forming a weir and waterfall, which was an awkward obstacle in the old times when barge traffic was in vogue, and was only passable near the right bank, and then only when the water was high and with the aid of pulley-blocks'. Just below the falls and an island was a fording place 'available at low water for the passage of horses and cattle' and a 'landing place on the gravel for the barges'. In 1801 lime was discharged for Mr. James at Monnington, 15 dozen costing £6 10s, in addition to which 14 men bringing the barge up were paid 5 shillings each, and the five men taking it down 2s 6d, and for unloading a total of 7s.[15]

The bargees that passed Moccas in the 1770s would have noticed the rebuilding of Moccas Court, 'pleasantly situated on an eminence, on the southern bank of the Wye, within a spacious park, and [which] commands a full and extensive view of the beautiful

A barge passing under Brobury Scar and heading towards Moccas Court,
as depicted in the 1780s

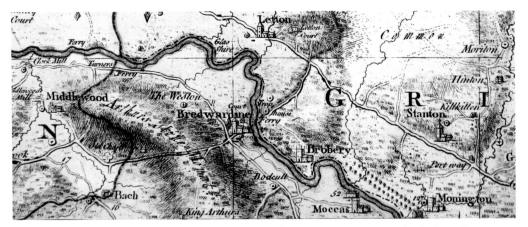

Taylor's map of 1754 showing the Wye between Monnington and Clock Mill

meanderings of the river'. In February 1772 'a barge with 15 tons of bark broke loose from her moorings, near Moccas and arrived about six o'clock on Saturday morning at our bridge [Hereford] but was prevented from passing through it by her mast, part of which was immediately sawed off, when she was taken through and safely moored'. She had travelled 16 miles undamaged, with 'not a soul on board!' In 1798 Moccas Court was the seat of Sir George Cornewall who took coal deliveries off the barges, and in 1826 John Easton was shipping 'Ash Timber' to Brockweir from Moccas Gardens.[16]

Bredwardine, Brobury and Whitney

From Moccas the Wye winds its way along a circuitous course below Brobury Scar which would have caught the bargees' attention with its 'bold and majestic roughness of its form, that contrasts beautifully with the views, more immediately upon the eye, on the bank of our river'. Below the lofty cliff a boathouse was occupied by the ferryman who carried passengers across to the Moccas Estate.[17] At Bredwardine, before the building of Bredwardine Bridge in 1769, the Trap House Ferry of 1754 took passengers across the river from the Trap Inn at Brobury. Although there is little evidence of barge activity at Bredwardine, there was a wharf by the bridge used for the delivery of coal. In December 1808 there was an auction at the Red Lion of 'Prime Naval Timber of the Largest Dimensions', comprising 'Five Hundred and Twenty large Oak Trees standing and growing in the several parishes of Moccas, Dorstone, Bredwardine, Blakemere and Monnington-on-Wye, within one mile of the River Wye'.[18]

From Bredwardine to Clifford the Wye twists and turns through a plain with few places for the bargees to rest and refresh. Before a 'new cut for river' at the 'Horse Shoe Meadow' at Letton was made to try to prevent flooding the barges negotiated a narrow and sharp meander of the river within distance of the Swan at Letton. Maybe a bargeman would have sighted a remote ferry crossing at Turner's Boat that connected Bredwardine with Willersley. As the Wye meandered between the parishes of Clifford and Winforton below Merbach Hill, the Merbach Inn may have been open, and then the barges would have reached Clock Mill on the south bank in Clifford parish.[19]

James Wathen's 1798 sketch of a barge with Bredwardine Bridge in the background

Here there was 'an ancient passage-way known as the Clock Mill Ford, with a right-of-way path from Winforton Village' where a boat was available 'for the conveyance of travellers'. In 1793 Clock Mill 'consisted of a water corn mill, grist mill, cider mill and clover mill' where coal was unloaded in 1798. In 1833 the mill was 'All that Messuage or tenement with the Water Corn Grist Mill and the passage thereunto belonging commonly called or known by the name of the Clock Mill' and 'Fullers Mill with the Garden' let to John Russell. At the riverside below Clock Mill there is evidence that during the 18th and early 19th centuries 'coal and other heavy articles from the Forest of Dean and Bristol were bought up the Wye by barge. Cider, bark and timber were sent back by the same conveyance to the River Severn.'[20]

From Clock Mill the bargees were faced by a haul past Lockster's Pool to the Boat Inn at Whitney on the north bank. This inn dates from 1801, when it was kept by Thomas Jones who would have served both the bargees and those travelling the road which went right past its door.[21] Beyond the inn, at 'what is known as the Cow Pond Pool, there is a ford which has been used locally for carting gravel from the right bank' and 'where the water is low or moderate, the river is capable of being forded, but it should at the same time be borne in mind that there have been many changes in the bed of the river, places which were formerly shallow being now deep pools, and vice versa'.[22]

The Wye at Whitney was indeed notorious for its drastic floods, changes of course and varying channels. In 1735 Whitney church and rectory were both swept away and since the first bridge of 1774 was destroyed by floods, three more followed the same fate in quick succession until the fourth toll bridge was constructed in the early 19th century. It is recorded that barge owners were to be answerable for any damage done to the first bridge, suggesting that 'goods such as coal from the Forest of Dean were being taken up the river to Hay at that time'. At the former ferry site a stone jetty existed on the right bank which may have served as a landing stage. When the horse-drawn tramway opened in 1818, its track was laid across the bridge, as negotiated by the company with the bridge owners.[23]

In 1772 John Stallard at Hardwick was seeking 'Barges to convey a large quantity of plank and converted navy timber from Whitney to Chepstow, for which freights will be paid on delivery' to Jaques and Dixon in Chepstow. Stallard was a descendant of Thomas Pennoyre, who had previously sold '500 cords of timber' in 1701 to Thomas Church and Samuel Bullock of Hereford. Although in 1701 provision had been made for the 'carrying away of the coles without horses or other beasts', as mentioned in chapter 2, it was not stated whether these were transported by water.[24] During 1772 and 1773 Stallard shipped tons of timber, planks, cordwood and chopped bark from his woods at Whitney and Hardwick to Chepstow by barge. He made payments for hauling, paying the bargemen, and carriage, which included 'Loading Timber upon the Meadow', 'halling out of Whitney Wood', and 'carriage of 8 Ton of Timber to Chepstow'.[25]

The timber from Whitney was shipped from several wharfs situated alongside the river below the ford, which was later replaced by the bridge. From Hardwick the timber from Stallard's 'timber yard' at the Moore was probably hauled by teams of horses across the Wye and shipped from the wharfs at Whitney to Chepstow. John Stallard paid £23 9s 6d to Thomas Jones in 1773 'for halling of 179 tons timber … and for halling two days with his team … at the same Time for Landing the Timber upon the Meadow' and 2s for '3 days halling with 6 horses in the yard'.[26]

Brilley and Clifford

At Brilley on the borders of England and Wales, the Rhydspence Inn, long associated with the drovers as an ale and cider house and locally known as the 'Cattle Inn', was near

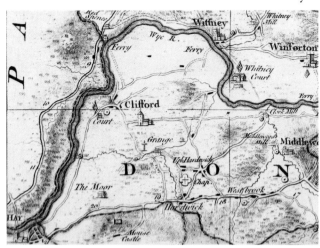

Taylor's map of 1754 showing the Wye between Clock Mill and Hay

enough to the river to be visited by the bargemen. Nearby at Wye Side, a cottage was occupied by William Goode employed as a bargeman in 1841.[27]

Further on still, Clifford village on the south bank was reached, and shortly before reaching the ruins of its castle the barges were able to pull in at the 'common and waste' alongside the river. Here, in 1817, the bargees would have seen the laying of the horse-drawn tramway leading from Brecon via Hay to Eardisley. The

Samuel Ireland's depiction of a barge passing under the ruins of Clifford Castle in 1797

tramway was built to provide a cheaper and more convenient means of transporting coal from south Wales, a real threat to the coal trade on the Wye from the Forest of Dean.[28] At Clifford Common timber was loaded onto William Hoskins' barge, the *Eliza*, in 1826 before heading downstream for another load at Canon Bridge. For the thirsty bargees at Clifford there was the Castle Inn kept by Thomas Norman in 1809 and a beer house later known as the Well Inn.[29]

Hay to Glasbury

Very few barges made the 34 mile journey up the Wye from Hereford to Hay, and even fewer to Glasbury, although, as mentioned in chapter 4, it is understood that the bell from Llywel church and the one from Hay church were transported by water from Hay to be recast at Chepstow in 1739 and 1740.[30] The barges crossed the boundary from Herefordshire into Wales at the mouth of the Dulas, where the Wye 'receives a considerable body of water ... thus assisted our river becomes a copious stream, and has been long rendered navigable in the winter seasons'. At Hay the bargees would have found a town 'happily situated on the declivity of a hill, on which the houses rising gradually, convey the idea of a place of infinitely more consequence than really it possesses, and in no small degree give the general outline of an Italian landscape'.[31]

In 1770 the barge owners were concerned about the state of the rivers Wye and Lugg including 'the greatest part of the River between Hereford and Hay'. They stated in a public notice 'That thro' length of time, since the navigation was first opened, many alterations

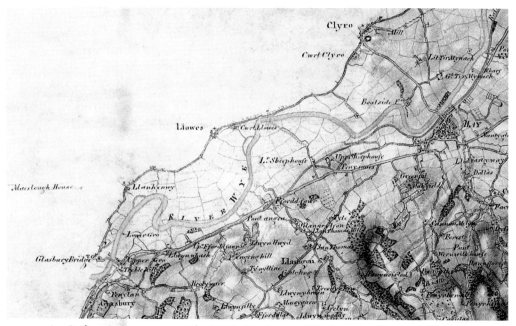

An Ordnance Survey map of c.*1812 showing the Wye between Hay and Glasbury*

have been made in the channel of the River Wye, occasioned by floods, the coming down of large quantities of ice, and various other causes'. Signed by the barge-owners and users, the notice continued 'that the navigation is by such means in many places so dangerous, as to make it impracticable for the most skilful barge-masters to pass and repass with their boats in safety'.[32] It is doubtful whether many improvements were carried out on the upper Wye as a result, but in 1772 'Ship Timber' consisting of 382 trees from the Hay Forest was

Hay as depicted by Samuel Ireland in 1797

151

advertised for sale being 'about one mile distant from Hay, where the River Wye is navigable'. In 1788 the Dean and Chapter of Hereford Cathedral paid for the 'Carriage of a stone from the Hay' and a load of birch poles from 'the Hay', in 1794 at a time when Greenly, Thomas and Goodman were freighting deals, oak boards, stone and alabaster to Hereford Cathedral from other sites on the Wye.[33]

It is understood that before 1800, Hay 'relied almost entirely on the River Wye for transport of coal and other necessaries, but pack horses were employed in small numbers bringing fuel from Wales'. At nearby Clyro in 1807 the occupiers of Cabalva transported 50 cwt of coal, which took two days for two boys to collect and deliver. Maybe it was the lack of coal transport that encouraged the building at Hay of a 39-ton barge in 1807 by Thomas Thomas who named her the *Penelope*.[34] Timber was still being freighted or floated down the Wye from Hay and Clyro in

An advertisement for a sale of timber to be held at the Swan Inn in Hay in January 1829. The timber is to be felled on the nearby Penyworlodd Estate, is noted to be 'well adapted for Building and Naval purposes', and it is pointed out that 'The Navigable River Wye is only two miles distant, to which there is an excellent road'.

1816 when several 'Lots of Timber' growing in Clyro were for sale 'Two miles of the Town of Hay, on Lands within half a mile of the River Wye'. Although the horse tramway reached Hay in 1816 to transport coal from south Wales, it did not deter Captain James Prout from building in Hay the *Liberty*, a 32-ton barge, in 1824. Prout was an experienced barge master who had worked the Wye since at least 1817.[35]

Lying east of Hay Bridge at Cusop was a wharf and timber yard probably reused by the tramway known as the Hay Railway. By the 1820s, when improvements had been made to the roads, more goods destined for Hay were conveyed from Hereford by various carriers run by Easton, Price, Prosser and Evans, which together with coal delivered by tram led to a reduction of trade on the Wye. Even so, in 1823 the *Lydney Trader*, a sloop, made the journey from Bristol to Hay, and during 1825 and 1826 small amounts of timber were conveyed downstream by bargemen who hauled, steered and sailed their loads of timber over a distance of 102 miles to Messrs. Watkins at Chepstow. In 1829 an auction took place at 'The Swan Inn, in the Town of Hay' of 'Valuable, Oak, Ash and other Timber', 'lengthy, and well adapted for Building and Naval purposes. The Navigable River Wye, is only two miles distant, to which there is an excellent road.'[36]

For the bargemen, Hay offered a number of inns and beer houses within a few minutes of the riverside and the barge moorings. In Newport Street there was the Lamb kept by David Morgan in 1802, the Ship kept by John Baker in 1815, and just over the border in Cusop was the Nelson, which opened opposite the tramway's coal wharf. Near Hay Bridge in Broad Street there was the Three Tuns of 1761 and the Seven Stars of 1776. The Red Lion of 1760 and the Wheatsheaf of 1775 were a little further away in the Pig Market. On the north bank of the Wye at Clyro and Llowes a few inns existed, but apart from the Radnor Arms at Llowes were situated too far from the Wye.[37]

The occasional barge that continued upstream from Hay had to navigate almost six miles over shallows and around meanders before reaching Glasbury. In the late 18th century the bargees were in 'the midst of this rich and beautiful valley, [where] an elegant stone bridge of seven arches is thrown across the river'. This, however, was totally destroyed by floods in 1795 when Hay and Whitney bridges met the same fate. In the early 19th century Glasbury was a village with 'no manufactures ... but the woolstapling business is carried on to a considerable extent. The Wye runs through the village, and divides the counties of Brecon and Radnor, the river being crossed by a neat bridge of wood, of great length and lofty.'[38]

The Wye at Glasbury as depicted by Samuel Ireland in 1797

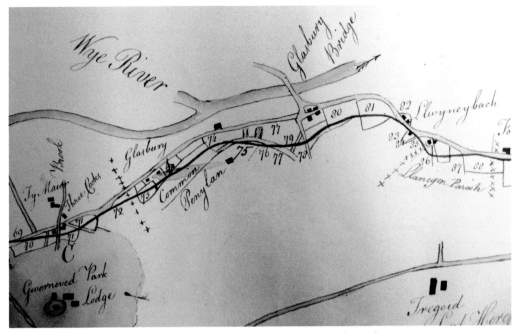

*A plan of 1812 showing the route of the horse-drawn railway from Brecon to Hay
as it passed through Glasbury. It continued from Hay to Eardisley.*

Despite the shallows and extreme floods of the Wye between Hay and Glasbury, a few barges made the long journey from the Forest of Dean to deliver coal at Glasbury during the 1770s, and timber was exported downstream, which possibly included 'all the Timber and Iron from the Old Bridge'. In 1794 it was recounted that the area up to 6 miles above Hay received some benefit from being close to the river when it was in flood, for it was then navigable. Thought of such benefit may have changed after the floods of the following year when there was concern about the Wye 'breaking out on the Radnorshire side, and is likely to leave Builth Bridge upon dry land; any person or persons conversant with Embankments, who will undertake to keep the river in its useful and proper channel are desired to attend with their Plans and estimates, at the next General Quarter Sessions'.[39]

Once the horse-drawn Hay Railway from Brecon to Eardisley opened in stages between 1816 and 1818 with its line straight through Glasbury, coal was available at a cheaper price from south Wales. In 1819 '84 Bags at 2/6 per Bag £10 10 0' of coal was delivered with other amounts to the Penlan lime kiln 'from the Railway'. Bags of coal were delivered the next year at the same price, when costs for nine horses working over six days were given as 11s 3d per day, and men were paid 1s a day. The Glasbury inns and beer houses, that served the occasional bargeman, continued their trade with the tramroad drivers and hauliers. There was the Maesilwch Arms and the Plough and Harrow of the 18th century, and in 1815 the Lamb, Six Bells and Hammer and Trowel. The Harp blossomed from a cider house into an inn frequented by the drovers during the 19th century.[40]

12 DECLINE OF THE RIVERS WYE AND LUGG NAVIGATION

The decline of the navigation on the rivers Wye and the Lugg from Symonds Yat to Glasbury was a gradual process due to road improvements and competition from canals and tramways, with the river trade's final demise caused by the rapid spread of an efficient railway system. During the 18th and early 19th centuries the turnpike trusts were established to develop the road network, and plans were contemplated to improve communications throughout the nation by constructing canals and tramroads which led to the railway age. The Wye, and to a lesser extent the Lugg, served as an important trade route but the rivers were often unpredictable with varying levels, fast-flowing water, numerous shoals and seasonal flooding.

In Hereford 'it was resolved, in 1790, after mature deliberation to cut a canal, which might open a communication with the Severn at Gloucester, and, by passing the collieries, afford the City of Hereford and its neighbourhood a more regular supply of coal'.[1] In 1828 Charles Heath referred to the coming of the tramroads after a long preamble about the difficulties of navigation on the Wye. He noted that many attempts had been made to 'render the rivers Wye and Lugg navigable, as well as for the sake of bringing up different articles from Bristol etc. at a small expense, as of finding a more easy and advantageous sale for the natural products of the county' but the 'capricious and headlong current of the Wye, seems indeed to bid defiance to every effort of control; yet it is, in its present unimproved state, very beneficial to the County in general'. To remedy 'the great privations the inhabitants of Hereford so often suffer, from the want of fuel, in times of long frosts, or high floods of this river, an Act of Parliament has been obtained, for making a tram road, from the extensive mines of Thomas Hill, esq., at the Blorens [Blorenge], near Abergavenny'.[2]

Canals

Canal mania spread across Britain during the 18th century, resulting in a network of waterways being promoted by 1789 that included the Severn and Thames Canal, the Staffordshire and Worcestershire Canal and the Oxford Canal. These waterways were followed by proposals for the Gloucester and Berkeley, the Brecknock and Abergavenny, the Leominster to Stourport and the Hereford and Gloucester canals, together with the Warwick and Birmingham Canal which later amalgamated to form the Grand Union Canal.[3] In 1830 the Lower Avon was leased to the Worcester and Birmingham Canal Company at a time when 'the new railway network was to provide serious competition for canal and river trade'.[4]

The Hereford & Gloucester Canal Act was passed in 1791 enabling a canal to be constructed between the two cities. It was opened from Gloucester to Newent in 1795, extended to Ledbury in 1798 and onto its Gas Works in 1832, although it was not until 1841 that the first barge-load of coal arrived at the town's Bye Street Wharf. The canal eventually reached Hereford in 1845. A gross tonnage of 43,000 was carried on the canal in 1848, and the construction of the Hereford to Shrewsbury Railway, the Newport, Abergavenny and Hereford Railway

Hereford and Withington Canal Wharfs.

EDWARD GEORGE,
TIMBER AND SLATE MERCHANT,
HAS CONSTANTLY ON SALE
FOREIGN TIMBER AND DEALS,
Of every description;
PRINCESS, DUCHESS, COUNTESS, & LADIES' SLATES;
RIDGE CRESTS, BROSELEY TILES, FIRE BRICKS, SQUARES, &c., &c.
AGRICULTURAL, FINE, AND ROCK SALT.

GOODS DELIVERRD TO ANY PLACE ALONG THE LINE OF THE CANAL.

Agent at WITHINGTON—WILLIAM BIRD, Canal Wharf.

An advertisement that appeared in the Hereford Journal *on 27 August 1851 concerning deliveries by canal*

and the Hereford, Ross and Gloucester Railway, saw a further increase in trade as the canal proved the most cost effective way of transporting the materials needed in their construction – which helped towards the demise of the canal.[5]

The trade on the upper Wye diminished as traffic on the canal increased from the Hereford and Withington Canal Wharfs where 'Edward George Timber and Slate

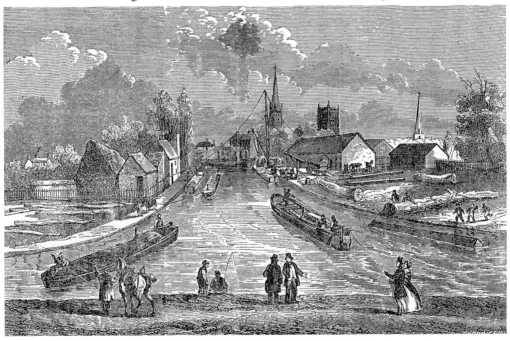

The canal basin at Hereford just after opening

Merchant' was offering 'Goods delivered to any Place along the Line of the Canal'. William Bird, a 'Timber & Coal Merchant', was a 'Commission Agent and General Wharfinger' based at Withington where he advertised that goods could be 'forwarded to all parts of the Kingdom'. At Hereford Wharf there were the 'Canal and General Carriers' of Gibson & Co., Joseph Holloway, Robert Smallwood and Joseph Trokes and Son. A few years later 'boats left Gloucester daily for Hereford from which latter place goods are conveyed expeditiously by railway'.[6]

The Leominster Canal was a further threat to the river trade. This canal was proposed to run from Stourport to Leominster and then on to Kington. It was suggested that the canal would allow the import of lime and coal from Shropshire, and the export of agricultural produce. Part of the canal was completed in 1796 when 'fourteen barges of coal arrived at the Wharf in Leominster' and sold 'at 15s. per ton which was half of what it had previously cost'. By 1805 it was confirmed that the Leominster Canal, even though it hadn't reached Stourport, had 'effected some reduction in the price of coal'. It appears that after this date trade on the River Lugg ceased.[7]

Tramroads

Tramroads carried wagons along tracks and rails similar to those used in later railways, but instead of having steam-powered engines to pull the wagons they were horse-drawn. During the first quarter of the 19th century three horse-drawn tramways were established to bring cheaper coal from the Forest of Dean and south Wales into Herefordshire. Although the tramways were competing for trade on the Wye, they also formed a wider transport network with connections to the wharves along the Wye at Lydbrook, Bishopswood, Hereford, Glasbury and Hay. In 1812 'barge owners in the Hereford trade urged completion of the [rail] road to Bishopswood' from where the coal was conveyed by barge to Hereford'.

A tramway connecting the Severn to the Wye was established after a meeting held in 1801 at the Swan in Ross. From the main line in the Forest of Dean a number of branches led to wharves on the Wye at Lydbrook. There was Teague's Railway of 1801 which transported coal from Perch Hill down to his quay at Lydbrook, an extension in 1814 to the Bishopswood wharves, and Scott's Tramroad of 1820 which served the Vention lime kilns. In 1821 The Lydney Trading Society was established as a goods and passenger service from the Severn to the Wye, and offered a reduced rate of transporting iron, tin-plate, sand, flour, grain and grocery from a siding near Bishopswood.[8]

From the beginning of the 19th century there had been proposals for a horse-drawn tramroad to Hereford from the Forest of Dean or the south Wales coalfields. A circuitous route from Lydbrook was dismissed in favour of an intended line from the Brecon to Abergavenny Canal in Monmouthshire. Construction of this tramroad was slow to progress. Even though plans were made in

FOREST OF DEAN RAIL-WAY.

THE Committee for carrying the said Rail-Way into effect, are desired to meet, at the Swan Inn, Rofs, on Thurfday, the Twenty-fifth inst. at Twelve o'clock, on particular bufinefs.

JOHN SCUDAMORE.

Hereford, March 16, 1802.

A notice referring to the horse-drawn tramway

1818 and 1825 for the route into Hereford, it was only opened at 10am on 21 September 1829 'when the first consignment of coal from Abergavenny arrived at the Wyebridge wharf. In all during the day thirty-four trams arrived at the wharf, fifteen from the Blaenavon collieries, and eighteen from Pontypool, and one of grain. Mr. Hill, the proprietor of the Blaenavon Collieries, gave orders for 10½ tons of the first coal consignment to be distributed among the poor of Hereford City. It is recorded that two horses drew twelve tons of coal from the tunnel at Haywood to the Wyebridge wharf.'[9]

The cause of the late arrival of the tramroad into Hereford was due to organised opposition from the barge owners and those with vested interest in the river trade. The rates of tonnage on the tramroad was 1½d per mile for minerals, manure, apples and cider, and 3d per mile for general merchandise, with passengers and animals charged at a different rate. The price of coal carried by tram from south Wales came to just over £1 per ton cheaper than coal transported on the Wye from the Forest of Dean. The tramroad proprietors soon established a dwelling house, counting house, tram house, stables, weighing machine, workshop, coal wharf and yard on a site previously used by the river trade.[10]

A horse-drawn tramroad known as the Hay Railway was established in 1811 connecting Brecon to Eardisley via Glasbury, Hay, Winforton, Clifford and Whitney. The tramroad company had been promoted by those associated with the Brecknock and Abergavenny Canal, the River Wye Horse Towing Path Company and coal merchants. A plan of the proposed line was made in 1812 and by 1816 it was passable 'from the Public Wharf at Brecon to the Town of Hay'. The problem of crossing the Wye at Whitney was overcome by using the existing road bridge after dismissing the idea of building a tramroad bridge or using 'Boats for passing the Tram Wagons over the River Wye'. In 1818 the tramroad reached Eardisley, and two years later was extended to Kington.[11]

The main traders on the Hay Railway were the Trusteds of Hay and Eardisley, and William Bridgewater of Glasbury. They both had teams of horses which generally worked in pairs 'pulling no more than six wagons' which held up to 2 tons each. James Spencer, a Hay solicitor, was the company's clerk from 1811 to 1847 and he kept meticulous accounts, not just of the tramway business, but also of his farming and lime burning activities. Apart from many records of coal deliveries, payments such as from the 'Tram Road Trust to John Dowell for repairing the hedges from Clifford Castle to Pontvain Bridge' in 1827 are noted.[12]

Very few barges on the Wye had conveyed goods to and from Whitney, Hay and Glasbury since the end of the 18th century, excepting some timber products during the 1820s. Previous to the tramroad, coal had been transported by road 'principally on mules' or horses' backs to the neighbourhood of Hay, Builth and other distant parts of the county

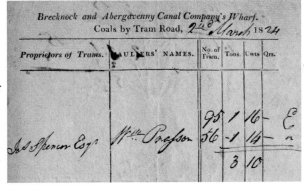

A record of coal delivered from the canal wharf on the Hay tramway from James Spencer's accounts

The trams on the horse-drawn tramway were described as follows in 1937 by F. Ellison: 'These were made with wood or iron bodies, and the whole were small and plain – no flanges – so they could leave the railway and deliver coal to a house. This was often done at the Six Bells at Glasbury, an inn gone long ago. Miss Honeyfield (aged 91 years) told me that she often watched the trams go bumping past, making a big noise, and that the horses always stopped at the Six Bells without being told'.[14]

where the inhabitants are happy at almost any rate to be supplied'. After 1800 it was unlikely that any coal had been transported by water to Hay and Glasbury, where it was an important product for the limestone industry. Therefore, there was little competition between this tramroad and the river trade on the upper Wye. By 1817 coal was sold 'at 18s per ton on the tram at Glasbury wharf, and at Hay at 20s per ton'.[13]

Railways

During the mid 19th century the railway network replaced the former tramroads and canals with swifter, cheaper and more convenient transport. Not long after the Hereford and Gloucester Canal was completed in 1845, the first railway was linked to the Wye at Hereford and the Lugg at Leominster in 1853, when the Hereford and Shrewsbury Railway was completed. This was followed in 1854 with the opening of the Hereford to Abergavenny and Newport line built partly along the route of the Abergavenny to Hereford Tramroad. The railway that had the most dramatic effect on the demise of the upper Wye river trade, however, was the Hereford, Ross and Gloucester Railway which opened in 1855. This line followed the valley of the Wye between Hereford and Ross where it continued across country to Gloucester.[15]

The Hereford to Gloucester railway was promoted as giving 'a boost to the agriculture, timber, brewing and manufacturing industries in Ross and Hereford', providing cheaper transportation of goods and giving 'tourists cheap and easy access to the tour of one of the finest rivers in Europe'. The first stations built between Hereford and Ross were at Holme Lacy and Fawley, where goods yards were constructed to house coal, lime, timber and other materials which had previously been shipped on the Wye barges. The railway network

HEREFORD, ROSS, & GLOUCESTER RAILWAY.
First General Ordinary Meeting.

NOTICE is hereby given, that the FIRST GENERAL ORDINARY MEETING of the SHAREHOLDERS in the HEREFORD, ROSS, and GLOUCESTER RAILWAY COMPANY, will be held at the GREEN DRAGON HOTEL, in the City of HEREFORD, on THURSDAY, the 4th day of SEPTEMBER, 1851, at One o'clock in the Afternoon, for the Election of Directors and Auditors, and for the transaction of the General Business of the Company.
By Order of the Board of Directors,
JOHN NASH, Secretary.
August 2nd, 1851.

continued to spread along the Wye, with the Hay Railway purchased and opened as the Hereford, Hay and Brecon line in the 1860s, and the opening of the Ross to Monmouth Railway in 1873.[16]

During the years that the railways were planned and constructed, the navigation continued on the Wye at Lydbrook, Ross, Foy and 'to Hereford in barges of from 18 to 40 tons, and sometimes lighter boats to Hay'. Bark, timber, apples, barley, fleece, meat, lambs wool

Barges at Hereford in 1854

and potatoes were shipped from Wilton to Hoarwithy, Glewstone Boat, Monmouth and Hereford, with slate, bark, cider, wines and spirits shipped by Pullings to and from Hereford and Bristol. Despite the publicity and excitement of the railways, the boatyards at Fownhope and New Weir were still building barges during the 1850s. The sacks of wheat and barley delivered by barge from Wilton to a corn dealer in Monmouth in 1853 and 1854 are the last known written entries of shipments on the upper Wye.[17]

Even so, barges were still sighted on the Wye at Hereford, Ross and Goodrich in 1861 and below Symonds Yat where the navigation continued until a later period.[18] In 1873 the 'cessation of navigation in the upper portion of the river has proved in one way injurious to the salmon fisheries in Herefordshire and the counties higher up. The barges, constantly passing over the shallow streams formed what was called the barge channel, and up this deepened stream it was inviting and easy for salmon to pass upwards even at low water.'[19]

On the upper Severn there was only a slight reduction of river trade taken by the canals, and in the 1840s the grain traffic even increased although the trade of shop goods diminished. When the Severn Valley Railway opened in 1862 it offered a far superior and more efficient means of transport than by river or canal, but even so trade continued on the Shropshire section until

The remains of a barge at Lydney c.1970

Pleasure boats making the Wye Tour in 1793

1895 when the last known barge was recorded at Bridgnorth. On the lower Severn the river traffic struggled on well into the 20th century.[20]

Recreational Boating

Since the Wye Tour had been established in the mid 18th century, there was a continuation of pleasure boating between Chepstow and Hay. In 1780 'a new pleasure boat with oars and mast' was available at Hereford to 'sail over the shallowest stream on the river Wye from Hay to Monmouth'. A 'complete pleasure boat, worked by three men, was to be had from

Pleasure boats at Hereford in 1850

Fownhope to Ross, Monmouth and Chepstow' in 1806, and in 1841 'the traveller may hire a boat' from Ross. In Hereford properties were advertised in 1853 as 'extending to the river Wye and affording excellent landing for pleasure boats', although it was Ross that had the greatest reputation for 'a choice of boats and the services of efficient, experienced, and trustworthy boatmen' supplied by Joseph Evans.[21]

Two Mast and Line	Two Windlasses
Two pairs Sculls	Five rollers
One pair oars	Box of grease
Paddle Boat Hook	Ball of string
Boat Hook	Lantern
Stern Cushion	Matches
Two Stretchers	Soap
Two Pads	Ordnance Maps
Three pieces matting	Tarpaulin
Two feather Pads	Flag
Bow lounge Board	Rug
Bow Cushion	Spare Cord
Two Cans (1 gallon each)	Dutch cheese
Two Pannikins	Six fenders

List of equipment taken on a rowing tour on the Wye and other rivers and canals from The Diary of a Rowing Tour*, 1875, by Howard Williams*

Similar to the decline of the barge traffic, the pleasure boat business was also affected by the opening of the railways. From 1873 tourists enjoyed the scenic Wye Valley from a comfortable seat on the Ross to Monmouth Railway, whilst those interested in rowing were able to join the Ross or Hereford Rowing Clubs. Further upstream R. Jordan at the Wye Bridge in Hereford was offering 'Boats from Hay and Hereford, to Ross, Monmouth, Tintern, Chepstow and all parts of the Wye' in 1890, and a few years later Thomas Dowell offered trips on his paddle steamer called the *Wilton Castle* from the Dock at Ross.[22]

The paddle steamer Wilton Castle *and various pleasure craft at Ross in 1905*

TOUR OF THE WYE.

BOATS from HAY and HEREFORD to ROSS, MONMOUTH, TINTERN, CHEPSTOW, and all parts of the WYE. SEASON COMMENCING APRIL 1st.—Terms on application.

R. JORDAN,

BOAT BUILDER AND PROPRIETOR,
WYE BRIDGE, HEREFORD.

The dinghy Shearwater *in which C.R. Shaw travelled from Hereford to Chepstow in 1948*

These days the Wye is much used by canoeists, here seen at Whitney (left) and Lydbrook

In 1931 holidaymakers in Hereford were informed that 'Hereford possesses a splendid safe boating stretch of river of 3 miles, and expert boatmen can go another 2 miles to Eaton Bishop. Boats can be hired very cheaply, a boat for one or two at 1s 6d the first hour and 1s per hour afterwards ... Mr. John Jordan is the proprietor and is very willing to advise about hiring for long or short boating trips. A great adventure is to row down to Chepstow.' Such a journey was undertaken by C.R. Shaw in a 16 foot out-rigger dinghy in early September 1948. A distance of 50 miles was completed at the rate of 16 miles a day in a loaded boat with a draught of about three inches.[23]

Pleasure boats at Hereford in 1870

Legacy of the River Navigation

From the late 1940s there was a certain amount of canoeing on the Wye, mainly organised by groups or by those wishing to explore the almost deserted river. This gradually became a more popular holiday activity, together with short riverside cruises available from Symonds Yat and briefly from Ross and Hereford. It was after a threat to introduce 'Hovercraft on the Wye' in 1985 that the rights of navigation on the Wye and Lugg became a controversial issue and discussed at a meeting hosted by the Ross & District Civic Society, which led to the formation of the River Wye Preservation Trust.[24]

During 1989 a 150-tonne Dutch barge renamed the *Wye Invader* was piloted by Frank Barton from Chepstow. It was a 'voyage he had to do in stages at weekends. It was only possible because the barge, unladen, draws on only three feet. Even so it got stuck at various places on its journey. One of them was at Symonds Yat. Looking on in amazement at this apparently foolhardy proceeding was Tony Gardiner, one of the fourth generation of his family to captain boats along this stretch of the river.' Although the barge reached Hereford there was opposition to it being opened as a 'floating bar'. So it remained moored just below Hereford.[25] Towards the end of 2012 the *Wye Invader* was steered downstream and sighted at Wilton and Symonds Yat before reaching Monmouth in February 2013.

Between 2008 and 2012 the Wye Valley Area of Outstanding Natural Beauty's 'Overlooking the Wye Scheme' carried out research on 'the fascinating and varied history and heritage in the Wye Valley' which resulted in identifying over forty heritage sites in the area. Information boards on 'river connections' describing and illustrating the river trade

Seen here at Symonds Yat in 2012, 'The m.v. Wye Invader *is a single screw, steel hulled, Dutch main river barge. She is of 38 metres length, 5.07 metres beam, 0.9 metres draft unladen and 1.9 metres fully laden. Her weight is 150 tonnes unladen, displacement, and 250 tonnes fully laden'*

A stylized representation of a ship by Mariele Neudecker in 2009 erected on the south bank of the Wye in Hereford

were installed at Chepstow, Brockweir, Llandogo, Monmouth, Wilton and Ross explaining the 'watery highway linking the riverside villages with the wider world', and about boatmen who 'navigated trows laden with cargo between the Wyeside wharves'.[26]

Plans were made in 2011 to build a scaled down replica of a Wye trow to feature in a pageant on the Thames to celebrate the Queen's Diamond Jubilee in 2012. The trow, based on a model at Monmouth Museum, was built by T. Nielson & Co. at Gloucester Docks. The trow, named the *Hereford Bull*, measures 36 feet in length with a 9 feet beam, and sports a sail, oars and a small outboard motor. When on the Thames it was not hauled in the traditional manner, but rowed with help from the outboard motor. After appearing in the pageant, the *Hereford Bull* featured at the Diamond Day community event in Hereford when the Queen and the Duke of Edinburgh visited Hereford on 11 July 2012.

In 2013 the trow team 'expect to take part in the Wye Festival in 2014, and hope to navigate part of the Severn in 2013 to take part in the Bewdley Art Festival', but keeping and using the trow on the Wye is their main aim. The balance of the money raised to build the *Hereford Bull* is held in trust with the Herefordshire Community Foundation who aim to make the trow 'available for educational and cultural use so that as many as possible can gain from the vivid reproduction of an element of our heritage that has long since passed into history'.[27]

The Hereford Bull *on display at the Diamond Day community event in Hereford in July 2012*

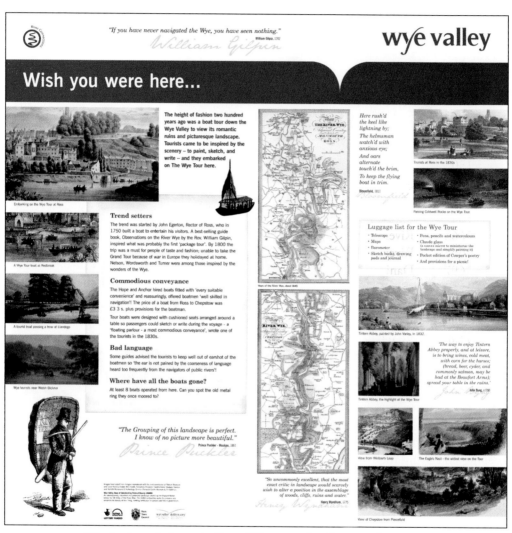

Display board about the River Wye erected at Ross Dock in 2012

Appendix I

The Rivers Wye and Lugg Navigation, Key Dates

1301	Survey of Weirs, Dykes and Stakes in the water of the Wye
1555	Hereford Mills Act
1597	Wilton on Wye Bridge Act
1641	John Taylor's Journey on the Wye
1662	Rivers Wye and Lugg Navigation Act
1695	Rivers Wye and Lugg Navigation Act
1697	Daniel Denell Survey of the Rivers Wye and Lugg
1727	Rivers Wye and Lugg Navigation Act
1763	Isaac Taylor's Survey of the Wye
1779	Robert Whitworth's Survey of the Wye
1786	Merchant Shipping Registration
1805	Report of William Jessop
1805	Henry Price Survey for making Towing Path
1809	Rivers Wye and Lugg Horse Towing Path Act
1855	Opening of the Hereford, Ross, Gloucester Railway

Appendix II

Bargemen, Owners and Masters etc. associated with the Wye between Symonds Yat and Glasbury

Balham, William	owner	1784	Baker, William	owner	1759
Barrow, Thomas	merchant	1798	Barrow, William	merchant	1811
Basset, Thomas	bargeman	1774	Bayton, Edward	bargeman	1811
Beale, John	owner	1722	Bennett, Richard	owner	1808
Biss, Charles	owner	1812	Biss, James	owner	1783
Biss, Susannah	owner	1835	Bloom, William	master	1755
Bonnor, William	merchant	1811	Bosley, John	merchant	1825
Bowsher, Thomas	owner	1825	Bowsher & Hodges	owner	1797
Bowsher, Hodges & Watkins	owner	1799	Brown, Samuel	master	1730
Bryder, George	owner	1822	Buckle, George	owner	1809
Bunning, William	owner	1835	Bunning & Gibson	owner	1843
Burgoyne, William	builder	1857	Burgum, Thomas	owner	1806
Bush, Elton & Bush	owners	1785	Butson, William	master	1771
Chapman, James	master	1825	Chapman, John	owner	1791
Chapman, Oliver	owner	1777	Cooke, Henry	merchant	1825
Cooke, William	owner	1822	Crompton, Adam	owner	1814
Crompton, Adam Sr	master	1796	Crompton, Henry	owner	1818
Crompton, John	master	1797	Crompton, Jonathan	master	1793
Crompton, Richard	master	1825	Crompton, William	master	1800
Crumpton, John	owner	1784	Crumpton, Jonathan	owner	1774
Crumpton, Thomas	owner	1784	Crumpton, William	bargeman	1784
Dale, John	bargeman	1771	Davies, John	master	1810
Davies, William	bargeman	1768	Davis, John	master	1789
Davis, William	owner	1801	Dibdon, Jonah	merchant	1744
Disney, Daniel	master	1730	Dowle, James	merchant	1830
Easton, John	builder	1822	Easton, John	master	1825

Eaton, Thomas	builder	1755	Eddy, Mr.	mariner	c.1800
Edwards, J.	owner	1847	Evans, George	builder	1730
Evans, John	owner	1866	Evans, Thomas	merchant	1800
Ford, Robert	master	1730	Gage, John	owner	1808
Gardiner, John	owner	1825	Garnons, Richard	bargeman	1770
George, James	master	1857	Goode, William	bargeman	1841
Goodman, Francis	master	1825	Gossing, John	owner	1730
Greenly, John	owner	1771	Greenway, John	bargeman	1766
Hale, Thomas	bargeman	1707	Hale, W.	owner	1795
Hale, Pride & Co	merchant	1801	Hall, Thomas	bargeman	1707
Hargist, John	bargeman	1835	Harris, George	master	1811
Harris, George	owner	1829	Harrison, John	owner	1801
Hartnell, William	merchant	1811	Hawkins, Mr.	owner	1803
Hobbs, John	owner	1730	Hopkins, Evan	boat builder	1822
Hopkins, James	boat builder	1730	Hopkins, William	master	1811
Hoskins, William	master	1809	Hughes, Charles	owner	1801
Hughes, Henry	owner	1825	Hughes, James	merchant	1795
Hughes, Luke	bargeman	1701	Hughes, Luke	owner	1735
Hughes, Robert	bargeman	1830	Hughes, Thomas	owner	1773
James, Charles	merchant	1780	Jenkins, Francis	bargeman	1728
Jenkins, William	bargeman	1796	Jones, Amos	merchant	1797
Jones, Charles	master	1810	Jones, John	owner	1784
Jones, Joseph	bargeman	1733	Jones, Philip	merchant	1810
Jones, Samuel	mariner	1730	Jones, Thomas	master	1809
Jones, Walter	bargeman	1804	Jones, William	owner	1812
Jordan, John	merchant	1809	Kelly, Joseph	boat builder	1827
Kyte, William	bargeman	1761	Lane, Thomas	master	1809
Lewis, John	master	1795	Lewis, Richard	owner	1818
Lewis, Thomas	owner	1796	Llewellyn, Elizabeth	owner	1797
Llewellyn, William	merchant	1754	Madley, James	owner	1810
Matthews, William	master	1825	Maund, Thomas	bargeman	1798
Maybury, P.	master	1811	Meredith, John	bargeman	1826
Moore, Edward	bargeman	1791	Moore, John	master	1798
Moreton, Henry	bargeman	c.1800	Morgan, Giles	bargeman	1736
Morgan, William	owner	1730	Morley, Captain	master	1826
Morse, George	owner	1799	Moxley, John	master	1825
Owen, J.	master	1823	Packwood, George	owner	1783
Packwood, James	owner	1801	Parker, Joseph	owner	1808
Peacock, George	owner	1825	Pearce, Daniel	owner	1783
Pearce, Daniel	owner	1829	Pearce, George	master	1825

Pearce, James	owner	1808	Pearce, James	master	1810
Pearce, Thomas	bargeman	1767	Pearce, Thomas	master	1809
Pewtner, Henry	owner	1810	Phillips, Francis Senior	owner	1772
Phillips, Francis	owner	1826	Philpott, John	bargeman	1826
Pitts, James	owner	1836	Platt, Daniel	master	1802
Platt, Henry	owner	1810	Platt, Mary	merchant	1795
Porter, William	merchant	1795	Porter, William	owner	1800
Powell, John	boat builder	1841	Powell, William	rafter	1729
Preece, John	bargeman	1820	Preece, Jude	bargeman	1754
Price, Francis	bargeman	1719	Probert, Richard	bargeman	1767
Prosser, Charles	merchant	1798	Prosser, Thomas	owner	1740
Prout, Captain	master	1846	Pugh, Thomas	bargeman	1761
Pulling, William	owner	1825	Purchas, Nathaniel	merchant	1775
Purchas, Nathaniel	owner	1787	Purchas & Skipp	owner	1787
Purchas, Robert	owner	1823	Purchas, Thomas	merchant	1796
Radford, Captain	master	1834	Reginald, Joseph	bargeman	1717
Reynolds, John	merchant	1838	Roberts, James	bargeman	1741
Roberts, Thomas	bargeman	1739	Rosser, John	bargeman	1817
Rosser, Roger	bargeman	1722	Rosser, William	bargeman	1803
Rosser, William	owner	1834	Russell, Thomas	bargeman	1780
Shellard, Joseph	master	1805	Sidway, John	bargeman	1789
Smith, William	merchant	1730	Smith, William	bargeman	1809
Stephens, John	merchant	1825	Swift, Henry	owner	1835
Swift, Hezekiah	merchant	1810	Swift & Co	owner	1822
Symonds, Philip	owner	1728	Symonds, William	bargeman	1753
Tamplin, Edward	master	1744	Tamplin, Edward	owner	1780
Tamplin, Joseph	master	1744	Tamplin, Thomas	master	1791
Tamplin, William	master	1827	Teague, James	merchant	1795
Terrett, Mark	bargeman	1828	Thackway, Joseph	bargeman	1828
Thirkil, John	bargeman	1841	Thomas, Francis	bargeman	1738
Thomas, Joseph	boat builder	1838	Thompson, Mr	merchant	1795
Trumper, Joseph	owner	1748	Trumper, Joseph	merchant	1790
Trumper, Thomas	owner	1728	Vaughan, John	mariner	1754
Vaughan, John	bargeman	1767	Ward, Edward	master	1851
Ward, James	owner	1823	Watkins & Morris	owner	1797
Watters, William	master	1809	Weare, Thomas	merchant	1795
Welch, William	bargeman	1701	Wells, Thomas	waterman	1702
Welsh, James	bargeman	1809	Wheatstone, Charles	master	1849
Wheatstone, George	master	1772	Wheatstone, John	owner	1773
Wheatstone, Richard	owner	1744	Wheatstone, Richard	owner	1851

Wheatstone, William	owner	1850	Wheeler, Thomas	merchant	1807
White, William	bargeman	1761	Whitefield, William	mariner	1730
Whittaker, John	master	1730	Williams, Edward	bargeman	1696
Williams, Henry	owner	1800	Williams, James	owner	1739
Williams, James	master	1825	Williams, John	owner	1808
Williams, William	bargeman	1696	Willmott, Edward	merchant	1796
Willmott, Elizabeth	merchant	1776	William, Thomas	merchant	1785
Wiltshire, William	merchant	1795	Wright, William	bargeman	1761
Yem, William	owner	1773			

Names collected from David Clark, Directories, Jean Dobson, John Eisel, Margaret Ellis, Grahame Farr, Gloucester Journal, *Percy Harris,* Hereford Journal, Hereford Times, *David Lovelace, Roz Lowe, P.J. Pikes, Parish Records,* TWNFC, *Barry Trinder, Ivor Waters and from archives at Gloucester Record Office, Hereford Cathedral Archives, Hereford Record Office and The National Archives.*

Appendix III

Sample of Barge Cargoes to and from Wilton and Ross
1744 to 1828

Wilton
1744 lime etc to Porter at Wilton
1789 wheat from Wilton
1790 barley from Wilton to Brockweir
1790 barley & wheat from Wilton
1791 iron hoops from Wilton
1792 barley and wheat to Wilton
1795 bottles from Wilton to Bristol
1795 oats from Wilton to Caple
1795 fire coal, hamper, cheese, peas & hair from Wilton to Caple
1797 freight from Wilton to Redbrook
1798 coal & wheat to Wilton
1799 salt fish, sugar, trefoil, cloth & lime
1800 lime from Wilton to Monmouth
1801 gallon of gin, sugar, linen & pantiles to Wilton
1801 hops, lime, seeds from Wilton to Bristol
1803 poles from Wilton to Bristol
1803 lime, flour & wheat from Wilton (some to Bristol)
1804 oil & peas from Wilton
1804 lime from Wilton to Bristol
1805 lime, casks, potatoes & cider from Wilton to Bristol
1805 poles & elm boards from Wilton to Bristol
1805 peas & rye grass from Wilton to Monmouth
1806 alabaster from Wilton
1806 grate, hamper, casks & pipe from Bristol
1807 bark from Wilton
1809 timber from Wilton to Chepstow
1809 corn & barley from Wilton to Bristol
1809 wheat & barley to Bristol
1809 deal & pantiles to Wilton from Chepstow
1809 wheat & barley from Wilton to Brockweir
1809 hops to Wilton from Hereford
1810 wheat to Wilton

1810 wheat from Wilton to Bristol
1810 flour from Wilton
1810 wheat to Bristol
1810 coal from Wilton
1810 coal, peas & pantiles
1810 peas to Wilton
1810 bark from Wilton to Chepstow
1810 wheat from Wilton to Bristol
1810 hampers of bottles from Wilton to Hoarwithy
1810 slate from Wilton
1811 herrings to Wilton
1811 stone & lime to Wilton
1811 lime & grain to Bristol
1811 coal from Wilton
1811 lime from Wilton
1811 slate to Wilton
1811 flax seed from Wilton to Monmouth
1811 lime, hoops & wheat from Wilton
1811 wheat from Wilton to Bristol
1811 hampers from Wilton
1812 lime, slates, chalk to Wilton Castle
1824 lime from Lydbrook
1828 barley from Wilton

Ross
1789 coal to the Rope Ross
1795 tiles from Ross
1796 hampers, pipes of wine, pantiles & bottles from Ross
1797 lime from Ross
1799 lime, ashes, oakum & lime to Ross
1799 potatoes, clover & wheat from Ross
1799 pantiles, kiln dust & cress from Ross
1800 ashes to Ross from Hoarwithy
1801 pantiles & lime from Ross
1801 twigs & lime to Ross from Backney
1801 ashes from Caple & lime to Ross
1801 soap to Chepstow from Ross
1805 lime & pantiles from Ross
1805 hampers, plain chimney
1806 lime & pantiles to Ross
1806 lime, oats & hay from Ross
1809 boxes & barley from Ross to Bristol
1810 freight flour from Bristol
1810 lime, wheat & flour from Ross
1811 flour to Monmouth
1811 paper from Chepstow
1811 oats, rye grass & clover from Ross
1824 lime from Lydbrook
1824 lime from Lydbrook to Wilton & Ross

Bibliography

Bewdley Historical Research Group, *Bewdley* 1999

Bick, D., *The Hereford & Gloucester Canal* 2nd ed 1994

Blount, T. (ed), *Manuscript History of Herefordshire* 1675

Brayley, E. & Britton, J., *The Beauties of England and Wales* 1805

Brian, A., *Six Walks of the Lower Lugg* 1993

Calderbank, G., *Leominster and its Waterways* 2000

Cassey, E., *Directory* 1858

Chandler, John, *Travels through Stuart Britain* 1999

Clinker, C., *The Hay Railway* 1960

Coates, S.D. & Tucker, D.G., *Water-mills of the Middle Wye Valley* 1983

Cross, A.G., *Old Industrial Sites in Dean* 1982

Crow, A., *Bridges on the River Wye* 1995

Druce, F., *A Good Plain Country Town* 1983

Duncumb, J., *General View of the Agriculture of Herefordshire* 1805

Eisel, J., 'Life on the River' in *A Herefordshire Miscellany* 2000

Eisel, J. & Bennett, F., *The Pubs of Hay-on-Wye* 2005

Fairs, G., *A History of the Hay* 1972

Farr, G., *Chepstow Ships* 1954

Farrant, A., *Rowing Holiday by Canal in 1873*

Finn, M., *Men of Iron* 1962

Fosbroke, T.D., *Wye Tour* 1823

Gale, E.B., *Farmers, Fishermen and Flax Spinners* 1983

Gilbert, H., *The Tale of a Wye Fisherman* 1959 ed

Gilpin, William, *Observations on the River Wye* 1782

Gorvett, David, *Bridge Over the River Wye* 1984

GWR, Routes and opening dates 1921

Green, Colin, *Severn Trader* 1999

Gwilt, C.F., *The Port of Bridgnorth* nd

Hadfield, C., *British Canals* 1974

       Canals of South Wales 1960

Harris, P., *Wye Valley Industrial History* 1968

Hart, C., *The Industrial History of Dean* 1971

Heath, Charles, *Monmouth* 1804

Heath, Charles, *Excursion Down the Wye* 1828

Hobbs, T., *The Pubs of Radnorshire* 2006

Holidays at Hereford 1931

Howse, W.H., *Radnorshire* 1949

Hughes, P. & Hurley, H., *The Story of Ross* 2009

Hughes, P. & Leech, A., *The Story of Worcester* 2011

Hurley, B. (ed), *Book of Trades* 1811

Hurley, H., *The Pubs of Ross & South Herefordshire* 2001

      The Pubs of the Royal Forest of Dean 2005

      Trackway to Turnpike 2007

      The Pubs of Monmouth, Chepstow and the Wye Valley 2007

      Landscape Origins of the Wye Valley 2008

      The Green Lanes of Herefordshire 2010

      The History of Shieldbrook 2010

Ireland, S., *River Wye* 1797

Kissack, K., *Monmouth* 1975

      River Severn 1982

Linn, M.W., *Men of Iron* 1962

Lipscomb, G., *Journey into South Wales* 1799

Lloyd, J. (ed), *History and Navigation of the Rivers Wye & Lugg* 1873

Lugwardine Historical Society, *Lugwardine in the 19th century* 1988

Marshall, W., *County Reports to Board of Agriculture* 1818

Mendelsohn, O., *The Dictionary of Drink* 1966

Myers, H., *W.H. Pyne and his Microcosm* 1996

Old Humphrey, *Country Strolls* 1844

Parr, H.W., *The Severn and Wye Valley Railway* 1973

      The Great Western Railway in Dean 1971

Price, J., *Account of Leominster* 1795

      City of Hereford 1796

Putley, John, *Riverine Dean* 1999

Rees, W.J., *The Hereford Guide* 1827

Reeves, N., *The Town in the Marches* 1973

Ritchie, L., *The Wye* 1841

Roberts, G., *The Shaping of Modern Hereford* 2001

Robinson, C., *A History of the Mansions and Manors of Herefordshire* 1872

Ross Guide 1827

Ross on Wye Civic Society, *Historical Aspects of Ross on Wye* 2000

Sanctuary, A., *Rope, Twine and Net Making* 1988

Shoesmith, R., *Hereford* 1992

Shoesmith, R. & Barrett, R., *The Pubs of Leominster & NW Herefordshire* 2000

Shoesmith, R & Eisel, J., *The Pubs of Hereford City* 2004

Smith, D., *Horse-drawn Vehicles* 1994

Stafford, H., *Treatise on Cyder-Making* 1753 (reprinted 2009)

Stockinger, V.R., *The Rivers Wye and Lugg Navigation* 1996

Strong, George, *Handbook to Ross and Archenfield* 1863

Taylor, E., *Kings Caple in Archenfield* 1997

Trinder, B., *Barges and Bargemen* 2005

Trinder, B. & Cox, N., *Miners & Mariners* 2000

Tweed, H., *Wilton Castle* 1884

Van Laun, John, *Hereford City* 2006

Walters, B., *Ancient Dean and the Wye Valley* 1992

Waters, I., *About Chepstow* 1952

      The Port of Chepstow 1977

Watkins-Pitchford, W., *The Port of Bridgnorth* 1935

Whitehead, D., *The Castle Green at Hereford* 2007

Whitehead, D. & Eisel, J., *A Herefordshire Miscellany* 2000

Whitehead, D. & Shoesmith, R., *James Wathen's Herefordshire* 1994

Willan, T.S., *River Navigation in England* 1964

      The Inland Trade 1976

Williams, H., *The Diary of a Rowing Tour in 1875* 1982

Wilson, D.G., *The Making of the Middle Thames* 1977

Wright, J.P., *A Walk through Hereford* 1819

VCH Gloucester Vol V 1996

Yarranton, A., *England's Improvement by Sea and Land* 1698

LOWV Barge Accounts

The Aramstone Archive 1744-1855

Barge & other Accounts 1790-1805

Ledger 1809-1811

Liverpool & Bristol Company Accounts 1825-1827

References

Abbreviations used

AONB   Area of Outstanding Natural Beauty
GRO   Gloucester Record Office
GSAI   Gloucestershire Society for Industrial Archaeology
Her Jnl   *Hereford Journal*
HCA   Hereford Cathedral Archives
HCL   Hereford City Library
HRO   Hereford Record Office
Her Times   *Hereford Times*
LOWV   Landscape Origins of the Wye Valley
OLW   Overlooking the Wye
OS   Ordnance Survey
RCS   Ross Civic Society
SMR   Sites and Monuments Records
TNA   The National Archives
TWNFC   *Transactions of the Woolhope Naturalists' Field Club*

Chapter 1 Rivers Wye and Lugg Navigation

1. Walters,1992, p.20
2. Putley 1999; *TWNFC* 1995; Shoesmith 1992
3. Herefordshire Through Time website 2011
4. CBA newsletter 28, 2003; Ross Civic Soc., *Historical Aspects* 2000, pp.217-222
5. Hurley 2008
6. Patent Roll 1301
7. Special Collections TNA; River Thames website
8. HCA 2393
9. Putley 1999
10. *VCH Glos* vol v p362; Willan 1976 p.25
11. Trinder 2005, p.76; Bewdley Vol 2 p.12
12. Willan 1964, p.119
13. River Thames website
14. Kissack 1996, p.132
15. Bewdley Vol 2, p.7; Willan 1964, p.120
16. Hughes & Leech 2011, p.251
17. Severn Navigation Restoration Trust website, Avon Navigation website
18. *VCH Glos* Vol V
19. Hurley 2007, p.20
20. Gerhold 2005 chapter III; Hurley 2007
21. Scudamore accounts CF60/5
22. Hurley 2010 chapter Four; Gerhold 2005 chapter V
23. Chandler 1999 editor of John Taylor's Travels chapter Five & Seven
24. Ibid. chapter Seven; author's local knowledge
25. Petition 1653 BG11/17/5/5
26. Articles of Agreement 1654 B47/H80
27. Wye & Lugg Navigation Act 1662
28. Willan 1964, pp.59, 146-150
29. *TWNFC* 1955, p.91
30. Broadsheet nd HCL; House of Commons Journal 1693-96; British History website
31. Hereford QSO/1 1673
32. *TWNFC* 1947, pp.154-157, 1955 pp.87-92
33. Shoesmith 1992, p.77
34. *TWNFC* 1905, p.219; Wye & Lugg Navigation Act 1695
35. Reputed to be a survey by Denell 1697, photocopy AP21
36. Survey 1697, AP21; *TWNFC* 1994
37. Hughes & Leech 2011, p.252; Trinder & Cox, *Miners & Mariners* 2000

38. Bewdley Historical Research Group, Bewdley Vol 2 1999, pp.9-14, Willan 1964, p.124
39. *TWNFC* 1955, p.90 (original not seen)
40. Scudamore accounts 1697-1703, TNA C115/114
41. Wye and Lugg accounts 1696-1700, K12/33
42. Hurley 2008, p.140
43. Kissack 1975, p.27, Willan 1964, p.99
44. Waters 1977, p.24
45. Taylor 1997, pp.232-3
46. Gerhold 2005, Ch III
47. Hurley ed. 2008, p.175
48. Info from Jean Dobson, Fownhope Parish Registers
49. *TWNFC* 1942, 1955, 1994
50. Scudamore accounts 1697-1703, TNA C115/114; Pennoyre accounts AD30/124
51. Tidnor Mill lease & papers 1714, F76/ii/361-362
52. Foley v Rea 1731, TNA E134/4
53. Wye & Lugg Navigation Act 1727
54. Defoe 1727; Vision of Britain website
55. Trumper Family D32/184; Guy's Hospital, AW28/46/212; Foley v Rea, TNA E134/4
56. Fairs 1972, p.266, *Herefordshire Miscellany* 2000, p.50
57. Reeve 1973, p.135; Calderbank 2000
58. Price, J., *City of Hereford* 1796, p.68
59. Parr 1973, p.21; GSIA 1980, p.51
60. Brayley & Britten 1805, pp.435-6
61. Duncumb 1805, p.14
62. Hurley 2008, p.167; River Wye Horse Towing Path Act 1809
63. *Her Jnl* 1 Jan.1814
64. *Her Jnl* 13 June, 17 Aug 1825 from P.J. Pike
65. Shoesmith 1992, chapter 11; GWR 1921 pp.67, 79
66. Lloyd 1873, pp.47-48

Chapter 2 Barges, Boats and Trows
1. Taylor Plan 1763; Brayley & Britten 1805, p.435
2. MDA Waterways website; Bewdley Museum leaflet nd; Colin Green info.; Trinder 2005, p.25
3. Harris 1968, pp.9, 45; Free Dictionary website
4. Bewdley Historical Res. Group 1999, p.5; Trinder & Cox 2000, p.196
5. Putley 1999, pp.36, 48
6. Barge accounts LOWV

7. Monmouth Museum display
8. Hurley 2008, pp.171-2
9. Barge accounts LOWV; Green 1999, p.159
10. Trinder 2005, p.76; Foley v Rea 1731, TNA E134
11. Kissack 1975, p.289
12. *Her Jnl* 24 Dec 1896 (from Jean Dobson)
13. Merchant Shipping Registration TNA; Farr 1954, pp.24-28
14. Trinder & Cox 2000, pp.25-26, 291; Bewdley 1999, p.3, Foley catalogue E12/VI
15. Trinder 2005, p.32
16. Foley v Rea 1731, TNA E134
17. The *York* galley carried 6 convicts to work on the Maryland plantations, but they all escaped, Q/SO/6 from J. Dobson
18. Foley v Rea 1731, TNA E134
19. *Glos Jnl* 14 Dec 1725 in Waters 1977, p.27
20. 1728 D32/184, 1735 AW28/46/212, 1772 AD30/124
21. Vicars Choral 1775 HCA3340/23, 1780 C99/III/16, 1785 AL24, 1788 AD30/124
22. LOWV barge accounts; Eisel 2000; Kissack 1975; Farr 1954; Fairs 1972; *Her Jnl* various
23. Farr 1954; LOWV barge accounts
24. LOWV barge accounts; Farr 1954; *Her Jnl* 15 Dec 1827
25. Farr 1954
26. Indented Inquisitions 1621
27. Harris 1968 pp.44-45, *Her Jnl* 24 Dec 1806 from P.J. Pike
28. Barge accounts LOWV; information from David Clark in *Her Jnl*, Kissack 1975, p.287
29. Summarised by D. Clark from A95/v/w/e/130
30. *Her Jnl* 16 Feb 1831
31. Country Strolls 1844, p.76
32. Information from P.J. Pikes
33. *Her Jnl* 21 Jan 1852
34. *Her Times* 7 July 1866
35. *The London Magazine* April 1752; Watkins-Pitchford 1935, p.22
36. *Her Jnl* 20 April 1796
37. *Her Jnl* 2 April 1800
38. *VCH* vol V, p.381; Hurley 2005, p.117; Hurley 2007, p.239; Farr 1954, p.81

Chapter 3 Barge Owners, Masters and Men
1. Trinder 2005, p.66; Farr 1954
2. Foley printed catalogue E12/vi/5
3. Bewdley 1999, Vol 2 p.3

4. Hurley in *Historical Aspects of Ross* 2000, p.37; info of Freemen from Jean Dobson
5. Hereford Corporation G.H. 1/146-183
6. LOWV barge accounts; Mortgage Q?RD/2/15; *VCH Glos.* 1996, p.309; AD30/124
7. Info from Jean Dobson from AA20/D/Vol 6
8. Lease BC1/25; Bark & timber accounts 1772/3 AD30/124/
9. Lease to N. Purchas 1775, HCA 3340/23
10. LOWV barge accounts; Farr 1954
11. LOWV barge accounts; Farr 1954, p.33; Woodhouse letter 1785, AL24
12. J. Eisel in *Herefordshire Miscellany* 2000, pp.52-53
13. LOWV barge accounts; Farr 1954, p.41
14. Waters 1977, pp.27-28
15. LOWV barge accounts
16. Farr 1954
17. Waters 1977, p.28; LOWV barge accounts; Farr 1954, pp.61, 77, 84
18. 1822 Directory; Pullings BB77; Farr 1954; LOWV barge accounts
19. Wilson 1977, pp.151-2
20. Luke Hughes will & Bonds G87; Bark & timber accounts AD30/124
21. LOWV Barge accounts; Guy's Hospital Records AW28; Aramstone Estate G87
22. Q/RD/2/14,LOWV Barge accounts; Guy's Hospital records AW28; Farr 1954
23. *VCH Glos* Vol V, pp.242, 309; Timber accounts 1772 AD30/124; info David Clark
24. Hurley 2008, p.168; LOWV Barge accounts; info from David Clark; Pullings accounts BB77
25. Trinder & Cox 2000, p.30
26. Hurley 2001, p.228; info Jean Dobson
27. Farr 1954, p.79; Crompton family see J. Eisel in *Herefordshire Miscellany* 2000, pp.53-4
28. *VCH Glos* Vol V, p.236
29. J. Eisel in *Herefordshire Miscellany*, p.54; Sale 1808 E59 SP 40; Farr 1954
30. LOWV Barge accounts; Waters 1977, p.28
31. *Her Jnl* June 1809
32. LOWV Barge accounts; Pullings accounts BB77; Farr 1954
33. Register of Freemen forwarded by Jean Dobson; *Her Jnl* refs from David Clark
34. *TWNFC* 1942, p.52
35. Kissack 1982, p.7; Green 1999, p.139
36. LOWV barge accounts transcribed by Mark Robinson
37. *Her Jnl* 30 June 1824 from P.J. Pikes
38. Heath 1804, p.194
39. Wages 1830 D48/47
40. Wilson 1977 Ch 8, info from Colin Green
41. Trinder 2005, p.68
42. Logaston Press' *The Pubs of ...* books
43. Heath 1804, p.194; LOWV Barge report by M. Robinson
44. Harris 1968, p.44
45. Jessop Report 1805 HCL
46. *TWNFC* 1955, p.101
47. Info from Jean Dobson, Maggie Ellis, Roz Lowe and David Clark
48. 1811 documents O68/III/6; Report 1828 A95/V/W/e/197
49. Lugwardine Hist. Soc. 1988, p.17; Census 1841, 1851; *Glos. VCH* Vol V

Chapter 4 Cargoes shipped on the Wye
1. Hurley 2008, p.168
2. Willan 1964, p.123, Shoesmith 1992, p.77
3. *VCH Gloucester* Vol V, pp.329-330
4. Barge accounts LOWV
5. Bringewood Chase, D. Lovelace mss 2005
6. Hart 1971, pp.63-7; Foley catalogue E12/VI/DGc; Harris 1968, p.9; Foley v Rea 1731, TNA E134
7. LOWV Barge accounts
8. Guy's hospital C/99/111/118
9. Taylor plan 1763; Trinder 2005, p.75
10. Putley 1999, p.34, Ireland 1797, pp.88-89
11. Lugwardine Hist. Soc 1988, p.10
12. LOWV barge accounts, Herefordshire Directories
13. *Penny Magazine* 31 July 1835
14. Scudamore accounts, TNA C115/114
15. Agreement 1701 AD30/124
16. Waters 1977, p.26
17. LOWV project 2008; Waters 1970, p.15
18. Foley v Rea 1731, TNA E134
19. Scudamore accounts from 1720 C115/115 TNA; Barge Accounts LOWV
20. *TWNFC* 1955, p.94
21. Transactions 1771-1775, AD30/124
22. Gorvett 1984, p.3
23. Waters 1977, p.28, Barge accounts LOWV; *Her Jnl* 7 Feb 1798
24. Hurley 2008, p.129; Barge accounts LOWV
25. Gill 1987; Hurley notes 2010
26. Barge accounts LOWV; Pullings accounts

1843, BB77

27. Trinder 2005, p.108; Hart 1971, p.313
28. Hurley notes 2010
29. Brat seems to be an unknown mineral, possibly a by-product of lime burning
30. Barge accounts LOWV
31. *Her Jnl* 5 May 1824
32. Barge accounts LOWV
33. Hughes & Hurley 2009, p.139, *Her Jnl* 12 Oct 1796
34. Barge accounts LOWV
35. Hurley 2001, p.15; Scudamore accounts CF60/6 & C115/114 TNA; Taylor 1997, p.233
36. Defoe from vision of Britain website; Shoesmith & Eisel 2004, pp.18-19, Stafford 2009, p.61; Reeves 1973, p.133
37. Barge accounts LOWV; Mendelsohn 1966; Pullings accounts BB77
38. *Her Jnl* 24 Oct 1771 from P.J. Pike
39. Hurley 2007, p.25, Waters 1977, pp.29-30
40. Barge accounts LOWV; Farr 1954, pp.31, 44
41. Pullings accounts BB77
42. Info from J. Eisel, Fairs 1972, p.266; *TWNFC* 1994
43. Q/SR/28 1740
44. Info from J. Dobson
45. Barge accounts LOWV; Letter 1785 AL24
46. Barge accounts LOWV

Chapter 5 Boat Buiulding and associated trades

1. Heath 1828
2. Trinder 2005, p.28; Heath 1828
3. Foley & Rea 1731, TNA 134
4. See chapters 2 & 3
5. Book of Trades 1811
6. Green 1999, p.120
7. Foley v Rea 1730 TNA
8. Info from D Lovelace; Green 1999, p.119; Farr 1954, p.4; www.thedearsurprise.com
9. Taylor 1997, pp.246-248, *Her Jnl* 2 Oct 1793
10. Hill Court records F8/iii/274
11. Farr 1954, p.72; *Her Jnl* 23 April 1772; Hurley 2010, p.111
12. Farr 1954; Herefordshire Directory 1793; *Herefordshire Miscellany* 2000, p.54
13. *Her Jnl* 22 June 1808
14. Farr 1954; LOWV barge accounts; Fairs 1972, p.265

15. Sale Particulars 1808, GRO D367/iii/8; List of houses at New Wear 1811, O68/iii/7; Coates & Tucker 1983, p.56
16. Harris 1968, p.18
17. Farr 1954; LOWV barge accounts; *Her Jnl* 18 Dec 1818
18. Farr 1954; *Her Jnl* 13 Feb 1822
19. Info from Maggie Ellis; Holme Lacy Tithe Map 1840
20. *Her Jnl* 12 Nov 1823
21. Farr 1954; *Her Jnl* 26 Jan 1825
22. *Her Jnl* 21 Dec 1825; Farr 1954
23. Hurley 2009, p.110; *Her Jnl* 16 May 1827 from P.J. Pike; Farr 1954, pp.14, 122
24. Farr 1954; Parr 1973, p.59; *Her Jnl* 11 July, 14 Nov, 15 Dec 1827; Lower Bullingham Tithe Map 1840
25. *Her Jnl* 11 Mar 1829
26. Hart 1971, p.417
27. *TWNFC* 1918, pp.86-87, 1936 p.74, 1958 p.78
28. *Her Times* 2 July 1836
29. *TWNFC* 1958, p.79; Druce 1980, pp.99-100
30. Green 1999, p.119; Foley v Rea TNA E134
31. Trinder & Cox 2000, pp.207-208; *Her Jnl* 16 Sept 1789 & 17 Apr 1793
32. Flinn 1962, p.199; Hart 1971, p.103; Harris 1968, p.19; *Her Jnl* 20 Jan 1790; Lugwardine Hist. Soc. 1988, p.10
33. Sanctuary 1988, p.3; Gale 1983, p.67; *Her Jnl* 12 Oct 1796; Hughes & Hurley 2009, p.139
34. *Her Jnl* 2 June 1774, 16 Nov 1775; Hughes & Hurley 2009, p.138; Cross 1982, p.70
35. Trinder 2005, p.30, Barge accounts LOWV
36. Hughes & Hurley 2009, p.138, Hurley 2008, p.134, Barge accounts, LOWV
37. 1822 Directories

Chapter 6 Wharves, Symonds Yat to Weiorend

1. Hurley 2008, p.168
2. Heath 1828; Dixton Tithe Map 1845; Leys Sale E59/SP/12
3. Barge accounts LOWV
4. Whitworth Navigation Plan 1779
5. Hurley notes 2012 for Wye Valley AONB
6. Gilpin 1782, p.25; Ireland 1797, pp.95-97
7. Cracklow Deeds CL59; Hurley 2001 chapter 14
8. Roz Lowe notes for Woolhope ARS 2, April 2009

9. Peter Dorling, Herefordshire Council information 2009
10. Accounts O68/11/53; Kissack 1975, p.27; info from Roz Lowe 2009; Coates & Tucker 1983, p.56
11. Heath 1803, 1828
12. Farr 1954; List of Houses 068/iii/7; Barge accounts LOWV
13. Symonds Yat Guide 1987, pp.16-18
14. *VCH Glos* Vol. V 1996, p.112
15. Commons Registration Act 1965; Hurley notes 2009
16. *Her Jnl* 27 Mar 1783; info from Roz Lowe; 1888 OS
17. Barge accounts LOWV; Road plan Q/RW/12; Goodrich Tithe Map 1838; Whitchurch Tithe Map 1847
18. Hurley notes 2008; Goodrich Tithe Map 1838; Heath 1828; Barge accounts LOWV
19. Parr 1971, p.14; info Colin Gibbons 2008
20. Barge accounts LOWV; Gilpin 1782
21. Ireland 1797, p.88; Sale 1808 E59/SP/40
22. Lease GRO D637/11/8; Sungreen website 2011; *Her Jnl* 5 May 1824
23. Hurley 2004, pp.81-87
24. Parr 1973, pp.59-60
25. Parr 1973, pp.57-59; Bryant Gloucester map 1824; Hill Court F8/iii/278
26. Fosbroke 1823
27. Hill Court F8/iii/278; Barge accounts LOWV, Farr 1954
28. Hurley 2007, pp.47-48
29. Strong 1863
30. Hill Court Records F8/iii/263, 258, 278
31. Barge accounts LOWV; Hurley 2001, p.232
32. Ross Turnpike Trust Minutes AM5/7
33. Hurley 2007, p.49, *Her Jnl* 13 Dec 1815; Hurley 2001, p.214
34. *TWNFC* 2007, p.97; Guy's estate records C99/111/105
35. 'A thin bed of coal mixed with pyrites', *Oxford Dictionary*. A local name for something else, Ian Standing 2012
36. Guy's Estate records AW28/47/5; Barge accounts LOWV

Chapter 7 Wharves, Wilton Quay & Ross Dock
1. Ireland 1797, p.70
2. Heath 1828; Hurley in *Historical Aspects* 2000, p.37

3. Leases AW28/46/212
4. OS 1888; Leases G87/7/34, G87/8/1-4
5. Guy's Hospital Reports AW28/47/5, AW28/2/5; *Historical Aspects* 2000, p.57
6. Guy's estate records C99/111/120
7. Farr 1954, p.14; Aramstone Records G87/9/2
8. Guy's Hospital Reports AW28/45/36, AW28/9/20
9. Guy's Hospital records C99/111/118
10. Guy's Hospital records C99/111/116
11. Guy's Hospital records AW28/9/20
12. Taylor 1997, p.284; Guy's Hospital catalogue entry C99/111/399
13. Guy's Hospital records AW28/45/64 & 66
14. Bridstow church, Monumental Inscriptions A88/266
15. Letter G87/52/201
16. Guy's Hospital records AW28/9/28-34
17. Barge accounts LOWV; Farr 1954
18. Barge accounts LOWV
19. Hurley, 'History of Orles Barn' unpub. 2011
20. Bridstow Tithe Apportionment and map; Barge accounts LOWV
21. Hurley in *Historical Aspects* 2000, pp.33-34
22. Information from Angus Watkins, May 2007
23. *Her Jnl* 29 Feb 1832
24. Tweed 1884, p.43
25. Hurley notes on Castle & River Crossing 2010; Barge accounts LOWV
26. Heath 1828
27. Ross Parish Boundaries BW14/42
28. Brayley & Britten 1805, p.436. Boundaries were altered in 1931
29. Guy's Hospital records AW28/47/5
30. Ireland 1797, p.70
31. Barge accounts LOWV
32. Terrier 1823 in Rectory Box now at HRO, Deeds L70/9
33. Ross Guide 1827, p.14
34. Hurley 2001, pp.41-43; Deeds and Sale Particulars L70/18
35. Druce 1980, p.96

Chapter 8 Wharves, Bridstow to Holme Lacy
1. Price 1796, p.2
2. Wye and Lugg Navigation Act 1695; Trinder 2005, p.20
3. Barge accounts LOWV
4. *Her Jnl* 5 May 1824; 1829 Survey BF21; Barge accounts LOWV

5. Foy Parish Recoirds
6. *ibid*
7. Red wine from Graves, info from Jon Hurley
8. Hurley 2008, p.170; Barge accounts LOWV
9. Old Humphrey 1844 chapter 6
10. Perrystone Sale M5/10/10; Timber sales TNA C115/115
11. Barge accounts LOWV; *Her Jnl* 5 May 1824
12. Hurley 2008, p.169; Barge accounts LOWV
13. Fawley Lease 1687; HRO A8/11/210
14. Abstract of Leases, Guy's Hospital Estate, 1735, 1737, HRO AW/28/46/212
15. A. Jones Agreement 1745, HRO AW28/31/22
16. *Her Jnl* 7 Aug 1799, 10 Mar 1802; Kynaston Sale 1863 M5/15/17
17. Hurley 2010, p.3
18. Barge accounts LOWV
19. *Her Jnl* May 1779 from David Clark; Hurley 2008, p.169
20. Letter 1799 A29/64
21. Barge accounts LOWV; Llanfrother Sale 1856; HCL PC3344; *Her Jnl* 3 Apr 1777
22. Hentland Tithe map & apport 1842; Barge accounts LOWV
23. Hurley 2008, p.157; 1809 Horse Towing Path Act; Towing Path plan 1808, Gwent RO P.BR 7/8
24. *Her Jnl* 10 Feb 1774; Barge accounts LOWV
25. LOWV barge archive 2006
26. Info from Tony Gardiner, May 2007
27. *Her Jnl* 1845 from David Clark
28. Dean & Chapter Registry Book 1841-1851, pp.100-101, HCA7005/7
29. Foley v Rea 1731 TNA E134
30. *Her Jnl* 5 Feb 1810
31. Squire Thomas Jones Day Book, 18 May 1793, Kington Historical Society
32. Barge accounts LOWV
33. Hurley 2001, chapter 9
34. Lipscomb 1802, p.70
35. Scudamore accounts 1717 TNA C115/68; Foley v Rea 1731 TNA E134
36. Barge accounts LOWV; Holme Lacy Tithe Map 1840; *Her Jnl* 5 May 1824

Chapter 9 Wharves, Mordiford to Leominster and to Rotherwas

1. Cassey 1858
2. Survey 1697; *TWNFC* 1994
3. Brian 1993, p.11; Price 1796, p.198

4. Barge accounts LOWV; Farr 1954
5. Smith 1994 pp.6-7; Barge accounts LOWV; Cassey 1858
6. Barge accounts LOWV; Hurley 2001, pp.156-159
7. Lipscomb 1802, p.76, Herefordshire SMR website; barge accounts LOWV
8. Duncumb 1805, p.18
9. Price 1795; pp.188-192
10. Duncumb 1805, p.18, Calderbank 2000
11. *Her Jnl* 22 April 1789, 11 Aug 1808, 25 Nov 1812, 4 Oct 1854
12. Lugwardine Historical Society 1988
13. Brian 1993. p.13, *Her Jnl* 21 Jan 1807; Eisel & Shoesmith 2003, p.291
14. Barge accounts LOWV
15. Lugwardine Historical Society 1988, pp.12-13
16. *Her Jnl* 18 Dec 1818
17. Quarter Session Index; Brian 1993; Barge accounts LOWV
18. Shoesmith & Barrett 2000, p.185; *TWNFC* 1994; pp.72-73; Brian 1993, p.30
19. *TWNFC* 1994 pp.76-79; QS index; Shoesmith & Barrett 2000, pp.175, 185; Barge accounts LOWV
20. Shoesmith & Barrett 2000, pp.211& 238
21. Woodhouse accounts AL24
22. Woodhouse accounts AL24, T72
23. Barge accounts LOWV
24. Duncumb 1805, pp.144-145
25. Price 1796, p.193
26. Barge accounts LOWV
27. Price, p.193; Towing path survey GRO Q-RU M 14
28. Rotherwas, Dinedor Heritage Group 2009; Barge accounts LOWV; *Her Jnl* 28 Nov 1810
29. Farr 1954; Barge accounts LOWV; Bullingham tithe map 1844
30. Tupsley documents G87/57/8; Tupsley tithe map 1839
31. Lipscomb 1802, p.76; Shoesmith & Eisel 2004, p.312

Chapter 10 Wharves, Hereford City

1. Wye & Lugg Navigation Act 1695
2. *TWNFC* 1955, p.90
3. Wye and Lugg accounts 1696-1700, K12/33; Register of Freemen AT49 from J. Dobson
4. Lease GH1/181
5. Shoesmith 1992, pp.77-78; Ireland 1797, pp.58-59

6. Ireland 1797 pp.58-59; Price 1796 p.75
7. See chapter 12
8. Barge accounts LOWV
9. St. Owens Tithe map copied by Geoff Gwatkin
10. SMR Herefordshire Archaeology, Shoesmith & Eisel 2004 p.312
11. Agreement 1809 HCA D196-98; Whitehead & Shoesmith 1994; Horse Towing Path 1805, GRO Q/Rum14
12. Horse Towing Path plan GRO Q/Rum14; Cole & Roper map HCL
13. See chapter 5
14. Leases HCA 3810; Lease A2A 1808 Shrop Archives
15. Her Paving Comm Mins 1783 (from J. Dobson); *Her Jnl* 15 Jul 1798
16. *Her Jnl* 19 Nov 1788, 15 July 1798, 22 Jan 1800, 21 Oct 1801, 5 May 1824
17. Van Laun 2006, p.13, *Her Jnl* 14 Jan 1829
18. *Her Jnl* 19th May 1801, 18th Nov 1801, 1st Jan 1806,; Horse Towing Path GRO Q/Rum14
19. Hereford Coal Wharf HCA 3826
20. Hereford Coal Wharf HCA 3826; Shoesmith 1992, p.85
21. Corporation deeds GH1/146, 1/181; Vicars Choral lease HCA3930
22. Trumper family D32/184, *Her Jnl* 18 Nov 1795 from J. Dobson; James Biss will AE38/11
23. Farr 1954; Waters 1952, p.24
24. Biss family at Wilton see Chapter 7; Bill of Complaint 1852 AE38/11; Vicars Choral lease HCA3930
25. Tanners history on website
26. Hereford Directory 1822; *Her Jnl* 21 Oct 1829
27. Eisel in *Herefordshire Miscellany* 2000, pp.52-53, Herefordshire Directory 1830, 1835; Pulling accounts BB77 (uncatalogued)
28. Barton map AA/59
29. *Her Jnl* 2 May 1798
30. Sun Fire Office BH31/8; *Her Jnl* 17 June 1801, 11 Oct 1809; *Herefordshire Miscellany* 2000, p.53
31. Taylor Map; *TWNFC* 1955, p.99; Van Laun 2006, p.13
32. *Her Jnl* 14 Aug 1799
33. *Her Jnl* 8 June 1803; Plan of Friars Wharf AL6/5
34. *Her Jnl* 15 July 1798
35. Shoesmith & Eisel 2004; *Her Jnl* adverts
36. Trumper deeds D32/184; info from J. Dobson

37. Info from John Eisel 2011; Woodhouse accounts L24; Leech account HCA 5715/3-
38. Barge accounts LOWV
39. QS BG11/5/56 Trans by R. Griffith
40. Barge accounts LOWV; Wright 1819, p.67; Rees 1827 p.76
41. Directories 1844, 1851; see chapter 12
42. Info from J. Dobson, P.J. Pikes, M. Ellis; 1793 Directory; Herefordshire Charities 1837, p.207; *Her Jnl.*
43. *Her Times* 1 Apr 1848 from Liz Pitman

Chapter 11 Wharves, Belmont to Glasbury
1. Price 1796, p.191; Barge accounts LOWV; Farr 1954, p.13
2. Price 1796, pp.190-191
3. Barge accounts LOWV; info from D. Lovelace
4. *TWNFC* 1922, p.80, Eisel & Bennett 2005, p.158; Eaton Bishop Tithe Map 1840; Sale E40/11
5. Barge accounts LOWV; *Her Jnl* 5 May 1824
6. Barge accounts LOWV; *TWNFC* 1922, p.80; SMR website
7. Price 1796, p.188; Letter F37/113
8. A.S. Wood 1954 typescript; Barge accounts LOWV
9. Timber yard BH19/1
10. *TWNFC* 1922, p.79; Bridge Sollers Tithe 1842; Shoesmith & Barrett 2000, p.38
11. 1730 plan D52/78; Lease F37/178
12. *TWNFC* 1922, p.79, Shoesmith & Barrett 2000, p.40; Barge accounts LOWV
13. See chapter 1
14. Note Dean & Chapter HCA3489
15. Survey of Wye & Lugg copy AP21; *TWNFC* 1922, p.78; Barge accounts LOWV
16. Ireland 1797, p.46, *Her Jnl* 13 Feb 1772 (from P.J. Pikes); Barge accounts LOWV
17. Ireland 1797, pp.44-5; *TWNFC* 1922, p.78
18. Taylor map 1754; Bredwardine Tithe Map 1840, *Her Jnl* 30 Nov 1808
19. Bredwardine Tithe map 1840; Taylor map 1754; Eisel & Bennett 2005, p.175
20. *TWNFC* 1922, p.77, Barge accounts LOWV; Clock Mill AE98/6; Clifford website
21. Ireland 1797, p.43; *Her Jnl* 21 Oct 1801
22. *TWNFC* 1922, p.77
23. *TWNFC* 1933, pp.121-2, Crow 1995, p.86
24. *Her Jnl* 2 April 1772; Agreement 1701 AD30/124

25. Transactions 1771-1775 AD30/124
26. Whitney Tithe map 1840; transactions AD30/124
27. Hurley 2010, p.111; 1841 Census
28. Clifford Tithe map 1840; Price map 1817; Fairs 1972, p.267
29. Castle Inn sale B29/1; Eisel & Bennett 2005, pp.179-80
30. Fairs 1972, p.266
31. Ireland 1797, pp.31-36
32. Public notice in Stockinger 1996, pp.159-160
33. *Her Jnl* 23 April 1772; Leech accounts HCA5715/3/11
34. Clinker 1960, p.5; Fairs 1972, p.258; Farr 1954, p.107
35. *Her Jnl* 20 March 1816; see chapter 4; Farr 1954, p.136
36. Tramway plan Q/RW/T4a D; Barge accounts LOWV; *Her Jnl* 26 Mar 1823, 14 Jan 1829
37. Ship Inn N44/12; Eisel & Bennett 2005; Hobbs 2006
38. Ireland 1797, pp.28-29; 1835 Directory
39. See chapters 1 & 3, *Her Jnl* 4 Feb 1779; Fairs 1972, p.265; *Her Jnl* 21 Sept 1796
40. Accounts N44/11, 12, 13; Hobbs 2006, chapter 13; Abstract of Title L79/13

Chapter 12 Decline of the Rivers Wye and Lugg Navigation

1. Price 1796, p.68
2. Heath 1828, referring to the Abergavenny to Hereford tram road planned in 1818, Q/RW/T8b
3. Hadfield 1974, p.109
4. Avon Navigation Trust 2012
5. Nigel Jefferies notes 1984
6. Bick 1994, pp.47-48, *Her Jnl* 27 Aug 1851, Herefordshire Directory 1851; Nigel Jefferies notes 1984
7. Duncumb 1805, pp.144-5; Reeves 1973, p.134; see chapter 9
8. Parr 1973, pp.15-61; Plan 1809 Q/RW/T14; Colin Gibbons notes 2008
9. 1802 Plan, Q/RW/T13; 1818 plan, Q/RW/T8; *TWNFC* 1939, p.101
10. Hereford Coal Wharf, HCA 3826; Roberts 2001, pp.46-7
11. Clinker 1960 chapter II; Hadfield 1960, pp.180-181; 1812 plan Q/RW/T4
12. Ellison in *TWNFC* 1937, pp.77-83; Spencer accounts N44/13
13. Fairs 1972, p.258; *TWNFC* 1937, p.82
14. 'The History of the hay Railway' in *TWNFC* 1937
15. Great Western Railway 1921
16. Shoesmith 1992 chapter 11; Hurley 2008 chapter VIII; Clinker 1960, p.47
17. Barge accounts LOWV; Pullings accounts 1843 BB77
18. Beddoes vol V, HCA; Green 1999, pp.149-50; James 1861 illus
19. Lloyd 1873, p.48
20. Trinder 2005 chapter VII; Williams 1982, p.59; Green 1999, p.18
21. Info from P.J. Pikes, David Clark from *Her Jnl*; Ritchie 1841, p.53, Druce 1985, p.99
22. *Her Times* 19 Apr 1890
23. *Holidays at Hereford* 1931, p.157; C.R. Shaw 1948, HCL LC387
24. RCS Archive CP26
25. Forest & Wye Valley Review 1989
26. Wye Valley AONB website
27. Info from Monmouth Museum; The Hereford Bull leaflet 2012; info from A. Wynn 2012

Index of Names

Index of Boats and Barges

General Index